PEOPLES OF THE WORLD SERIES

THE PEOPLE
OF AFRICA

PEOPLES OF THE WORLD SERIES

Editor: *Sonia Cole*

THE PEOPLE
OF AFRICA

Jean Hiernaux
Director of Research at the
National Centre for Scientific Research, Paris

Weidenfeld and Nicolson
London

Weidenfeld and Nicolson
11 St John's Hill London SW11

ISBN 0 297 76831 X

Printed in Great Britain by
Cox & Wyman Ltd
London, Fakenham and Reading

Contents

Figures

Tables

THE PEOPLE
OF AFRICA

Preface

Some ten years ago I wrote a short handbook for the sub-department of anthropology of the British Museum (Natural History). This was in the days when the word 'race' was innocent of many of its present connotations and the booklet was entitled *Races of Man*. After it had been published, and as a result of my frustrations when trying to compile it, I realized that outside the major groups of Caucasoid, Mongoloid and Negroid there are no such things as 'races of man'. There are populations, there are ethnic groups, but they grade into one another to such an extent that races or sub-species, as normally defined in zoology, are really meaningless when applied to anthropology.

So, out with races, on with peoples. But call them what you like, there are obvious differences between them. You don't have to be a physical anthropologist to recognize that a Japanese, an Englishman and a Kikuyu don't *look* alike (probably they won't think alike either, but that is a question of culture and not genetics). Yet, as a statement drafted for UNESCO by fourteen physical anthropologists put it: 'Some biological differences between human beings within a single race may be as great as, or greater than, the same biological differences between races.'

There is no problem in finding a book on the birds of Europe or the mammals of Africa, but when it comes to human beings it is quite a different matter. Man is seldom included with other mammals, partly because of our conceit but mainly because the book would burst its binding. It was this lamentable lack which made me realize the need for world-wide coverage on people. To do justice to the subject, it would have to be in several volumes. As divisions based on 'race' presented such difficulties, the boundaries would have to be geographical.

The books would have to be written by specialists. Clearly they would have to be trained in physical anthropology, but they would need to be far more than just skull-measurers.

They would have to describe characteristics and relationships of the present populations of each continent, based on the latest findings of human biologists and geneticists. They would have to try and discover how people got where they are and how they coped with and were moulded by their environment. This would involve the whole pageant of migrations and invasions, conquest and trade, throughout history. It would also mean examining the hardware of preliterate societies, their tools, weapons, art and other artifacts. The origins of the diverse populations of today would have to be traced back to a handful of bones in the grey mists of prehistory.

The setting would also be important, taking in geology, climatology, ecology and many other -ologies. The animals man hunted, the vegetable foods he gathered and later cultivated, would all have to be brought in.

It would be hard enough to find authors competent to discuss all these varied aspects; but the geographical boundaries of the proposed volumes presented yet more difficulties. An anthropologist who had specialized, say, in the sophisticated cultures of Chinese or Indian civilizations might have little knowledge of, or interest in, the seal hunters and reindeer herders of northern Siberia; yet all these peoples, and many more, would have to be included in the one volume on Asia.

There was still another very important qualification that these paragons of authors would have to possess, perhaps more daunting for some than anything else. This was the ability to turn a mass of scientific data and statistics into a readable and stimulating book, of real value for serious students and at the same time appealing to non-specialists.

Naturally, each author would ride his favourite hobby-horse to a certain extent; indeed one would want them to, for enthusiasm is infectious. Each author in this series has in fact treated his subject with a different emphasis, one underlining the historical background, another the genetic aspects and so on. These various approaches emphasize the wideness of the topics under discussion and perhaps enhance the interest.

SONIA COLE

Introduction

Africa is said to be the cradle of mankind, that bough of the evolutionary tree which depends on culture for its survival; certainly this seems to be the most reasonable hypothesis that can be made at present. The oldest and simplest stone tools have been found in Africa, as well as the earliest known hominid who systematically made such tools. Culture, to which man owes his biological success, is the sum of all that individuals acquire by communicating with their fellows – behaviour, objects, ideas, knowledge and beliefs – and its development began in Africa.

The present peoples of Africa can thus trace their ancestry back to an original stock, common to the whole of mankind, which emerged in their continent. The story of man in Africa is one of changes, both biological and cultural: the change from a relatively small-brained biped to modern man, from a hunting-gathering way of life with a limited set of simple tools to the sophistication of modern culture. Evolution is the key to this story. Its two fields interact so much that an understanding of biological evolution, the main concern of this book, requires at least a schematic knowledge of cultural evolution, with which we shall also be concerned.

Mechanisms of Biological Evolution

A few general mechanisms govern biological evolution and, since they will be evoked again and again in this book, a bit of theory is needed before plunging into the story of man in Africa.

The biological characters of an individual are determined jointly by his heredity and his environment. This is equally true for measurements like those of stature or weight, for observed features like ear form or pilosity (hairiness), or for traits tested in the laboratory (although some aspects of these, like the qualitative aspect of blood groups, are strictly determined by heredity alone).

In other words, environment influences the way in which an individual expresses his genetic heritage or *genome*. This influence is not transmitted to the offspring and biological evolution, therefore, concerns only the genome.

Genetically, an individual does not evolve: he was born and will die with his genes. Nor does he transmit his genome as a whole; his offspring inherit half of it, but in each parent there are so many ways of splitting the genome that no siblings will ever be genetically identical (except monovular twins who develop from the same fertilized egg). Evolution is a matter of groups, not of individuals.

Human groups tend to evolve independently according to the measure in which they refrain from exchanging mates with other groups. No human group ever keeps genetically closed for long periods. However, at all times except perhaps during the very earliest period, mankind has been fragmented into breeding populations which kept closed enough to maintain or develop some genetical differentiation from each other, while practising no systematic barrier within their own, thus keeping fairly homogeneous. These are the units of human evolution.

A large closed breeding population in a stable environment tends to remain genetically constant along the generations. Genetical change in a population results from one or a combination of four processes: selection, interbreeding, mutation, and random genetic drift. These change the frequency of the *alleles*, the variants of a gene (for example, the M and N alleles which determine the three MN types: M (genotype MM), N (NN), and MN (MN).

Selection, and inequality of the contribution of the alleles to the next generation, occurs when the population leaves or modifies the environment to which it was adapted. Such a population will change genetically until it reaches a new equilibrium, the best that it can reach with its stock of genes. In man, the equilibria for many characters usually maintain genetic diversity: for example, all populations have the three types of MN blood groups, at different frequencies, and in the case of the four types of ABO blood groups only a minority of populations are completely lacking in one or the other of them. All are inherited from pre-human ancestors but some have been lost by some populations.

Interbreeding means the incorporation of fertile mates from another breeding population. No two breeding populations being genetically identical, this will induce a change, however slight it may be.

Mutations, the transformation of a gene or group of genes transmitted to the offspring, create new variants or increase the number of individuals having a variant which already exists in the population. If recurrent, mutations exert a systematic pressure in favour of the mutant allele. This pressure is very slight, because all mutation rates are low, and because reverse mutations may occur. Generally, selection will act on the frequency of the mutant in one or other direction: keeping it down to a very low value, or bringing it up to a steady value in equilibrium with other alleles, or causing the mutant to replace them.

As long as their pressure keeps constant, selection, interbreeding and mutations produce a genetic evolution whose direction, speed and final state can be predicted. In contrast with these directional processes, *random drift* is a product of chance; its intensity can be estimated only in terms of probability.

In small breeding communities, especially in a species like ours in which average family size is low, the hazards of the transmission of the genes from one generation to the next result in a random fluctuation of the allele frequencies; some alleles may even disappear in the process. This is *genetic drift senso strictu*, its intensity being an inverse function of the size of the breeding population.

Certain single events also are likely to result in random changes of allele frequencies. This is the case when a small group leaves a community and founds a new breeding population somewhere else; the chances are low that the migrant group has the same allele frequencies as the original population. This sudden random differentiation is called the *founder effect*. A drastic reduction in the size of a population – by war, pestilence, famine or other catastrophe – will result in a similar sudden genetic change; this is known as the *bottleneck effect*. In each case, with the population size keeping low for at least a few generations, the sudden effect is likely to be followed by genetic drift *senso strictu*.

The largest breeding population that can be described is the species itself. By definition, a species is genetically cut off from all other species by a total (or quasi-total) absence of fertile cross-matings. When the species is not in a state of genetical equilibrium with its environment, and if the circulation of genes between its populations is intense enough, it will evolve as a whole towards a

3

new equilibrium. This evolution may have gone so far that biologists consider that the descendants would not be interfertile with the original species; *speciation*, or the emergence of a new species, has taken place by a process of linear evolution which will possibly continue. When a breeding population happens to be subjected to strong selection, or intense drift, or both, during a number of generations in severe genetic isolation, it may become so different that it is no longer interfertile with the rest of the species and therefore becomes a new species. This is speciation by branching.

This is enough theory for now. When the necessity arises, one or other of these points will be developed further.

I

The Physical Environment, Past and Present

Structure and Drainage

Africa is the second largest continent next to Asia. It is three times as big as Europe, but has a shorter coastline; its contour is bulky, with few deep bays or gulfs. Much of the continent is far from the ocean and this had the effect of isolating its human populations from that of the other continents. This is especially so south of the Sahara, where the coast approaches another continent only in a limited eastern sector: that which faces southern Arabia across the Red Sea and the Gulf of Aden. The Sahara, now a hot desert, crosses Africa from coast to coast at latitudes which include the Tropic of Cancer. A barrier to migration, the severity of which varied with time, it divides Africa into two sub-continents: North Africa and sub-Saharan Africa. The only river to cross it is the Nile, which descends through the desert in a series of steps. North Africa, a part of the Mediterranean area, is more open to contact with Europe and Asia than the rest of the continent.

Most of Africa consists of a plateau with only a narrow coastal plain. The rivers descend from the hard rocks of the plateau to the coast via a series of rapids and cataracts. Until recently, this hindered penetration far inland and was a further factor of continental isolation, together with the rarity of harbours except along the western Mediterranean coast.

Most of the major rivers have long navigable upper courses on the African plateau and, since remote times, they have facilitated human migration within the continent. The most important ones are the Nile, flowing northwards into the Mediterranean; the Senegal, Niger, Congo and Orange draining into the Atlantic; and

Figure 1. Major rivers and lakes of Africa

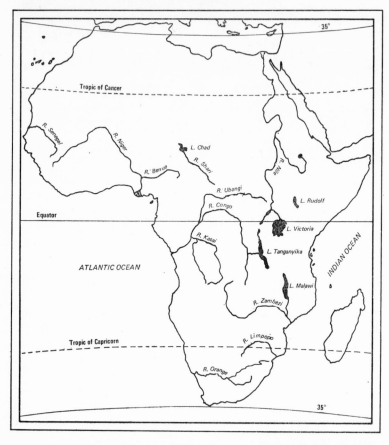

the Limpopo and Zambezi flowing into the Indian Ocean. A third of the continent has no outlet to the sea and large areas drain into inland basins. The main ones are the basin of Lake Chad, into which the Shari flows from the south, and that of Lake Rudolf in Kenya and Ethiopa, which collects the water from a long section of the eastern branch of the rift valley system (Figure 1).

The African plateau is higher in the south than in the north. Its higher portion stretches nearly as far north as the Equator and is then deeply cut by the basins of the Congo, the Nile and the Shari, so that tongues of the high plateau extend northwards, separating the river basins.

6

Figure 2. Relief of Africa

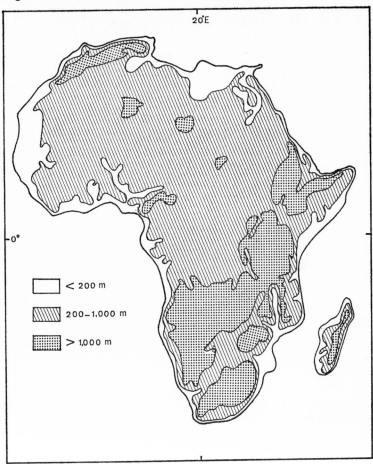

The eastern and broadest limb is the chief exception to the topographic monotony of Africa. Here tensile forces in the earth's crust have resulted in the formation of a series of rift valleys and of high volcanoes and mountains. The western branch of the rift valley system extends from south of Lake Malawi through Lakes Tanganyika, Kivu, Edward and Albert to the Upper Nile. Less continuous, the eastern branch can be traced from the northern end of Lake Malawi to Lake Rudolf and across to the southern end of

7

the Red Sea. Associated with the faulting of the eastern branch are the volcanic highlands of Kenya, which culminate in Kilimanjaro, Mount Kenya and Elgon, and the dissected basalt plateau of Ethiopia and Eritrea. The western highlands culminate in the Virunga volcanoes (in the borderland area of Rwanda, Uganda and Zaire), and in the Ruwenzori range, an uplifted block of the crystalline plateau.

The central limb of the high plateau extends north-westwards across the Sahara as the Tibesti and Tassili massifs. The western limb follows the trend of the west coast round the Gulf of Guinea, forming the mountains of Cameroun and the interior highlands of West Africa. The same stresses that caused the rifting and vulcanism in East Africa were responsible for the volcanic masses of Darfur in the central limb and of Cameroun peak in the western limb.

The Atlas range in North Africa is not part of the African plateau, but really belongs to the European Alpine system of folded mountains.

Present Climate and Vegetation

Africa is the only continent to be almost cut in half by the Equator. Though more of it lies to the north than to the south, its most northern and southern points are at an almost equal distance (36°) from it.

As a consequence, climate tends to change gradually in a similar way as one moves northward or southward away from the Equator. Symmetrical climatic zones lie on either side of a central zone of equatorial climate, with two tropical, two hot desert, and two Mediterranean zones (Figure 3).

The equatorial climate is characterized by heavy rainfall and constant high temperature and humidity. It extends over much of the Congo basin, along the coast of West Africa, a small part of the east coast and, somewhat modified by altitude, in parts of the East African highlands.

North and south of this belt, the tropical climate extends over a broad zone. It has a marked dry season during the cooler half of the year and, in general, the length of the dry season increases as one proceeds away from the equatorial belt.

The northern zone of hot desert climate covers a large area from the west to the east coasts, between the tropical belt and the

Figure 3. Broad climatic zones of Africa

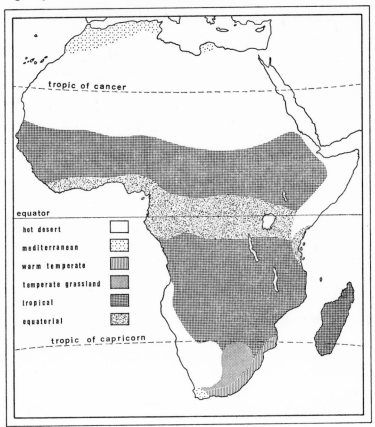

tropic of cancer

equator

hot desert
mediterranean
warm temperate
temperate grassland
tropical
equatorial

tropic of capricorn

Mediterranean coastlands. There is an extension southward over the eastern Horn of Africa (the Somaliland desert) due to the prevailing winds being parallel to the coast for most of the year. The southern zone, the Kalahari desert, is much smaller and is limited to the western part of the continent. Rainfall is very scanty and falls mainly in thunderstorms during the hottest part of the year. The range of temperature is considerable, both between seasons and between day and night.

At the latitude of the Kalahari desert, south of the Tropic of Capricorn, the south-east coast has a warm temperate type of climate resulting from the narrower width of the continent and the

Figure 4. Broad vegetation zones of Africa

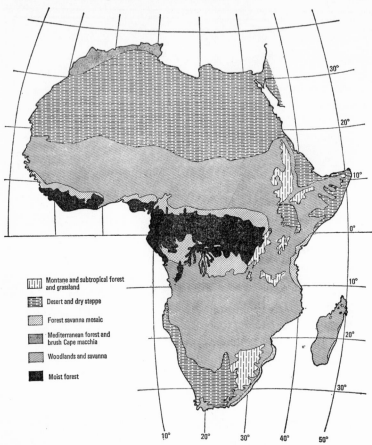

vast expanse of the ocean lying to the east. It receives a fairly heavy trade wind rainfall during the hot season.

West of this coastal area, in the interior – where altitude considerably reduces the temperature – the climate can be classified as of the temperate grassland type. This covers a rather narrow area, the rainfall decreasing fairly rapidly towards the western desertic zone.

In the north, the Mediterranean climate occurs along the coastlands and on the northern slopes of the Atlas. It is characterized by winter cyclonic rainfall and an almost complete summer drought, the length of which increases rapidly as one proceeds eastwards from Tunis. The Atlas Mountains attract occasional summer storms, but beyond their summits to the south the climate quickly approaches that of the Sahara.

The extreme south-western corner of Africa also experiences conditions akin to those of the Mediterranean as regards the temperature and rainfall regime. However, the area having a real summer drought is very limited and the south coast of the continent, with a very even rainfall, deserves to be classified as a warm variety of the temperate forested type of climate.

In the main, the natural vegetation reflects climate, varying from absolute desert to luxuriant moist forest. Although it depends mainly on the amount and distribution of the rainfall, altitude also exercises a control.

The equatorial climate corresponds with the distribution of the rain forest, which covers a large part of the Congo basin and a strip along the west coast from Sierra Leone to the mouth of the Congo River. In Dahomey, Togo and eastern Ghana, this strip of moist forest is interrupted by savanna.

The tropical climate corresponds with various forms of savanna, which cover an enormous area (over 40 per cent of the whole continent). All are characterized by the dominance of annual grasses, with trees occurring sporadically, either scattered or in clumps in the wetter areas, especially along watercourses. Corresponding with increasing rainfall is a sequence of steppe, grassland with scattered trees or shrubs, and dry deciduous forest with a substantial grass cover under and between the trees. Forest-savanna mosaic marks the transition to the moist forest. At high altitudes, savanna is replaced by upland grasslands and forests.

When one adds dry steppe and montane grasslands to the various types of savanna, the proportion of the surface of Africa which can support herbivores is really extraordinary. To the primitive bands of evolving men it offered an immense hunting ground, and to later food-producing communities vast grazing fields for their cattle.

With decreasing rainfall and a longer dry period, the savanna merges gradually into semi-desert and finally into absolute desert. Semi-desert vegetation leaves most of the soil bare. It consists of scattered woody plants or succulents which look all but dead for the greater part of the year; but after rain, the plants and grasses burst into new growth, hurrying through their life-cycle. This type of vegetation is found in an enormous area in the Sahara and the

Figure 5. Political map of Africa

Horn of Africa, with a large patch in northern Kenya. Absolute desert is confined to certain parts of the Sahara and to the coast of South West Africa, the Namib.

The Mediterranean vegetation of the Atlas lands and the Cape region share the characteristic of drought resistance. However, drought is not so pronounced at the Cape as in the Atlas and the flora of the Cape is therefore richer.

Climate and Vegetation in the Past
Many branches of the natural sciences co-operate in reconstructing the past climates of Africa during the Pleistocene, the Age of Man.

12

Geologists trace the past extension of sands. Mineralogists study the nature and surface texture of sand grains which provide evidence about the action of wind. The study of chemical alterations of fossil soils provides estimates of rainfall intensity. Fossil pollens tell the botanist about past vegetation. Remains of animals which are restricted to specific conditions indicate past climates. In some areas, rock paintings or engravings left by artists of several millennia ago depict a fauna which could not live there nowadays. Accumulations of pottery sherds in areas which are now desert bear witness to a settled way of life in the past.

Such accumulated evidence suggests that rainfall and temperature have changed significantly several times in Africa since the emergence of man. Rainfall may have fluctuated by as much as 40 per cent from its present mean, and temperature up to 6°C lower than the average today. As a result, the vegetation zones, together with their specific faunas, shifted and changed in size and degree of continuity.

During such periods of change, human communities, whose culture was adapted to their biotope, either had to move in order to keep in a similar environment, or adjust to new conditions. Migrating communities were brought into contact with others which had developed different techniques and ways of life, and they exchanged genes and cultural items. Like biological progressive evolution, cultural progress resulted from two broad factors: adaptation, and selection of elements from societies which had evolved in different ways.

Savanna and grasslands were the only types of environment to have been permanently occupied by man until somewhere between 100,000 and 50,000 years ago. They covered an immense area on the African plateau, without presenting any severe geographic barrier to migration.

The Sahara, which has severely hindered communication between North Africa and the rest of the continent in recent times, was entirely covered with a Mediterranean flora some 50,000 years ago. Places which are now absolute desert were inhabited by farmers and herdsmen no more than 4,000 years ago. Only around 3500–2500 BC did pastoralists leave the desiccating Sahara. In this desert, which today is dotted with oases supporting intensive irrigated agriculture, important routes of communication have persisted long after its desertion by pastoralists.

2

From Hominids to Men

The Branching of the Hominids

Some twenty million years ago in the Miocene, the Hominidae – that limb of the evolutionary tree whose only living offspring is man – branched off from the Hominoidea, the superfamily which includes both the Hominidae and the Pongidae, or apes.

Some palaeontologists are inclined to push this date further back. On the other hand, some geneticists claim that the affinities between man, the chimpanzee and the gorilla are so close that a much shorter time would suffice for acquiring the present differences in the genetical traits of the blood found in man and the African apes. The date proposed here cannot be pushed back very far: a recently discovered Primate, *Aegyptopithecus*, which lived in Egypt approximately twenty-nine million years ago, looks like being a possible common ancestor of the great apes and the hominids, but is more primitive than any known member of either line. Neither can the date be much more recent, since a Primate which lived some four-teen million years ago in East Africa and India, *Ramapithecus*, is generally considered to be a hominid.

The particularly tight affinities between man and the two African apes, the existence of an early hominid in East Africa, and the many discoveries in Africa of *Australopithecus* – a group of hominids which immediately preceded man – all speak for locating in Africa the whole sequence of transformations leading from the first hominids to man, despite the fact that some groups spread to Asia.

Whatever the exact date of the branching, comparative anatomy helps us to guess what the common ancestor of man and the African apes was like. Apes live in the forest. They move about in the trees by brachiating, that is, hanging from the boughs by the arms, with the trunk vertical. This mode of locomotion made the apes diverge morphologically from their quadrupedal ancestors. The upper limbs grew longer in comparison with the lower limbs. The body weight now bore more on the lower part of the vertebral column and on the pelvis; the lumbar vertebrae, which were reduced in number, became bulkier; the sacrum broadened out and the strengthened pelvis expanded laterally.

Figure 6. Evolutionary tree of the Hominoidea

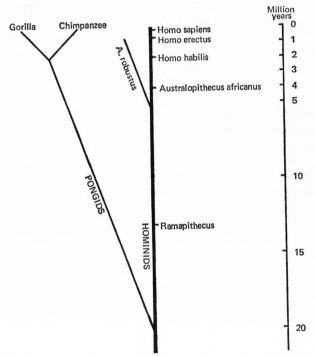

In his anatomy, modern man retains several traces of an ancestral brachiator stage. Relatively to the trunk, his upper limbs are as long as those of the chimpanzee and much longer than in quadrupedal monkeys. Like that of the apes, the human arm can move laterally as well as backwards and forwards, and the human forearm can rotate through nearly 180°, twice the capacity of rotation in

¹Much of this chapter is based on Campbell (1966) [26].

quadrupedal monkeys. Such characteristics of the upper limb are highly adaptive for survival in the trees. Also reminiscent of an arboreal way of life is the reflex of the human baby of grasping firmly any cylindrical object presented to his hand. The common ancestor of man and the African apes must have been, at least during part of its history, a tree-living brachiator.

Many characteristics which resulted from brachiation would later prove useful for hominid evolution. The strengthening of the lower part of the vertebral column is required for erect locomotion as well as for brachiation. The high rotating capacity of the forearm makes it easier to manipulate objects, as well as to swing from bough to bough. The shift of the main anterior support of the foot, from the level of the third toe in the quadrupedal monkeys to between the first and second toes in the large apes, brings it near to its human position, at the level of the first toe.

Of course the common ancestor did not look like a chimpanzee or a gorilla. The lineage which recently (a few million years ago) split into these two forms of apes specialized further in brachiation. A group of fossil primates of Miocene age, *Dryopithecus*, whose position on the tree is near to the base of the great apes' branch, resembled man in having a relatively short forearm and a straight femur. We may guess that the common ancestor was better able to brachiate than man, and to move along the ground in an erect posture better than the African apes. These walk semi-erect, on the soles of the feet and the knuckles, with the trunk oblique.

The prime distinction of the hominids, the character that made them diverge from the apes, is erect locomotion. Man is the only living being to walk perfectly erect, with the head positioned vertically above the feet. Very early on, man's ancestors acquired the gross anatomical transformations associated with erect walking; only slight improvements were made later.

These transformations concern a large part of the skeleton. In the hominids, the femur is long, straight and robust. The foot, which now bears the full weight of the body, is a sturdy arched buttress, with a strong big toe, in line with the others, which has largely lost its capacity of grasping. The pelvis has broadened out and has acquired the form of a basin: it now has to carry the weight of the viscera and has to provide a wider base for the insertion of the powerful muscles required for erect equilibrium and loco-motion. The vertebral column, further strengthened in its lower

Figure 7. Sagittal profiles of the skull vault of the chimpanzee, *Australopithecus africanus*, *Homo erectus* and *Homo sapiens*

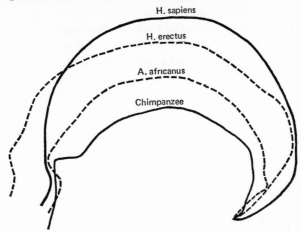

part, describes a series of compensating curves. During the process of evolution leading to man, the foramen magnum – the hole through which the brain passes into the spinal cord – migrates towards the centre of the base of the braincase. By the end of this process, in man, the head stands in equilibrium on the column. It no longer needs to be attached to the neck by powerful muscles and these, together with the ridges of the skull to which they are attached, became gradually weaker as man evolved.

Recession of the face under the braincase, a response to a diminished demand on the masticatory apparatus, is a characteristic trend of the Primates in general. The hominids extended it further and in man it became extreme, so that the area of least shrinkage appears to be the chin. The recession of the face in man is one of the factors which allowed the mechanical equilibrium of the head on the vertebral column.

The dentition of the hominids contrasts with that of the pongids in forming a rounded arch instead of being U-shaped as in the apes. The overlapping of the upper and lower canines, separated from the adjacent incisors by a gap, is characteristic of the pongids but not of the hominids. The canines were probably never so developed in the ancestors of man as they are in male chimpanzees and gorillas. The pongids have accentuated large canines and sexual dimorphism during the course of their separate evolution, but the abnormally strong development of the roots of the canines in man gives evidence of longer and sturdier canines in his ancestry.

Erect posture gave the hand complete freedom from any duty in locomotion; henceforward it would be used only for grasping, handling and carrying objects. These functions of the hand were already highly developed in the ancestral primates, but their anatomical basis was further refined in the human lineage. The widest freedom of movement of the thumb is achieved in man.

The brain, of course, is much more developed in man than in the apes, but this is not an early distinction of the hominids. Erect walking was the basic development which made them diverge from the pongids (enlargement of the brain came later). Such a major change can result only from strong new selective forces, triggered off by a marked modification of the environment. Most probably the impetus was due to the fact that our ancestors were forced to abandon their arboreal way of life and to adapt to the savanna. This must have happened only in areas where the forest was diminishing in response to climatic fluctuations, or even disappearing completely during the drier phases – not in the central equatorial forest, but in the peripheral forest-savanna mosaic. The complete disappearance of the patches of forest in which they lived, or strong population pressure in a shrinking forested habitat, pushed bands of hominoids – the stem ancestral to both hominids and pongids – into the savanna. Many of them probably died out, but the fact that we exist today proves that some successfully met the challenge.

The most immediate challenge to survival was concerned with food. The forest abounds in relatively rich vegetable food on which the pongids base their diet: fruits, seeds, sprouts and leaves. The edible vegetable resources of the savanna are quite different and only some of them could be digested by our ancestors, mainly Graminaceae and roots. The emergent hominids had to feed on these; but at least some started to exploit regularly that nutriment in which the savanna is much richer than the forest: meat. They became omnivorous (at all stages in the evolution of the hominids, vegetable food remained an important item of their diet).

Forest primates do not disdain animal food when they find an opportunity to get hold of it. Occasionally they eat insects and eggs, and some species will even eat lizards, frogs and young birds. But they lack the means which allow the carnivores to tackle bigger animals: the speed, the claws and the fangs. In any case, the forest provides enough good vegetable food to cover their needs.

In the savanna, the survival of vegetarian hominoids was most hazardous. Two groups apparently adapted themselves to such a diet: *Gigantopithecus* of India and China, an ape which is probably descended from *Dryopithecus indicus*, and the robust variety of *Australopithecus*, a hominid. Both died out, while omnivorous hominids evolved into that extraordinary biological success, modern man.

At first, the meat in the diet of this group probably consisted only of small prey that could be captured by hand; perhaps scavenging was also a source of animal protein. At a time still unknown with any precision, hunting began. It might have started very early, since chimpanzees living in a savanna/forest mosaic environment have been observed to hunt and kill fairly large animals for food. [127]

The Transition to Man: Why?

The response to the selective pressure in favour of hunting resulted from those special attributes of the newcomers to the savanna: tapering fingers, associated with acute vision in the recording of the outer world; social organization – the mutual interests of members of the same band; and the importance of an acquired component in their behaviour: learning. (Young hominids are apt to learn much by imitating their elders and exploring their physical and social environment by playing, an activity devoid of any immediate purpose.)

Possibly the pressure in favour of hunting was a factor of the shift towards erect locomotion which, on the ground, is more efficient than the semi-erect posture of the apes. It allows its possessor to observe possible prey and predators above the high grass cover and also, it has been argued, makes it possible to carry heavy haunches of meat over long distances. Most of all, probably, the pressure acted strongly towards complete freedom of the hand, which can be realized only by erect posture.

Physically, primitive hominids were poorly endowed for hunting. They could hardly succeed individually and success could be achieved only by collective effort. The survival of primates in the savanna, where there are few high trees in which to sleep safely or to serve as refuges, required co-operation in defence against big carnivores. In hunting, co-operation had to be extended to the strategy of attack, whereas non-human primates usually collect their food individually. Surely, the need pressing the hominids to shift towards regular co-operation in obtaining meat strongly stimulated evolution in both the genetical and cultural fields. All genotypes which induced a more social behaviour were favoured by selection and the pool of acquired behaviour, transmitted by imitation, was rapidly enriched by the adoption of those individual discoveries which the community found useful. Perhaps the reduction of the canines resulted (at least partly) from this need for tighter social cohesion: in the apes, strong canines and their sexual dimorphism are associated with a marked social, and sexual hierarchy.

Besides their social co-operation, the hominids could rely for survival on their free hands, their acute vision, and their brain (a well-developed one, although at first not more so than that of a pongid). By themselves, these were not very efficient weapons. But the hand–eye–brain complex of the hominids initiated a new way of responding to the challenge for survival. Through apparently purposeless play, the proto-hominids had already acquired the habit of handling objects. They thus came to discover the properties of hardness and sharpness of natural objects, to explore their possible use, and to benefit from this acquired experience in becoming more efficient in the exploitation of their biotope. Objects selected by experience would be used as rudimentary tools or weapons.

Through multiple trials and observations made during their leisure time, progressive hominids discovered how to improve hard natural objects (like pebbles) by striking them against another hard material, in order to give them a fresh sharp edge or a more functional shape. Once the greater efficiency of such modified objects had been recognized by the community, their manufacture became a regular activity of at least some of its members.

This behaviour – the repeated manufacture of preconceived artifacts, which soon became the specific solution of the hominids to the challenge for survival – is such a unique innovation that it is now widely accepted by anthropologists as the hallmark of man. A chimpanzee will sometimes manufacture a very simple tool, but this activity will be occasional rather than regular; the survival of the species is not based on such behaviour, which does not tend to progress with time.

Ever since the emergence of the human line, discovery and communication between members were vital necessities. Communication was involved in the trial of individual discoveries by the community, followed by the adoption of the beneficial ones and the transmission of culture from one generation to the next. These needs exerted a strong selective pressure in favour of everything in the genome that could enhance such processes. Like collective hunting, communication of discoveries requires social cohesion and both needs concurred in inducing genetic evolution towards tighter socialization. This concerned not only the endogamic bands, but also the species as a whole. Since remote times, assimilation of cultural items developed by other communities has played an important role in the progress of any culture; cultural isolation is highly dangerous for any human society and usually leads to backwardness. The selective pressure in favour of socialization acted against any genetic factor that could promote hostility between communities.

Selection was no less active in increasing intellectual endowment, lengthening the period of high educability, and improving the biological basis of communication. In this field the human line developed a major innovation: speech. Anatomically, this required relatively minor modifications of the larynx and pharynx and the development of speech centres in the cerebral cortex.

We do not know when speech appeared, but we may state that a pressure in favour of it was present since the most incipient stages of the human line. Co-ordination of hunters, education and adoption of discoveries soon called for more elaborate means of communication than the vocalizations and mimicry used by non-human Primates.

Language is closely related to conceptual thought. Both require a highly developed brain, especially in the cortex. This need was responsible for a tremendous increase in brain volume. However, the brain of a modern man, although nearly three times as big as that of a chimpanzee, shows no new structure: it is only superior in overall size and particularly in some areas of the cortex.

The Transition to Man: How?

Up to now, only one genus of extinct hominids is represented by a collection of fossil bones large enough to give a fair idea of the skeletal anatomy: the genus *Australopithecus*. Its earliest known members were discovered in the Omo valley, in southern Ethiopia, in deposits between three and four million years old; the latest known specimen lived in Tanzania some 700,000 years ago, at a time when man was already present in the area.

Remains of hominids from the period between the time of their branching off from the ancestral stock and the appearance of *Australopithecus* are very scarce. They consist of teeth and parts of the jaws of *Ramapithecus*, a genus found in the Siwalik Hills in India and at Fort Ternan in Kenya. When the late Dr Louis Leakey described the first African specimen, he called it *Kenya-apithecus wickeri*. Professor Elwyn Simons later produced evidence to show that it belonged to the same genus as the previously discovered Indian *Ramapithecus*; according to the rules of zoological nomenclature, this generic name should therefore be given to the African fossil. The African *Ramapithecus* lived approximately fourteen million years ago, a date somewhat earlier than the presumed age of the deposits containing its Indian relative.

We do not know if *Ramapithecus* walked erect: teeth and jaws have little to tell about posture. To most palaeontologists, the dentition of *Ramapithecus* looks typically hominid and they therefore assume that its possessors walked erect.

Recently at Fort Ternan, Leakey found a naturally flaked pebble in a layer contemporary with *Ramapithecus*. Apparently it had been brought to the site, since there is no similar rock in the vicinity. Leakey hypothesized that a *Ramapithecus* had picked it up and used it. Moreover, he suspected that broken bones of other species also present in the layer might represent remains of the meals of *Ramapithecus*. The evidence for such hypotheses is very tenuous, but they imply a tool-using hominid hunter or scavenger, conforming to the behavioural stage that we have supposed to precede the human.

We are on much surer ground when discussing the australopiths (let us use this contraction which avoids long Latin names). This group is now represented in the collections not only by a number of well-preserved skulls and jaws, but also by bones from all parts of the skeleton.

There is no doubt that the australopiths walked erect: the foramen magnum is horizontal, the vertebral column shows the characteristic compensating curves, the lumbar vertebrae are strong, the pelvis, limbs and extremities are nearly human in their

Figure 8. Localities of the sites mentioned in Chapters 2 and 3

general adaptation to erect locomotion, although they differ from man's in many details. The australopiths are near to man also in their dentition; the teeth form a parabolic arch and show no gap (diastema) between incisors and canines, which are of moderate size.

Up to now, all the remains of this group have come from sub-Saharan Africa, except for a fragment of jaw found at San Giran, Java, first named *Meganthropus palaeojavanicus* by the late Professor Weidenreich, but considered by Professor J. T. Robinson to be an australopith. This specimen, which is late compared with the antiquity of the group in Africa, is the only evidence for the spread of australopiths outside sub-Saharan Africa. The claims that fossils found at Ubeidiya, in Israel, and in the now desertic region of Lake Chad (a specimen named *Tchadanthropus uxoris* by its discoverer, Professor Y. Coppens), might belong to the australopiths have been discarded. Sub-Saharan Africa was evidently the cradle of this group.

The first discovery of an australopith was recorded in 1925, when Professor Raymond Dart described the skull of a child from Taung, Botswana. He named it *Australopithecus africanus*. At the time, most palaeontologists were sceptical about his contention that the new fossil was much nearer to man than any Primate ever found. In his country, South Africa, the late Dr Robert Broom backed Dart's interpretation and encouraged the search for more fossils of this type. Soon the Transvaal started to produce a number of specimens. Most of them came from ancient caves being worked for limestone; the fossils were embedded in a hard breccia left aside by the limeworks and were brought to light by dynamite, followed by patient disencrusting by specialists.

The names of these sites, all in the Transvaal, are now familiar to palaeontologists: Sterkfontein, Kromdraai, Swartkrans and Makapansgat. The study of the many fossils akin to the Taung specimen that were recovered from them confirmed Dart's interpretation and today nobody doubts that the australopiths are the nearest to man among the Primates.

Ten years ago the focus of interest in australopith studies moved from the Transvaal to Tanzania. At Olduvai Gorge, in the Serengeti Plains, the excavations conducted by Leakey and his family produced a number of spectacular discoveries which threw light not only on the significance of the australopiths, but also on the coming of man.

While the Transvaal and Olduvai surely have an immense potential for important discoveries, the focus of interest has shifted once again in recent years: first to the Omo valley, north of Lake Rudolf in southern Ethiopia; and even more recently to sites east of Lake Rudolf in Kenya. Not only has the Omo region produced a number of remains of australopiths, but also the time-span covered by its Pleistocene deposits extends into a much more remote past than the oldest bed at Olduvai. Bed I at Olduvai has been dated to 1,800,000 years, while the Omo sequence starts approximately four million years ago. Some of the numerous finds of hominids east of Lake

Rudolf are also older than those of Olduvai Bed I, having been dated to more than 2.6 million years.

Absolute dating in these sites is made possible by the nature of their sediments; in each case, lake or river deposits alternate with tuffs. This volcanic material can be dated by the potassium-argon method, based on radioactive decay. Temporary recession of the lakes created fresh soils, on which the hominids lived and left their bones and traces of their activities. These habitation surfaces were later covered by other deposits and their possible date is limited by the age of the tuffs between which they are sandwiched.

As usual, Latin names flourished in the first descriptions of the fossil remains. Besides the original *A. africanus*, four other names were bestowed on the Transvaal specimens. The two forms present in Bed I at Olduvai were called *'Zinjanthropus' boisei* and *Homo habilis*. The first mandible discovered in the Omo beds got the label *Paraustralopithecus aethiopicus*. By now, most palaeontologists agree in seeing only one major subdivision in this material: a gracile and a robust form, making two species. In this classification, the Taung fossil belongs to the gracile form and its name *Australopithecus africanus*, which has priority, also covers the former *'Plesianthropus'* from the Transvaal and probably *Homo habilis* of Olduvai Bed I. The robust form, *A. robustus*, includes the former *'Paranthropus'* of South Africa and *'Zinjanthropus'*, also possibly the Javanese *Meganthropus*.

The two forms, or species, of australopiths differed in size, the gracile one being about 1.25 m tall and the robust one about 1.55 m. However, their main anatomical distinction lies in the dentition. That of *A. africanus* is nearer to the human, while the robust form stands further apart in its powerful molars, its molar-like premolars, and its small canines which are even more reduced than in man.

The massive dentition of *A. robustus* was associated with powerful masticatory muscles: their area of insertion on the skull is strongly corrugated. In some individuals the temporal muscles were so massive that they met on the top of the skull, where a sagittal crest developed in response to the need for a larger area of insertion, as is also the case in some male gorillas.

The skull, although generally similar in the two forms, is also nearer to the human in the gracile australopith than in the robust one. The skull of *A. africanus* shows a distinct forehead; 61 per cent of its dome rises above the orbits, a value which comes near to the lower end of the range in modern man (between 64 and 77 per cent). The corresponding value in *A. robustus* is 50 per cent, only slightly higher than the average in the chimpanzee, 47 per cent.

Following Robinson's hypothesis, palaeontologists today generally agree that the difference in face and skull between the two forms of australopiths reflects differences in diet and behaviour. The very great similarity in dentition and skull structure between the gracile form and man suggests that, like man, *A. africanus* was an omnivore. The relatively large anterior teeth of the gracile australopith were needed for meat-eating until tool-making had reached a fairly advanced level, and until fire came into use. The dentition of *A. robustus*, on the other hand, is adapted to crushing and grinding, strongly suggesting a vegetarian diet. The massiveness of the whole masticatory system and the greater body size are also consistent with this supposition.

The anatomical features, as well as the inferred behavioural characteristics, all point to *A. africanus* as a possible ancestor of man, with *A. robustus* an evolutionary sideline. The two forms could co-exist because they occupied different ecological niches. Both are present at sites east and north of Lake Rudolf, and in the Omo beds australopiths have been traced back to about 3,300,000 years. A mandible of *A. robustus* from Peninj, west of Lake Natron in Tanzania, is a powerful argument in favour of a strong ecological distinction between the two forms: about 700,000 years old, this specimen shows that the robust form could survive long after the emergence of man, which would be hardly conceivable in the case of direct competition.

A. africanus being anatomically so near to man, on which criteria are we to base the boundary between the two? The major anatomical difference concerns the development of the brain: cranial capacity varies around 500 cc in *A. africanus*, around 1,300 cc in modern man. The gap to be filled is large; but, since evolution proceeds in a continuous way, it is impossible to fix a critical value below which a fossil would be 'animal' and above which it would be 'human', especially since, in the past as now, the members of every population varied considerably in brain size. The field in which evolution, in spite of being continuous, produced something strikingly new was not in anatomy, but behaviour. As already stated, the hallmark of man is the regular manufacture of preconceived tools, attesting the existence of a cultural tradition. Therefore, a crucial question in defining the status of *A. africanus* is 'was he a tool-maker?'

No clear answer to this question has come from South Africa, where there is no clear situation in which *A. africanus* is associated with an undoubted stone industry. Stone tools are present in some breccias, but not in those containing numerous bones of *A. africanus*. The deposits in which the tools occur, or deposits of presumably similar age at a neighbouring site, also contain bones of a more advanced hominid. This was first named '*Telanthropus*', but was later considered to be *Homo erectus*, a stage of human evolution with a long-established tradition of tool-making behind it. It now seems possible that this hominid is similar to those known as *Homo habilis* in Bed II at Olduvai (see p. 28).

At Makapansgat, the remains of *A. africanus* are associated with a large number of bones of other species. Dart is convinced that some of the horns, mandibles, and whole or fractured long bones of large animals were used as tools or weapons by *A. africanus*, to whom he attributes an 'osteodontokeratic' culture. However, his claims are not found convincing by all.

The evidence from Olduvai, though not absolutely certain, is much clearer. The oldest bed, Bed I, contains the Oldowan industry, which consists of pebbles from which a few flakes have been removed in order to give them a sharp edge. Flakes are also worked and these simple tools of various sizes and forms may be grouped into a few functional classes.

At a site near the base of Bed I, where the skull of a robust australopith was found (see below), careful excavation by the Leakeys revealed an occupation floor about 1,700,000 years old. An oval area about seven metres wide was scattered with stone flakes and small tools, while blocks of unworked stone predominated in the peripheral area. Animal bones were numerous within the central oval, mostly of small species like rodents, amphibians and birds, or of younger specimens of larger mammals whose long bones had been broken, presumably in order to extract and eat the marrow.

Without any doubt a tool-making hunter, hence a man, had lived there. His stone industry is present at Olduvai throughout the whole of Bed I and, in developed form, in the lower part of Bed II. During the time-span represented by these sediments, nearly a million years, the Oldowan industry changed little. One line of evidence for cultural progress, however, is that the proportion of bones from large, mature animals increases with time, an indication of more efficient hunting.

Had a single hominid species been found in Bed I, there would have been little hesitation in attributing the Oldowan industry to him. This was indeed the situation in 1959, when Dr Mary Leakey discovered the skull of an australopith in Bed I. The Leakeys named him *Zinjanthropus boisei* (from *Zinj*, the ancient name given by the Arabs to East Africa) and considered him to be the maker of the stone tools. But less than a year later they discovered a different fossil hominid from a slightly older level which was subsequently named *Homo habilis*. Further discoveries showed that the two species co-existed throughout the time covered by the Oldowan.

This reopened the question of who was the maker of this industry, the oldest known human culture: '*Zinjanthropus*', *Homo habilis*, or both? Most palaeontologists are now convinced that it was the second species, on the basis of anatomical characters. '*Zinjanthropus*' belongs to the line of robust australopiths and is now assigned to *A. robustus*, while the affinities of *Homo habilis* are more with the gracile australopith, *A. africanus*. If the inference from the dentition is correct, the first was a vegetarian, the second an omnivore, and hunting can be attributed only to the second. Morphologically, as already pointed out, *A. africanus* resembles modern man more than *A. robustus*. This resemblance is even more striking in *Homo habilis*; while falling within the range of variations of *A. africanus* for most characters, he stands a good deal nearer to our species than the average of this group in several features which strongly differentiate modern man. For example, his cranial capacity amounts to 639 cc, according to Professor P. V. Tobias [209]. Anatomically, therefore, *Homo habilis* may be seen as an advanced australopith, a member of the line which was evolving into man. This status makes him by far the most valid candidate to the paternity of the Oldowan industry, which gives evidence of a decidedly human behaviour.

Is all this enough for classifying *H. habilis* within the genus *Homo*, which includes modern man? Leakey, Tobias and Napier answered positively when they gave him this name. Other specialists believe that there is no good reason for removing him from the species *A. africanus*. Such differences of opinion between taxonomists are not exceptional: evolution is a continuous process, and the cutting up into discrete species and genera for the purpose of classification necessarily makes the status of transitional forms ambiguous.

The industry present in the deepest layers of Olduvai, approximately 1,800,000 years old, is already too elaborate to be at the roots of culture. It surely goes back into a remote past, judging by the very slow rate of its progress. This deduction makes the excavations in the Omo valley especially interesting in further unravelling the story of incipient mankind. In this area, layers much older than Bed I at Olduvai contain gracile as well as robust australopiths. Recently, Dr Jean Chavaillon [32] described what he interprets as a living site from Omo Bed E, which is sandwiched between two tuffs dated two million and two and a half million years respectively. It contained a worked pebble of Oldowan type, broken pebbles, and a fragment of worked bone. No doubt the Omo valley will be the scene of major discoveries in the future.

Still more recent evidence suggests that the whole area of Lake Rudolf, into which the Omo River flows southward, is of immense potential interest for the study of the beginnings of man. In the Koobi Fora area, east of the lake in Kenya, excavation of layers between one and 2.61 million years old has unearthed a number of flakes and choppers whose manufacturing technique is at least as elaborate as those of Bed I at Olduvai, according to Dr Mary Leakey. From this site and from Ileret, about thirty miles farther north, numerous hominid specimens have been recovered, including well-preserved crania. Preliminary study by Richard Leakey – of the second generation of the extraordinarily successful discoverers in this family – shows that one type is similar to the robust australopith of Olduvai (*A. robustus boisei*), while others are very early representatives of the genus *Homo*. A relatively large-brained skull, known so far simply by its number, 1470, was found in August 1972 and has been dated to more than 2.6 million years.[1]

[1]LEAKEY, R. E. 1973. 'Skull 1470'. *National Geographic* **143**: 819–29.

3

From the First Men to African *Homo Sapiens*[1]

Homo habilis

From the time of the first tool-makers up to the appearance of *Homo sapiens*, the two fields of human evolution, the cultural and the physical, have interacted in a mutual feedback. As already mentioned, the survival of incipient mankind relied on culture and this strongly favoured any genetical change that improved the capacity for communication, co-operation, learning and invention; and the most spectacular response was the enlargement of the brain, especially the cortex, which plays a prominent part in intellectual processes.

The head of modern man differs strikingly from that of his predecessors not only in its much higher braincase, but also in the greatly reduced face, produced by a diminishing demand on the chewing mechanism. As a result of softer food, the dentition, the teeth-bearing bones and the brow ridge (a bony bar above the orbits which serves as an upper buttress to the muscles concerned with chewing) all diminished in size. Development of the braincase, especially in the frontal and lateral regions, and recession of the face finally resulted in a rounded head. Perched in quasi-equilibrium on the vertebral column, it required but little strength in the muscles of the back of the neck to keep it straight. Eventually, the place of insertion of these muscles on the back of the skull was situated lower down and became less rugged.

Palaeontologists have subdivided the continuous evolution from first men to modern men into grades, which inevitably makes some specimens difficult to classify. If we accept the advanced australo-

[1]Much of this chapter is based on Clark (1970) [34].

pith present in Bed I at Olduvai as human, it represents the first grade, *Homo habilis*. Up to now, he has been found only in Africa south of the Sahara, where his industry is widespread in the African savanna. An Oldowan-like industry is present in North Africa where, as at Olduvai, it predates the more evolved lower Acheulian industry, but no hominid remains have been found associated with it. All known or suspected members of this first grade occupied a semi-arid environment of park-savanna and grasslands, with plenty of permanent water and large quantities of game for food.

Homo erectus

The second grade, which many specialists consider to be the first undoubtedly human stage on anatomical grounds, is *Homo erectus*. He lived in Africa, in Asia (where his remains have been found in Java and in China), and most probably in Europe.

For this evolutionary step, Olduvai is again unique in providing indications about the transitional stage, represented in Bed II. It contains various stages of the Acheulian industry, the earliest

Figure 9. Oldowan tools from Bed I, Olduvai

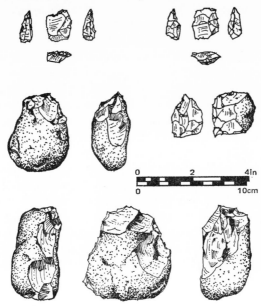

Figure 10. Upper Acheulian tools from Kalambo Falls, Zambia

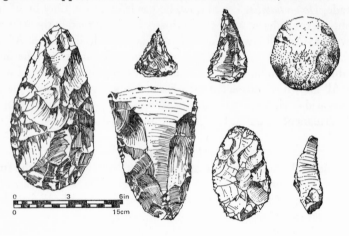

of which were contemporaneous with the developed Oldowan [129].

All the basic technological processes of the Palaeolithic – cutting, smashing, chopping, scraping and piercing tools – seem to be already represented in the tool kit of the Oldowan; this equipment was suitable for collecting vegetable food as well as for preparing meat. A digging stick, pointed by means of a stone chopper, could greatly increase the variety as well as the quantity of vegetable food by unearthing roots and bulbs, which could then be rendered more palatable by being softened or pulped by bashing between two stones. This simple stone equipment would also have been effective for breaking long bones to get at the marrow, and the flakes would have greatly facilitated skinning and scraping meat from bones. What occurred later was merely a series of modifications in the direction of more specialized and more refined tools to do the job. The most characteristic tool that the Acheulians added to the Oldowan assemblage was the handaxe, or biface. These were accompanied by other large tools such as choppers, cleavers and polyhedral stones, as well as a number of small tools.

It would be inconceivable that such cultural continuity, based on transmission by education from one generation to the next, should not be associated also with continuity in biological evolution. A good specimen of *Homo erectus*, dated at roughly 500,000 years, came from about half way up in Bed II. Anatomically, there is quite a step from *Australopithecus* to *Homo erectus*, but extensive excavation in the lower part of Bed II provided teeth and skull fragments of an intermediary being, thus partly filling the gap between the two grades. At first provisionally described as a more evolved form of *Homo habilis*, it may perhaps be regarded as an early and primitive member of *Homo erectus*. Its date may be approximately 900,000 years and the accompanying industries are said to be 'indeterminate' [129].

As already mentioned, the Swartkrans cave in the Transvaal has produced a more advanced hominid than *Australopithecus*. Very recently, a piece of bone from the same site among the collections in the Pretoria Museum was found to fit perfectly with the fragment already described. The more complete piece reinforces the diagnosis of *Homo*, but the authors hesitate to add *erectus* to the generic name. Perhaps this specimen is similar in status to those in the lower part of Bed II at Olduvai. As at Olduvai, the Swartkrans deposits contain a developed Oldowan assemblage with a few crude bifaces and heavy duty picks.

Fossils found at Ternifine in Algeria (three mandibles and a parietal bone), first named *Atlanthropus*, undoubtedly belong to *Homo erectus*. They are associated with an early Acheulian industry, tentatively dated around 350,000 years. Fossils from several places in Morocco (Sidi-abd-er-Rhaman, Rabat and Temara) are assigned to the same grade by most authors, although some would rather classify them with Neandertal man [64].

Compared with modern man, *Homo erectus* had a smaller brain (the mean cranial capacity was near to 1,000 cc). He had heavy brow ridges, his forehead was sloping, his skull was greatly constricted behind the brows, and his jaws were massive. Bigger-brained than *Australopithecus*, he was also taller and was a better walker and runner; the few bones of his legs to have been recovered are within the range of variation of modern man.

In early Acheulian times, the occupation sites were still close to water, along the edges of lakes and rivers. Remains of large animals are associated with the artifacts, including elephants, rhinoceroses, hippopotami and large antelopes, as well as smaller animals. Evidently *Homo erectus* was well organized for group hunting.

From the smaller development of the brain compared with modern man, especially in the frontal and parietal areas, one may deduce that his capacity for thinking was lower. We have no direct evidence that he could speak; however, the degree of complexity of communication between individuals implied by the successful collective hunting of big game, as well as by the teaching and learning of already elaborate techniques of tool-making, makes it appear probable that he had developed a language. *Homo erectus* had learnt the use of fire some 400,000 years ago in China, but so far in Africa traces of its use are much more recent (at the end of Acheulian times).

Homo sapiens

The third grade of the human lineage recognized by modern palaeontologists is the one to which we belong, *Homo sapiens*. Anatomically, the evolution from *Homo erectus* to *sapiens* concerned mainly the enlargement and rounding of the braincase and the reduction in size of the dentition, together with its supporting facial architecture and related parts of the skull like the brow ridges. The area and ruggedness of the place of insertion of the nuchal musculature in the occipital region diminished at the same time.

The braincase and the face did not evolve at the same pace; modern cranial capacity was attained before the reduction of the face. Such a stage was formerly given the rank of a species, *Homo neandertalensis*, or Neandertal Man, though nowadays most specialists consider him to be a subspecies of *Homo sapiens*.

This former classificatory distinction was mainly due to the fact that the first specimens from Western Europe were of the 'extreme' type. Dating from about 50,000 years ago, they had retained dentitions and faces not far removed from *Homo erectus*, although their braincase was fully modern in size. As a group, they showed little variation. Apparently they were replaced suddenly by populations of nearly modern aspect. It is hard to imagine this group of Neandertal men as possible ancestors of modern man and they were considered by many to be a sideline in human evolution.

Later, a number of discoveries in the Near East (Tabūn and Skhūl in Israel), Middle East (Shanidar in Iraq), and North Africa (Jebel Irhoud in Morocco) showed that less extreme Neandertaloids had lived in these areas. Unlike the homogeneous West European group, they display great diversity, combining in various ways features characteristic of the 'classic' Neandertals of Western

Europe with modern-looking features. Most authors now see the populations to which such individuals belonged, especially the Skhūl population, as transitional to modern man.

In Africa far south of the Mediterranean, several skulls of a rather extreme form of Neandertaloid have been found. This group is often called the Rhodesioids, from the name given to the first to be discovered. It was found in 1921 during the mining of lead and zinc ores in the Broken Hill cave in Zambia. First labelled *Homo rhodesiensis*, his status was later lowered to that of a subspecies, *Homo sapiens rhodesiensis*, and some see him as just a southern variant of Neandertal Man. This skull shows the most strongly developed brow ridges ever seen in man. Its walls are extremely thick, the forehead is receding, and the face is very long. A very similar skull was found at Saldanha, north of Cape Town. A skull from deposits at the north-eastern end of Lake Eyasi in Tanzania, reconstructed from a large number of fragments, is also grouped with the Broken Hill and Saldanha Rhodesioids.

The Rhodesioids were more or less contemporary with the extreme or classic Neandertalers of Western Europe, although they may have persisted until more recent times. Their industry belongs to cultural stages which are later than the Acheulian sequence – the Fauresmith and Sangoan. Also post-Acheulian is the Levalloiso-Mousterian industry associated with the Jebel Irhoud Neandertaloid in Morocco.

In time and cultural development, there is a large gap between the two undoubted specimens of African *Homo erectus* (that of upper Bed II at Olduvai, dated at about 500,000 years, and that of Ternifine, dated at about 350,000 years, both associated with early Acheulian industries) and that of the African Neandertaloids or Rhodesioids. In Europe there is only one well-preserved skull, dating from between 100,000 and 200,000 years ago, which partly fills this gap: the Steinheim skull. By its combination of archaic and advanced characters, it may be considered transitional between *Homo erectus* and the Neandertaloid stage leading to modern man.

Very recently in the Omo valley, which had already revealed such crucial evidence about the earliest phase of hominization, equally spectacular discoveries have been made about the transition to *Homo sapiens*. In a layer called Member I of the Kibish Formation, two skulls of late Pleistocene age (probably around

100,000 years old) were found. Although roughly contemporaneous, they differ markedly from each other. Both combine archaic and advanced features and, according to Dr Michael Day who described them, they belong to the *Homo sapiens* grade. In many features, he says, the skull known as Omo II resembles Solo Man (a Javanese form of Neandertaloid rather similar to the Rhodesioids) and, less markedly, it resembles the Rhodesioid from Broken Hill. Omo I looks more modern; it shows similarities with the Skhūl group, which is transitional between the Neandertaloids and modern man. Apparently in Africa as in Europe, as early as 100,000 years ago, there were populations whose very varied gene pool was able to give rise to both modern man and the extreme Neandertaloids (the classic Neandertal Man in Western Europe, and the Rhodesioids in sub-Saharan Africa).

By the time of the early *sapiens* of Omo, the cultural stage was late Acheulian. This culture showed little regional variation and its tool kit was still relatively restricted and unspecialized. Compared to the Oldowan kit, the two most typical Acheulian tools, the hand-axe and the cleaver, seem to be connected with the better exploitation of the meat supply provided by large animals. The settlements of the Acheulians were still tied to sites immediately adjacent to water, and the uniformity of their culture throughout the continent seems to reflect their restriction to one main type of environment – savanna and grasslands. If climatic change altered their surroundings, evidently they did not adapt to the new conditions, but moved with the biotope. Acheulian assemblages have been found in the peripheral areas of the moist forest and in the desert, but in Acheulian times these areas were in savanna country: the environment has changed since.

The first evidence for the use of fire in Africa dates from the latest stages of the Acheulian, before a climatic change to cooler and wetter conditions.

This change, which marks the beginning of the Upper Pleistocene, was accompanied by considerable cultural evolution and diversification. This resulted from adaptation to different types of environment, including the moist forest which had never previously been occupied.

Climatic change, the use of fire, and the attainment of a fully modern cranial capacity are probably the factors whose combined effects precipitated cultural evolution during this period. The same factors may also explain why, about this time, man began to make permanent use of caves and rock shelters as regular places for habitation, and also extended his occupation sites to places at some distance from water.

Between 60,000 and 40,000 years ago, three broad cultural traditions developed in Africa. North of the Sahara was the Mousterian or Levalloiso-Mousterian, an industry of light flake tools, associated with the local Neandertaloids. In the grasslands and dry savannas of the south and east of the continent was the Fauresmith culture, a continuation of the Acheulian handaxe tradition which persisted in the unchanged ecological conditions of these areas. The third tradition was the Sangoan, a culture which included many heavy duty tools like picks and choppers, as well as light duty tools with denticulated edges, many of which would have been suitable for woodworking; this culture developed in the marginal zones of the equatorial forest. This cultural stage, the Early Middle Stone Age, is associated with the Rhodesioids from Broken Hill and Eyasi (the Sangoan) and from Saldanha (the Fauresmith).

Later in the Upper Pleistocene, perhaps from about 35,000 to

Figure 11. Sangoan/Lower Lupemban tools from the Congo Basin

Figure 12. Middle Stone Age tools from the Orange River

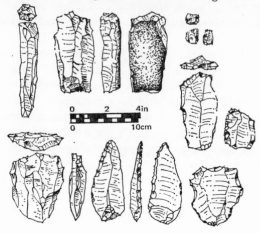

12,000 years ago, a variety of specialized regional forms developed from the three earlier complexes. The Levalloiso-Mousterian produced the Aterian, characterized by tanged points. The Fauresmith was followed by the Stillbay, with leaf-shaped points; and the Sangoan evolved into the Lupemban, which showed a continued emphasis on woodworking tools.

A skull from Singa beside the Blue Nile is associated with a fairly early phase of the Middle Stone Age. It was originally regarded as showing affinities with the Bushmen, but re-examination by Don Brothwell of the British Museum (Natural History) suggests that it is rather akin to the Rhodesioids.

The number of Middle Stone Age sites in Africa is enormous. During the cooler and wetter climate of the Later Pleistocene, man could occupy regions that today are among some of the most inhospitable on the continent. Within the three broad cultural divisions already mentioned, a considerable degree of differentiation existed. The equipment shows a much larger range of specialized stone tools than that of previous cultures. The relative importance of one form of tool with respect to others varies from place to place. This, according to Professor J. Desmond Clark, results from the interaction of cultural traditions and inertia in cultural evolution, whereas ecology encouraged change by selecting for greater efficiency. He suggests that the greater degree of specialization in the material culture at this time is connected with greater specialization in the diet.

No human remains worth studying have been found associated with either the Aterian or Lupemban and we know little about the physical status of African man during the Middle Stone Age except that, in a few places, Rhodesioids were the makers of an early phase of this cultural stage. This does not exclude the possibility that more advanced human beings were present in Africa by that time. The advanced aspect of some features of the Omo I skull, which belongs to a considerably earlier period, makes it even probable. Possibly, the remains from Kanjera in western Kenya represent such early forms of the last stage of human evolution, *Homo sapiens sapiens*, but unfortunately their dating and associations are still uncertain.

At Kanjera, on the Kavirondo Gulf of Lake Victoria, Leakey found fragments of four human skulls, some on the surface, others in the ancient lake beds. Apparently the fragments found in situ were associated with a late Acheulian industry. The uncertainty about their age comes from the fact that they consist of broken and scattered material that had been washed into the lake from the surrounding land in Late Pleistocene times. However, uranium tests speak in favour of their association with the extinct fauna.

Two crania could be partly reconstructed. Although their walls are very thick, their outline looks modern and the brow ridges are very poorly developed. Brothwell suggests that these remains might represent a basal stock ancestral to the Negroes as well as to the Khoisan people (Bushmen and Hottentots).

An early date has also been assigned to the Florisbad fragments, which consist of parts of the face and skull vault of an adult. They were found in the deposits of a mineral spring, north of Bloemfontein in the Orange Free State, embedded in layers about 40,000 years old according to radiocarbon dating. However, it has been suggested [37] that this fossil may be much more recent and might have dropped down the eye of the spring as late as 7,000 to 5,000 years ago. The first reconstruction by Professor Dreyer, he admits, was influenced by the supposed great antiquity of the skull and it appeared to resemble one of the Rhodesioids. According to Professor Carleton Coon, the fragments patently belong to an ancestral Bushman. Brothwell [20] has proposed a middle view: Florisbad man, possibly like other fossils discovered in South Africa, might have belonged to a population resulting from the mixture of ancestral Bushmen and Rhodesioids (who might have persisted late in the southern part of the continent). In any case, the Floris- bad skull could be used as evidence of an early form of *Homo sapiens sapiens* only if both the dating is correct and if a modern component in his gene pool really exists, which seems improbable.

For reconstructing the evolutionary history of the living popula- tions of South Africa, the existing skeletal material allows this to be done only for the Khoisan peoples – and even here some aspects remain hypothetical. Brothwell has proposed the following sequence. A large Khoisan (full-sized in stature and large-headed) stock was present from Zambia southwards 10,000 years ago. It is often labelled 'Boskop' in the literature, a reference to fragments of a braincase found at this site in south-western Transvaal, whose age and associations are unknown. Some populations of this stock are believed to have mixed with residual Rhodesioids, who had persisted in the southernmost part of the continent up till that time. This view would explain the presence of fairly recent robust skulls with marked brow ridges in South Africa, like the specimens from Cape Flats and Border Cave (Coon even proposes that these are descended from the Rhodesioids without any considerable Khoisan admixture). From an examination of the human remains from Mapungubwe, on the Limpopo, Professor Galloway [61] con- cluded that the Large Khoisan stock persisted in Rhodesia as late as the fourteenth century AD. A re-examination of the evidence by more objective methods showed Dr G. Rightmire [175] that these remains fall within the range of recent Bantu populations and may not be classified as Khoisan. Nearly all authors agree that the living Khoisan peoples are descended from the Large Khoisan stock and that the reduction in size occurred quite recently (a few thousand years ago), and that this happened only in South Africa.

According to Brothwell, the source of the Khoisan people was in East Africa. The skeletons found associated with a Late Stone Age industry in the Homa shell mounds, on the shore of Lake Victoria in Kenya, have been described as belonging to the unreduced Khoisan. If this is correct, it would confirm that Khoisans lived until recently in East Africa. Coon, however, traces their original area of differentiation much farther away, in North Africa; but the evidence in favour of this view seems very tenuous.

Although the available skeletal remains permit a fairly consistent reconstruction of the evolution of the Khoisan people, this concerns only a rather short span of time; it probably does not go much further back than ten thousand years ago, if as long. The more remote ancestry of the Khoisan people is unknown, apart from the hypothetical view that they could be descended from the stock to which Kanjera man belonged, the age of which is still debatable.

The oldest known remains of *Homo sapiens sapiens* from North Africa are not early either: they are dated at 10,000 BC and are associated with a blade and microlith culture called the Ibero-Maurusian (or Mouillian). They have been found at a number of sites in north-west Africa, of which the two most important are Taforalt in Morocco and Afalou-Bou-Rhummel in Algeria. More than a hundred individuals are represented and they are usually described as the Mechta or Mechta-Afalou group.

This group, which is generally believed to have come from Spain or the Near East (although it could have evolved locally), resembles the Cro-Magnon population of Europe. They were tall and robust people, with a very large skull displaying heavy brow ridges, and a short and broad face. The main difference between them and their European counterparts lies in their wider nose.

The Ibero-Maurusian culture persisted in north-west Africa, especially along the coast, until well into the time of Neolithic culture elsewhere. Several authors recognize a 'Cro-Magnoid' or Mechta component in Berber populations still living in relatively inaccessible regions along the Mediterranean, particularly in Kabylia and the Moroccan Rif. It has also been claimed that by the time of the Spanish conquest of the Canary Islands during the fifteenth century, some of the Guanches (the native Canarians, who practised an advanced Neolithic culture) were physically akin to the Mechta group of Ibero-Maurusian times, and that this component is still recognizable in the living population of the islands. However, Professor Hooton in his analysis of Guanche crania concludes that their greatest similarity lay with the early historic populations of north-west Europe; they even show close resemblance to seventeenth-century Londoners! A recent survey of six blood group systems in a large sample of the rural population of Gran Canaria shows a much closer resemblance to north-west Europeans than to either Berbers or Spaniards.

A second Mesolithic blade and microlith culture, the Capsian, was also present in north-west Africa. Its oldest-dated site, at 6500 BC, is considerably later than the beginning of the Ibero-Maurusian. This, however, is an Upper Capsian site; the Lower Capsian, though still undated, seems to be later than the early Ibero-Maurusian. The Capsian sites lie east and south of the Ibero-Maurusian area and at some of them, Capsian levels overlie Ibero-Maurusian deposits.

The makers of the Capsian are less well known physically than the makers of the Ibero-Maurusian. They are Mediterraneans, whose lighter build contrasts with the robustness of the Mechta people. Probably the Berbers are their descendants, with a possible admixture of the Mechta element in some places.

Figure 13. Upper Kenya Capsian tools from Gamble's Cave, Kenya

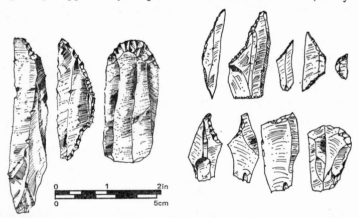

The oldest remains of *Homo sapiens sapiens* found in East Africa were associated with an industry having similarities with the Capsian. It has been called the Upper Kenya Capsian, although its derivation from the North African Capsian is far from certain. At Gamble's Cave in Kenya, five human skeletons were associated with a late phase of the industry, Upper Kenya Capsian C, which contains pottery. A similar association is presumed for a skeleton found at Olduvai, which resembles those from Gamble's Cave. The date of Upper Kenya Capsian C is not precisely known (an earlier phase from Prospect Farm on Eburru mountain close to Gamble's Cave has been dated to about 8000 BC); but the presence of pottery indicates a rather late date, perhaps around 4000 BC. The skeletons are of very tall people. They had long, narrow heads, and relatively long, narrow faces. The nose was of medium width; and prognathism, when present, was restricted to the alveolar, or tooth-bearing, region.

Many authors regard these people as physically akin to the Mediterraneans, hence the label of 'Caucasoids' (or European-like) generally attached to them. However, all their features can be found in several living populations of East Africa, like the Tutsi of Rwanda and Burundi, who are very dark skinned and differ greatly from Europeans in a number of body proportions. For these people, a large Caucasoid component has also been claimed; the whole question will be discussed when dealing with the living populations, which provide much wider evidence than skeletal material from the past.

The Capsians in North Africa, the Large Khoisan in South Africa, and the Gamble's Cave people in East Africa, all appear to be ancestral to populations still living in the same areas. The descendants of the first clearly belong to the Mediterranean world. Those of the other two groups differ in physique from the most numerous and most widely spread African stock which prevails in West and Central Africa. Until recently, representatives of this stock appeared very late in the fossil record, and far away from its present area of maximum concentration. The best-preserved skeleton was from Asselar in the Sahara, dated by radiocarbon at 4440 BC. But in 1965, Professor Thurston Shaw found a human skeleton near to bedrock while excavating the Iwo Eleru rock shelter in the forests of south-western Nigeria. It was associated with a microlithic industry and charcoal collected around it gave a date of 9250 BC. Brothwell and Shaw [21] described it and compared it with a number of early and recent African series. Its postcranial part was in a state beyond useful reconstruction; all that they could say about it was that the Iwo Eleru man seems to have been of medium height and build, with a stature unlikely to have been greater than about 165 centimetres. In a number of traits, the skull would qualify for being ancestral to the present West Africans. However, when eighteen measurements are considered simultaneously, the Iwo Eleru skull is widely separate from Early Egyptian samples and from a recent series of Teita from East Africa, and it has a marginal position in relation to the scatter of

43

positions for East Africans, early and modern Khoisan, and recent West African series from Gaboon.

Like their Middle Stone Age predecessors, all the populations represented by these fossils were hunter-gatherers, but they had improved hunting techniques, particularly in the use of the bow and arrow. Their industries include a variety of small worked flakes, or microliths. Such Later Stone Age hunters continued to roam parts of South Africa until recently and their way of life must have been essentially the same as that of the living Bushmen. Some communities had adopted more permanent settlements, near to lakes, rivers, or the sea shore, and for the first time exploited fresh water or sea foods – snails and fish – on a significant scale. Such an economy elsewhere is known as Mesolithic.

There is a complete gap in the fossil record between the Rhodesioids and the earliest specimens of African *Homo sapiens sapiens*. These appear suddenly, already differentiated in a way similar to that of the living populations. We have no material evidence on which to reconstruct the origins of their differentiation. The only hypothesis based on skeletal data is the view of Brothwell, already cited, that the Kanjera skulls belonged to a stock that could have been ancestral to both the Large Khoisan and the West Central African.

How much indigenous evolution was affected by mixture during this period we can only guess. From the cultural evidence, we may suspect that some intrusion from Asia took place in East Africa. In

Figure 14. Later Stone Age tools from the Orange River

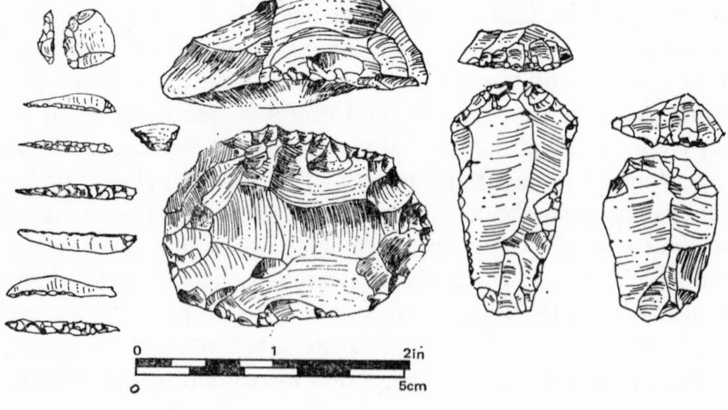

44

Figure 15. Tools and 'dotted wavy line' pottery from Khartoum Neolithic

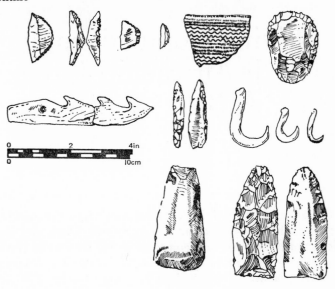

Kenya, a blade and burin industry, apparently foreign to the autochthonous African industries of the area, seems to have been present by about 20,000 years ago. It is called the Lower Kenya Capsian, a misleading name since the genuine Capsian of North Africa is much later. By about the same time, wetter conditions in the Sahara had made it a favourable region for hunter-gatherers. The Aterian industry moved southwards, the Lupemban northwards, and in some places the two traditions blended. Then the Sahara became desiccated again, squeezing out its populations in both directions.

The Sahara again absorbed human populations in neolithic times, and again squeezed out most of their descendants at the time of its last desiccation. These and other late events in other parts of Africa will be discussed later. They are so recent that a description of the living populations of the continent is needed in order to explain their influence on the present diversity of African populations.

4

Living Populations of North Africa and Egypt: A Brief Sketch

In this book the emphasis is on sub-Saharan Africa, the specifically African anthropological area. Because North Africa and Egypt belong much more to the Mediterranean and the area of Western Asia than to Africa in that which concerns physical anthropology, these regions will be touched on only very briefly. The living populations of the Sahara will not be described at all; owing to the complexity of interbreeding in this region, the subject would require a substantial account of the genetic traits of human populations in North Africa and the Near East. In this outline, Africans living south of the Sahara are referred to as sub-Saharans or simply as Africans; the great diversity covered by these loose terms will be developed later.

As pointed out in the preceding chapter, the mesolithic inhabitants of North Africa were physically akin to the populations of Europe and the Near East. They left their trace in the gene pool of the living North Africans, especially in those Berber groups which have been less influenced by later invaders. During later periods, North Africa repeatedly received a flow of genes, as well as cultural elements, from the same two foreign areas, Europe and Western Asia.

Neolithic agriculture and domesticated animals were introduced into Egypt from adjacent South West Asia by about 4500 BC and then spread westwards along the Mediterranean coast to the Atlantic. Metallurgy also came to Egypt and North Africa from the East. Phoenicians and Greeks colonized the North African coast, which was later incorporated in the Roman Empire when political rule shifted from Rome to Byzantium. In the seventh century, Moslem Arabs conquered the area. These were mostly city dwellers and traders. A second wave of Arabs arrived in the eleventh century and entire tribes of Bedouin moved in from the Syrian desert, with their sheep, camels and horses. A large amount of intermixture took place between the indigenous Berbers and the Arab new-comers, especially in the lowlands. Along with many Berbers, some Arabs of the first wave passed into Spain, whence these Moslems (as well as Sephardic Jews) were ejected in AD 1492. Many returned to North Africa, bringing back a gene pool which had meanwhile absorbed an important Spanish element. Clearly, since the intro-duction of Arabs in the area, historical events have favoured genetic homogenization in North Africa. Nowadays, as Coon [38] has pointed out, it is easier to tell a Berber from an Arab by dress and behaviour than by external physical characteristics. But there are still statistical differences, particularly between the tribal Arabs of Bedouin origin and the mountain Berbers. In the latter, blond hair is by no means rare; in some tribes, 25 per cent of the people have it. In the Rif, 4 per cent have red hair, as in Scotland and Ireland. Light and mixed (with green or blue elements) eye colours are also frequent in the mountain Berbers; the lightest pigmented tribe has an incidence of 9 per cent of light and 73 per cent of mixed eyes. Many city Arabs are also blond, while the Arab tribes of Bedouin origin tend to be darker-skinned and less frequently light-eyed than the mountain Berbers; they are rarely blond, and more of them have convex nasal profiles.

The relatively high incidence of blondism in North Africa has raised much speculation. Has it evolved locally, or does it represent an admixture of European elements from an area where blondism has a high incidence? Both views are tenable. Those who favour the second see the supposed European blond component as having been introduced quite a long time ago. The osteological affinities of the ancient Guanches of the Canary Islands with North West Europe, together with the serological affinities of present rural Canarians with the same part of Europe, might be considered as strong evidence for an ancient settlement in North Africa of Europeans coming from farther north than the Mediterranean region.

Statistically, North Africans are very different from sub-

Saharans; however, their gene pool has absorbed a far from negligible amount of sub-Saharan elements, which are conspicuous everywhere. All the living Berbers have a symbiotic relationship with Africans of sub-Saharan origin [38]. In the Rif, these serve as smiths, butchers, town criers and musicians. The part-time and full-time Berber nomads have Haratins, of sub-Saharan physical affinities, to do agricultural work for them. The slave trade has also substantially contributed to a gene flow from sub-Saharan to North Africa. However strong may be the barriers to mating between socially contrasted groups, some mixture inevitably occurs wherever they are in contact over a number of generations.

In Egypt, which by the end of prehistoric times was inhabited by an essentially Mediterranean stock, written history tells of a number of invaders from Western Asia who settled in the delta and on the banks of the Nile. The newcomers were either rather similar physically to the indigenous population, or were numerically unimportant; they have little modified the physique of the Egyptian farmers. The present fellahin are people of medium stature, with brown skin, and most of them have curly hair and dark eyes.

The relative anthropological stability of the farming population of Egypt has been traced back for at least five millennia. No major discontinuity appears in the osteological record between predynastic and dynastic skeletons, and between these and recent series.

From a typological analysis, Wiercinski [233] concludes that in predynastic as in recent times, the Negroid component in the Egyptian population decreased in importance from south to north. In recent series, the Negroid component accounts for 1 per cent of the anthropological picture in the northern provinces, 4 per cent in middle Upper Egypt, and 16 per cent in the Southern provinces. In terms of population genetics, this cline could represent a gene flow from the Sudan, whose intensity would decrease with distance down the Nile. Or it could represent a cline in selective forces, favouring a sub-Saharan physique increasingly with decreasing latitude, whereas in the opposite direction a Mediterranean physique would be favoured. Possibly both factors might act simultaneously.

Similar factors may be invoked for explaining the slight decrease in the frequency of Negroid characters in Egypt since predynastic times, a tendency whose reality is supported by Crighton's recent analysis [44]. It might result from a gene flow from the north, or represent a reduction of sub-Saharan traits with time as an effect of selection where this favours a more Mediterranean physique. It is also possible that the adaptive equilibrium shifted in response to a change in the environment; for example, that desiccation of the climate since Neolithic times favoured a narrower nose.

5

Living Populations of Sub-Saharan Africa: Their Biological Diversity

The Evolutionary Units

As stated in the Introduction, human populations evolve independently according to the measure in which they are endogamous (that is, to the extent to which they refrain from incorporating mates from outside).

In sub-Saharan Africa, many ethnic groups, whether tribes or castes, practise a high degree of endogamy, without having any strong internal barrier to mating. They therefore constitute suitable units for describing human biological diversity and attempting to explain it in terms of the theory of genetical evolution. For example, the Moyen-Chari province of southern Chad is inhabited by about ten tribes in which the mean endogamy rate is 97.5 per cent (in each tribe, on an average, only 2.5 per cent of the males marry a girl from another tribe; tribal affiliation of the children is that of the father). In the largest of these groups, in terms of territory and population size, no conspicuous regional differences appear for anthropological characters [100]. The same rate of endogamy has been reported for the Bedik, a population of eastern Senegal [73]. The Shilluk and Dinka, two contiguous Sudanese tribes, intermarry at a frequency of two per cent [18].[1]

Where several castes co-exist in a political unit, caste endogamy

---

[1] Throughout this book, the recommendations set forth by the International African Institute [116] in 1933 are followed in naming ethnic groups and in the spelling of their names. In particular, the communities usually referred to as Fulani are named Ful.

is usually strong also; each of them must therefore be sampled separately. For example, endogamy rate, though not precisely known, is certainly high within each of the three castes which inhabit Burundi: the Tutsi, Hutu and Twa. Although they have co-existed for a number of centuries, they still differ strongly from one another in their physique. It would completely obscure reality to pool two or three of them in a single sample on the basis that a common designation Barundi – meaning the inhabitants of Burundi – covers the three castes, just as the term Banyarwanda covers all the inhabitants of Rwanda, a neighbouring country where the same three castes show similar striking physical differences.

The probability of biological heterogeneity is high also in those large political units which result from the conquest of a number of endogamous populations by a warlike group. This applies, among a number of other cases, to the Lunda, who occupy a large territory which includes parts of Zaire, Angola and Zambia. They owe their unity of designation to the foundation of a vast empire a few centuries ago by a group which never made up a high percentage of the population outside a limited area around the royal residence, and has little interfered with local customs. Marked biological differences might exist between distant local groups of Lunda.

Another example of heterogeneity is the Kuba kingdom, south of the Sankuru River in Zaire. It consists of a federation of tribes under the rule of one of them, the Bushong, to which the king belongs. In its biological features, one of the Kuba tribes, the Twa, strongly differs from all the others. It is one of the socio-political manifestations of the many bands of Twa who live, or lived until recently, a predominantly hunting-gathering way of life in the equatorial forest, and whose physique shows a marked degree of convergence towards that of the Pygmies. Here, as in the case of the castes of Rwanda and Burundi, pooling the tribes in a sample aimed at representing the Kuba in general would completely obscure the picture of the real anthropological diversity in the area.

How much unjustified pooling biases the published anthropological means and frequencies is impossible to tell. Many authors are vague about the mating structure of the units for which they give average values. Often the investigator has sampled a local community, a village for example. This is all right so far as it goes, but to take the sample as representative of a large unit without evidence of the homogeneity of the whole may be misleading. Quite a number of samples have been drawn from particular groups, like soldiers or prisoners, which may be far from representative of the unit being described.

There is certainly no hope of approaching objectivity unless the description and analysis of human diversity is based on quantified data; the comparison of populations, each made up of biologically diverse individuals, cannot be anything other than statistical. But however correct the statistical procedures, we must remember that the poor validity of a number of samples will reduce the soundness of some of our statements.

Human biological units in sub-Saharan Africa may be roughly estimated to number around a thousand. At present, quantified data (means and/or frequencies) are available on less than half this number of units and, in most cases, the characters measured or tested are very few. Large areas have never seen a physical anthropologist at work, while detailed investigations covering most units have been made in only a few regions. Where such detailed research has been carried out, it often shows a large biological diversity between neighbouring populations. This implies that, in general, it is unwise to extrapolate from studied units to unstudied ones. Where the anthropological map is blank, we must accept our ignorance.

Variation in Anthropological Characters

In sub-Saharan Africa, many anthropological characters show a wide range of population means or frequencies. In some of them, the whole of the world range is covered in the sub-continent. Here live the shortest and the tallest human populations, the one with the highest and the one with the lowest nose, the one with the thickest and the one with the thinnest lips in the world. In this area, the range of average nose widths covers 92 per cent of the world range: only a narrow range of extremely low means are absent from the African record. Means for head diameters cover about 80 per cent of the world range; 60 per cent is the corresponding value for a variable once cherished by physical anthropologists, the cephalic index, or ratio of head width to head length expressed as a percentage.

In the field of serological traits, the frequency of the alleles which define the S and C haemoglobins (to which we shall return later) vary in sub-Saharan Africa from naught up to the highest recorded values in the world. Variation in the frequency of the commonest alleles of the Rh system of blood groups covers from 24 to 84 per cent of the world range, depending on the allele concerned. In their variation in sub-Saharan Africa, the frequency of the alleles responsible for the ABO blood groups (the *A*, *B* and *O* alleles) respectively cover 38, 48 and 64 per cent of the world range. For the *M* allele of the MN blood group, the corresponding value is 49 per cent.

In another rather widely investigated field, that of fingerprints, the variation in the frequency of loops and whorls in sub-Saharan Africa covers 51 and 37 per cent respectively of the world range.

Less rigorously quantified characters which have been frequently recorded in sub-Saharan Africa also prove to be far from uniform over the sub-continent. This is the case for skin colour. Until recently, it was recorded by reference to a set of coloured plates, which was not very satisfactory. The characteristics of the surrounding light, and even subjective factors of the observer, might interfere with the evaluation; an exact match to the observed skin could not always be found in the plates and their numerical scaling was arbitrary. Nowadays a more objective and consistent evaluation of skin colour may be obtained by using a reflectometer. This apparatus measures how much a beam of light, whose wave length has been focused by a standard filter, is reflected by the skin (hence the name 'reflectance' for the reading). The few studies made so far in sub-Saharan Africa with this equipment confirm that quite a large variation in skin colour is present both within and between populations. To the eye, the range runs from brownish yellow to very dark brown.

Hair form has rarely been quantified by physical anthropologists, who usually content themselves with broad divisions like 'straight', 'wavy', 'curly' and 'spiralled'. Only the last two categories are frequent in the populations of sub-Saharan Africa, and spiralled hair, which may be more or less tightly spiralled, occurs in many more populations than curly hair. An extreme is the 'peppercorn' hair of the Khoisan people, in which spiralling is so tight that the hair forms tufts which appear to leave bare patches on the surface of the scalp.

One of the features that physical anthropologists measure on skulls is prognathism, or facial protrusion. A straight face is said to be orthognathous. Prognathism may be total or subnasal, that is restricted to the region below the nose. This character is hard to evaluate on the living, except in radiographs. In sub-Saharan Africa, individuals vary from orthognathism to extreme prognathism and large population differences may be observed between skull series.

All this is evidence of the great biological diversity of the peoples living in sub-Saharan Africa. But let us make it clear that the diversity discussed here is that of 'native' Africans, in the sense that communities which arrived during the last centuries from other parts of the world, like Europeans or Indians, are excluded from this analysis. Also excluded are those groups which resulted from such newcomers mating with the indigenous inhabitants, and which later attained the status of a biological population by genetic isolation (that is, they were closed to mating with outsiders). The Reheboth Basters are an example of such a group. They originated in South Africa from a community of Dutch settlers who took wives from among the Hottentots; later genetic isolation, resulting in a new biological population, was due to religious causes (these people belonged to an exclusive Protestant sect). Another example is the Cape Coloured people, whose ancestral ingredients are of African (Hottentot, Bushmen and others), Asian (mainly Malay) and European origin; today the socio-political system of apartheid keeps them genetically isolated.

Outside Contributions to Sub-Saharan Diversity

Confronted with such a wide variation in biological characters in the native populations of sub-Saharan Africa (and, to be frank, with the stereotyped idea that most of us have about what a 'true' African looks like), one is inclined to ask whether all this diversity originated in sub-Saharan Africa. If not, how much of it was the result of gene flow into the area, and where did it come from?

Owing to their rarity and purely osteological nature, fossil remains do not help much in answering these questions. Data on the living are much more numerous and varied, but when analysing them we must be aware that the older the genetic admixture, the more its impact may be blurred by the other factors of genetic change, drift and selection.

Ethnological and historical data show that, through its northern and eastern fringes, sub-Saharan Africa has absorbed important cultural elements from the two regions with which, geographically, it is most in contact: North Africa and Arabia. In the northern fringe live a number of groups which claim to be descended from Moslem Arabs and speak Arabic dialects. History and culture show Ethiopia and the Horn of Africa to be strongly impregnated by Arabic influences.

During the first millennium BC, the Sabaeans of southern Arabia enjoyed a flourishing agricultural civilization. Around 700 BC, a wave of Sabaeans crossed the Red Sea from Yemen and settled in north-eastern Ethiopia and adjacent Eritrea. They established a powerful state whose capital was at Axum, where excavations have revealed a complex civilization of southern Arabian type. After they had adopted the Christian faith in the fourth century, the Axumites conquered Yemen twice, each time holding the country for a period. Later, encircled by Moslems, Axum disappeared as a power. During the Axumite period, a second and smaller band of immigrants from Arabia invaded south-eastern Ethiopia, from whom the Gurage are said to be descended. A third immigration from Asia brought Judaism to Ethiopia and this religion is still practised by one Ethiopian ethnic group, the Falasha, or 'Black Jews'. The most numerous populations of central Ethiopia – the Amhara (the dominant group today), the Gurage and the Tigre – speak Semitic languages, the group to which Arabic belongs. Traditions of the Afar (or Danakil) and Somali of the Horn of Africa trace their ancestry back to Arab founders and tell of a substantial infusion of Arab blood.

These are very useful indications but, when trying to assess the importance of genetic mixture, we must rely only on biological characters. The proclaimed ancestors of a population may represent only a 'glamorous' group whose contribution to the present gene pool was trifling. Similarly, the language of a small group of immigrants may be totally adopted by a large population; and cultural traits may travel and be widely adopted with a minimum of corresponding gene flow, which may have been too modest to be detectable.

This last point can be exemplified by the case of a third area which has culturally influenced sub-Saharan Africa. According to George Murdock, Malaysian food plants played a major role in the development of agriculture in the African equatorial forest and were introduced by Indonesians settling on the East African coast during the first millennium BC [157]. The wide presence in Africa of food plants of Indonesian origin is a fact; but no trace of an Indonesian admixture has been detected in the gene pool of any East African population. On the other hand, such an admixture is clear and important in Madagascar, off the East African coast. We may therefore be sure that Indonesians migrated in numbers towards East Africa. Did they ever found large settlements on the coast? Only future archaeological research can provide the answer. If they did, they left the continent (presumably forming one of the waves of Indonesians who settled in Madagascar) without leaving any conspicuous genetical trace.

We may therefore restrict the question of exotic genetical influences in sub-Saharan Africa to the impact of Arabs and North Africans. For this purpose, Berbers and North African Arabs may be pooled, since they resemble each other much more closely than they resemble sub-Saharan Africans. Suitable biological data on this question are scanty. For example, they are practically non-existent on Arab tribes south of the Sahara, which must therefore be left out of the discussion.

For the present purpose, the most useful biological characters are those in which sub-Saharan Africa as a whole contrasts most with North Africa and Arabia. Perhaps the most promising one is the system of hereditary variants of blood serum substances known as the Gm groups. Few African populations have been tested for it so far (no one in Ethiopia, unfortunately). The more we know about it, the more complex it appears to be, making previous studies look partly obsolete. One of the hereditary factors of the system, called Gm (x), is present in Europe and North Africa, while it is absent or very rare in the populations of sub-Saharan Africa where it has been searched for. Four populations of Senegal, at the northern fringe of sub-Saharan Africa, have been tested for it. The factor is present with a frequency of 0·3 per cent in Wolof and Tukulor samples, and is absent in samples of Serer and Ful (Fulani) [121]. This indicates that genetic influences from across the Sahara have been very limited, at least in Senegal. Particularly striking is the absence of the Gm (x) factor in the Ful sample, since many authors see an important 'Caucasoid' (or European-like) element in this group.

Where the factor is present, the existing data do not permit us to quantify safely the exotic influence. Very large samples are needed in order to estimate with enough accuracy such low frequencies as those recorded in Senegal. North of the Sahara, which frequency should be considered as representative? On large samples, the Gm (x) factor is present in 1.2 per cent of the Algiers population, 6.8 in Rabat. These figures are considerably lower than in Europe (the factor is present in 20 per cent of Frenchmen). Does this indicate a strong genetic influence from across the Sahara in the populations of North Africa? Possibly; but it must be stressed again that drift, or selection, or both, might have intervened to complicate the picture.

Another genetic system of serum groups, that of the transferins, also provides a contrast between sub-Saharan Africa and the adjacent areas. One of its variants, transferrin D_1, is very rare outside sub-Saharan Africa except in Australia and New Guinea [67], while it is present in all populations of the subcontinent in which it has been searched for, except in small samples of the three Ethiopian populations tested for it, the Amhara, Tigre and Billen. Where present, transferrin D_1 attains only very moderate frequencies: from one to seven per cent, in terms of allele frequencies. Its absence from the three Ethiopian samples is a strong indication of an important exotic element in them (presumably from Arabia), but is by no means a proof that their gene pool is essentially of exotic origin. In a small sample of sedentary Ful of northern Nigeria, the only sample of Ful to have been tested for transferrins so far, the D_1 allele frequency is 3 per cent, a value also observed in the Nzakara of the Central African Republic, where no trace of an Arabic element is reported or even suspected.

Compared to the two systems of serum groups just reviewed the Rh system of blood groups displays, in its commonest variants, a genetical contrast of a lower order between sub-Saharan Africa and the surrounding areas: the same variants (or alleles) are present at considerable frequencies in each, but for some alleles the range of frequencies in sub-Saharan Africa does not overlap that in the surrounding areas. The R_0 allele provides the strongest case. Its frequency varies between 33 and 95 per cent in sub-Saharan Africa, while it never attains the lowest of these values in North Africa or Arabia, and in Europe it does not rise above a few per cent. The R_0 frequency is therefore useful for tracing an exotic influence in sub-Saharan Africa (within the limits of the existing

data, which are confined to less than forty well identified populations). However, it would be misleading to accept the scale of
decreasing African R_0 frequencies as indicating increasing exotic
influence. Certainly genetic drift, and possibly selection, accounts
for part of the variation. Moreover, in small samples – alas, the
most numerous – the sampling error around the computed frequency covers an important part of the total range, which introduces a serious uncertainty in the observed sequence.

Moderate frequencies of R_0 – below 50 per cent – have been
found where we might expect them on the basis of history – in
central Ethiopia. They are also found in some populations in which
an exotic influence has been suspected, in the pastoral Ful of
northern Nigeria and in the Hima of Ankole (Uganda), but also
where there was no reason to suspect such a low value, as in the Eve
of Ghana. High frequencies of R_0 – above 65 per cent – have been
found in populations far removed geographically from possible
sources of exotic influences: in the Mbuti Pygmies, in the Bushmen
and Hottentots of southern Africa, and in the Mano of Liberia; but
also in the Wolof of the Senegal, at the northern fringe of sub-
Saharan Africa, and in the Nuer and Shilluk of the Nile valley in
the Sudan, not far from Ethiopia.

The MN blood groups are also useful for assessing a genetic
influence from Arabia. The M allele has a high frequency in Arabia,
above 65 per cent; in sub-Saharan Africa its frequency varies
between 31 and 73 per cent. This highest frequency is displayed by
a sample of Nama Hottentots. They are followed by all populations
in central Ethiopia which have been tested for the MN blood
groups: the Tigre, Billen, Gurage, Falasha and Amhara, and by the
Danakil of the eastern Horn. The only other sample to show an M
frequency above 60 per cent is a small one of Tutsi from Rwanda
and Burundi. At the other end of the African range, those nine
populations whose M frequency lies below 45 per cent all live on
the West African coast or not far from it; they include populations
of Ghana (the Eve), Liberia (among them the Mano), and Senegal
(here we again find the Wolof and the Senegalese Ful).

It is clear that we may not consider the scale of decreasing M
frequencies as one of decreasing genetic influence from Arabia.
Other factors of variation certainly intervene. Nama Hottentots
surely do not represent an extreme of Arab genetic impregnation.
Some authors have speculated that Hottentots have mixed some-

LIVING POPULATIONS OF SUB-SAHARAN AFRICA

what with Ethiopian herdsmen in the past, but such a view has never been held about the Bushmen, who stand rather high in the scale of M frequencies.

Outside the serological field, hair form appears to be the character which shows the most sharply marked contrast between sub-Saharan Africa as a whole and surrounding areas. Over most of the subcontinent, spiralled hair is the only category to be observed. Were it to be quantified, it would surely display quite a wide variation between individuals and populations. Its most intense expression, peppercorn hair, attains its highest frequency in Bushmen and Hottentots. At the opposite end of the scale, the lowest frequencies of spiralled hair in sub-Saharan Africa have been observed in Ethiopia and Somalia, with a minimum in the Somali. Its frequency is still lower in Arabia, where spiralled hair presumably represents an import from sub-Saharan Africa.

As repeatedly stressed here, reliance on a single indicator of an exotic genetic influence can be misleading. We are on much firmer ground in the case of populations which exhibit values near to the 'Arab' end of the scale for a number of independent traits: the probability that factors other than genetic admixture might generate such systematic affinities with Arabs is very low. Such is clearly the case for the populations of central Ethiopia. Unfortunately, no population in the surrounding areas has been tested for the set of most useful indicators determined in these people.

For extending the question to a wider area, may we rely on other sets of indicators, like anthropometric measurements, which have been recorded in many more populations than a suitable set of serological indicators? As a rule, yes, if we use a large and varied set of relatively independent measurements. Where selection or drift have not blurred the picture, means of metrical characters in a cross-bred population tend to lie between those of the parental populations.

The 'Hamitic' Concept

Many authors have used some measured or observed external characters (mostly facial features such as long, narrow and prominent noses) as indicators of a 'Caucasoid' element in sub-Saharan Africa. In the anthropological literature, this European-like element is very often called 'Hamitic', extending this originally linguistic term to the field of physical anthropology. In *Races of*

59

Africa, a widely known work by C. G. Seligman [188], a large number of populations of sub-Saharan Africa are seen as 'Hamiticized' to a greater or lesser extent; only the Bushmen and the populations of the West African forest belt are said to be free from Hamitic admixture. Such a view therefore claims to detect exotic influences over a much wider area than the one identified here on the basis of a set of serological traits.

Are the facial features considered to be characteristic of the Hamites necessarily of Caucasoid origin? If so, they should tend to be associated in sub-Saharan Africa with other traits which strongly differentiate the two main proposed contributing stocks: the Caucasoid and the West African.

In discussing this question, let us compare the two most numerous populations of Rwanda, a country which lies deep in the interior of sub-Saharan Africa, a little south of the equator east of Lake Kivu. There live the Tutsi, a pastoral people, intermingled with the much more numerous Hutu, who are predominantly agriculturalists. The Tutsi are the latest comers in the country. They entered it from the north-east, started to found a kingdom there about six centuries ago, and gradually expanded their rule over most of the country (this hegemony was put to an end in 1962, when Rwanda became a Republic ruled by Hutu). The more remote history of the Tutsi is unknown. Like all inhabitants of Rwanda, they speak a Bantu language, Kinyarwanda, which they presumably adopted from the Hutu.

The Hutu are descendants of waves of Bantu-speaking earlier immigrants, whose ultimate origin lies in West Africa; they still resemble closely in physical appearance the peoples of the southern Nigeria–Cameroon area. Before the arrival of the first agriculturalists, in the first few centuries of the Christian era, Later Stone Age hunter-gatherers were sparsely occupying Rwanda. Probably the small minority of Twa, the third ethnic group of the country, are their descendants.

The Tutsi and Hutu have intermixed to some degree but, as groups, they remain strikingly different. The Tutsi exhibit 'Hamitic' facial features to a marked degree. Do they systematically differ from the Hutu in the direction of Caucasoids?

The Tutsi are taller than the Hutu by nearly ten centimetres; the average male stature is 176 cm. Such tallness is by no means characteristic of North Africa or Western Asia: for example, the inhabitants of the central plateau of Yemen have an average stature of 164 cm. In skin colour, the Tutsi are darker than the Hutu, in the reverse direction to that leading to the Caucasoids. Lip thickness provides a similar case: on an average the lips of the Tutsi are thicker than those of the Hutu. In most cases, however, they are not everted as in many West Africans. Like that of the Hutu, the hair of the Tutsi is spiralled (perhaps less tightly so, but this has not been quantified).

In a detailed study, relative growth in the two groups and in Europeans has been compared. In the development of a number of body proportions with age, which appears to be largely determined by heredity, the Tutsi are more different from Europeans than the Hutu [96]. In cephalic index, the Hutu are nearer to Yemenites than the Tutsi, whose long, narrow head makes their index lower than that of the other two groups. Existing serological data, based on rather small samples, are equivocal; the Tutsi are higher in M frequency, but do not differ significantly from the Hutu in R_0 frequency nor in the frequency of transferrin D_1.

These comparisons do not lend support to the idea that the Tutsi are a mixture of Caucasoids and West Africans. If the West African element, introduced recently by mixing with the Hutu, were subtracted, their physique would differ even more from North Africans or Western Asians. Apparently, either 'Hamitic' facial features developed in the Tutsi's ancestral line independently of any exotic source or, if an exotic element really was introduced, it was such a long time ago that selection has thoroughly remodelled the resulting gene pool. Even if the second hypothesis were correct, the physical appearance of the Tutsi would result from evolution which took place in sub-Saharan Africa.

Now, the Tutsi are not a physically aberrant group in East Africa. When we consider a number of anthropometric characters simultaneously, and compute the general difference between the Tutsi and other East African groups, the Tutsi do not appear to differ significantly from the Galla of southern Ethiopia. They differ more from the Somali. The set of general differences between the Tutsi, Galla, Somali and Yemen Arabs is compatible with seeing the Somali as the result of a mixture of Yemen Arabs and a Tutsi-like population, and the Galla as intermediary between the Tutsi and Somali. Nor do the Tutsi differ significantly from the Masai, who live in Kenya and Tanzania at approximately the same latitude. However, whether it be a matter of lesser differentiation or of a higher mixture rate with populations of West African affinities, the Masai are closer to the Hutu than are the Tutsi.

The Tutsi are found not only in Rwanda but also in Burundi, the country bordering Rwanda to the south. The differences between the Tutsi of the two countries are very slight. North of Rwanda, in south-western Uganda, Hima shepherds live intermingled with populations akin to the Hutu. Few measurements have been made on them, but they do not look very different to the Tutsi who acknowledge kinship with them.

What the Tutsi and related populations have in common is a tendency towards general elongation of the physical features: long and narrow heads, faces and noses, narrow thorax and shoulders relative to the stature; even the limb diameters are small when related to limb length. 'Elongated East African' would best designate this tendency.

From the foregoing, it is tempting to locate the area of differentiation of these people in the interior of East Africa. Now, as mentioned in Chapter 3, the fossil record tells of tall people with long and narrow heads, faces and noses who lived a few thousand years BC in East Africa at such places as Gamble's Cave in the Kenya Rift Valley and at Olduvai in northern Tanzania. There is every reason to believe that they are ancestral to the living 'Elongated East Africans'. Neither of these populations, fossil and modern, should be considered to be closely related to Caucasoids of Europe and western Asia, as they usually are in the literature.

How far geographically can we trace physical affinities with the Elongated East Africans? West of the great lakes, some genetic influence of the Tutsi-Hima can be detected, but it falls off sharply over a short distance. Beyond this fringe, the immense area of central Africa occupied by Bantu-speaking tribes shows no trace of an Elongated East African element. There is no base to Seligman's view that all Bantu populations are 'Hamiticized' to some degree. As already stated (and the arguments will be developed later), Bantu expansion originated in the west. Only the waves which reached East Africa picked up an 'elongated' element. From there, it was carried down as far south as South Africa by later advances of the Bantu expansion.

North of the Galla, affinities with the Elongated East Africans are observed in the arid crescent which borders sub-Saharan

Africa to the east and north. (The lack of quantified comparable data hinders the evaluation of this element in the central Ethiopian populations; if, as Coon states, the Amhara strongly resemble the Galla, it could be important). In northern Ethiopia and eastern Sudan, the Beni Amer and the Hadendoa, who resemble each other and are considered by ethnologists to be sub-groups of the Beja, do not differ highly from the Galla and Warsingali, a northern group of Somali; they differ considerably more from the Tutsi. Still farther north, the Bisharin, who live near the Red Sea coast at a latitude of 19°N, differ markedly from all the groups cited.

West of the Nile valley, similarities with the Elongated East Africans are seen only in populations who live near to the southern fringe of the Sahara, or are presumed to have migrated from this area. The second case is represented by the numerous Ful communities, who differ from the surrounding populations in their leaner body build and narrower face and nose. The first case refers to a sample of Moors of southern Mauretania, who are anthropometrically close to the Warsingali Somali and, to a lesser degree, to the Beni Amer and Hadendoa. It is amazing to find such similar people on the west and east coasts of Africa at a latitude where the continent is at its widest. Moor society is highly composite; its ingredients are of Berber, Arab and sub-Saharan origins, variously represented in hierarchical castes. The resemblance of the measured Moors to the Somali probably reflects a similar mixture: an exotic element (from Arabs, Berbers, or both) added to a sub-Saharan one, like the one present in the Somali.

If this is correct, has the second element come from the east? Not necessarily: it could have evolved in a broad area under similar selective pressures. It seems therefore more accurate to name this element 'Elongated Africans', without special reference to East Africa. Coon believes that it was first concentrated in the cattle breeders of the neolithic Sahara, whose inhabitants dispersed because of progressive desiccation, giving rise to the herdsmen of East Africa (the Tutsi, Hima, Masai, Galla and Somali are all pastoralists). However, the Gamble's Cave men were already there in a mesolithic stage of culture, before the time of animal domestication. We shall come back to this question when dealing with migrations and expansions in sub-Saharan Africa.

Possible sources of 'Hamiticization' (in the sense given by Seligman to this term) are plentiful in sub-Saharan Africa west of the Nile valley: in some populations, like the Tuareg, of predominantly North African origin in the Sahara; in the Moors, some groups of whom live in Senegal; in the 'Arab' tribes north and east of Chad and in eastern Nigeria; and in the numerous Ful groups now scattered in a wide belt from the west coast to the Sudan. However, no gene flow of any conspicuous importance which could be attributed to Caucasoids has been detected in the western half of the sub-continent. The case of the Wolof is striking: although a few Moor and many Ful communities live in their territory, they have a high R_0 and a low M frequency, opposite to that of the Arabs; only the possession of the Gm (2) factor indicates a Caucasoid admixture in them, a very slight one indeed. Genetic influence seems rather to have flowed the other way, incorporating a strong West African element in most Arab and Ful communities living south of the Sahara.

In concluding these remarks about the Hamitic concept, let us leave to sub-Saharan Africa what belongs to it. Recent exotic influences play a minor and localized role in the biological diversity of its populations. If ever, in the remote past, migrations from Western Asia brought a more substantial Caucasoid element to East Africa, local evolution has subsequently reworked the gene pools so much that their present state largely reflects a genuine African history.

6

Factors of
Biological Diversity

Human populations of sub-Saharan Africa, we have seen, are highly diverse; how much of this diversity is due to gene flow from outside was discussed in the last chapter. Let us now analyse the other factors of the present picture.

The Influence of Environment on Growth and Adult Physique[1]
When we find two populations differing in the frequency of blood groups, we know for sure that the difference is genetical: blood groups are strictly determined by heredity and no circumstance in the life of an individual can change his blood group. This holds true for all systems of hereditary variants of blood substances cited in this book.

On the other hand, environment interacts with heredity in determining the course and end point of growth, and influences some adult measurements (like body weight) after growth has stopped. Variation between populations in adult measurements is therefore only partly genetical.

For those who wish to use measurements in assessing genetical variation, this introduces a complication. Some situations, however, are of particular help in estimating its intensity: those in which genetically similar populations are living in different conditions; and those in which genetically different populations have been brought to live in similar conditions.

Three broad categories of environmental factors may interact with heredity in the control of growth and adult physique: climate, nutrition and disease. Nutrition and disease, of course, are largely

[1] This section leans on Hiernaux 1970 and 1971. [101, 102].

65

dependent on human culture. Perhaps cultural behaviour itself is a direct factor of growth. On a world basis, Landauer and Whiting [126] claim that male adult stature is positively correlated with the rate of stress in infant care practices; they observe an especially high correlation in the set of fifteen African populations included in their study.

Within the limits of its variation in Africa, climate does not interfere much with heredity in determining growth and adult physique. Contrary to popular belief, the surrounding temperature has little, if any, effect on the rate of growth. On a world scale the onset of puberty does not appear to be particularly early or late in hot regions, after taking into account the influence of nutrition and hygiene. Menarche, or first appearance of the menses, is later in most samples from sub-Saharan Africa than in Europe or North America, where it is now about thirteen years (it is near to seventeen years in Rwanda, as it was in Scandinavia a century ago). However, better-off segments of African populations show mean values nearer to the present European ones, as has been observed in Nigeria and Uganda.

Such differences in adult body build have been observed in mice of the same strain, one group reared in the heat, the other in the cold, but no influence of this kind has been proved in man. Living at very high altitudes is known to depress human growth and modify some body proportions, but no African population lives as high as those in the Andes where such influences have been observed.

Nutrition and disease, on the other hand, do influence the rate of growth and adult measurements under certain conditions. As noted above, the age of menarche is sensitive to socio-economic factors, which act mainly through nutrition and hygiene. Adverse conditions in these fields, either permanent or occurring during especially critical periods, stunt physical development.

Evidence of this is given by observations made in Rwanda. Hutu, living at higher altitudes, enjoy a more abundant diet, dependent on more rainfall and better soil, and suffer much less from malaria. They surpass their lower-altitude relatives in adult weight by seven kilograms, but they are not significantly taller. Their skeletal frame is wider – they have wider shoulders, thorax and hips – and their head is bigger. They are far more muscular, their handgrip strength being four kilograms higher. The difference in altitude between the homes of the two groups is less than three hundred metres, too trivial to play a direct role [94].

A study of growth in two groups of Hutu children contrasted in nutrition and hygiene shows how early is the impact of these factors on measurements and proportions. Already by the age of six years, the better-off group is in advance for all measurements; for an equal stature, children of this group weigh more, have wider shoulders and hips, and larger limb circumferences; these differences in proportions do not tend to get wider with age [96].

The most sensitive period is apparently the perinatal one. In a general growth survey of Tutsi and Hutu in rural Rwanda, one age class, the same in both groups, showed a depressed value for all measurements in the male sex. The boys belonging to this class were either in the last months of intra-uterine life or in the first months of post-natal life when a terrible famine struck the country. They remained permanently stunted, while older boys caught up after restoration of normal conditions. No such depression was observed in girls of the same age: the female sex resists environmental handicaps better [96].

Diets vary largely in sub-Saharan Africa. At least during part of the year, between one harvest and the next, many populations have a caloric intake below what international health authorities consider to be an optimum. In some years these lean months are prolonged or intensified and famine sets in, as in the Rwanda case just mentioned.

Protein deficiency is common among agricultural African populations, especially those whose diet consists mainly of vegetables that are poor in proteins. There is a strong contrast between the populations who eat mainly peas and beans, which are rich in proteins, and those for whom cassava, very poor in proteins, forms the basis of the diet. Among the latter, if no protein-rich foods are added to the cassava, protein deficiency becomes so serious that kwashiokor, a nutritional disease usually fatal in the absence of adequate treatment, strikes a variable percentage (sometimes very high) of the children. Those who do not die, or those who show only slight symptoms, are no less indelibly marked by it; as adults they are far from showing a physical development (and without doubt also a psychical one) corresponding to their genetic potential. Since individual differences in diet are usually slight, whole rural populations carry the scars of protein deficiency acquired in childhood.

Pastoral populations, or those that carry on agriculture and cattle herding simultaneously, have a vital source of proteins in beef and milk – however the meat is not always eaten, and the production of milk is often inadequate. In Rwanda, where cattle are super-abundant, cows have primarily a social value: a large part of the population never eats meat, or does so only a few times per year. The milk yield is so poor that its consumption, although highly prized, is very low in most families.

The other domestic animals, goats, sheep, pigs, fowls etc., are rarely a satisfactory source of protein, since they are either not raised in sufficient numbers, or their products do not feature in the nutritional habits. Many populations milk neither goats nor sheep and consume no eggs; in Rwanda, the Tutsi and the Hutu consider eating mutton to be repugnant – only the Twa do it.

In numerous and vast regions, game is actually too scarce to provide sufficient protein. The contribution of insects (termites, caterpillars, grasshoppers etc.) is very moderate.

Populations that have access to abundant fish have a great advantage from the point of view of animal protein consumption compared with other African groups, and their physical condition reflects this.

Vitamin deficiency has a high incidence in many regions, particularly in vitamin A, where the diet is poor in fat and vegetable carotenoids – palm oil saves huge areas of central Africa from this deficiency – and also multiple vitamin B deficiency. It is probable that the intense ultra violet radiation compensates for the vitamin D deficiency of many diets, which would explain the rarity of rickets.

The dietary intake of soluble salts depends in part on the nature of the soil. Iodine deficiency, with its often dramatic physical and psychic consequences, appears where the soil is very poor in this element. Calcium intake depends both on the composition of the water and the presence in the diet of foods rich in calcium.

Numerous pathological factors are also capable of influencing the average physique of the populations of huge regions of Africa; it is mostly a matter of chronic parasitic diseases. When not fatal, malaria, ancyclostomiasis, bilharzia, onchocerciasis, to cite only a few, have the tendency to chronically debilitate their carriers and thus produce an effect similar to that of malnutrition. Very often parasitism and malnutrition are synergetic: parasites consume energy, and malnutrition lowers resistance to disease.

In certain biotopes favourable to *Glossina*, the tsetse fly, sleeping sickness is so severe and widespread that human occupation is all but impossible.

This large variation in diet and disease obviously accounts for part of the anthropometric diversity of the populations of sub-Saharan Africa. Fat and muscle are the most sensitive, and the skeleton is more sensitive in its lateral development than in its growth in length. Some proportions, like the ratio of lower limb length to stature, and the classical indices of the head, face and nose, are hardly influenced by diet and disease.

On the other hand, heredity certainly accounts for an important part of the observed variation, even in characters which are highly sensitive to diet like body weight. Rwanda again provides nearly ideal experimental conditions for studying this question. At the times when they were measured, the Tutsi enjoyed better nutritional conditions owing to their aristocratic status; in particular they were much leaner than the Hutu: for equal stature, their weight was much lower, their trunk narrower, their limbs slenderer. Clearly, the Tutsi's leanness is largely genetical [96]. Roberts [182] reached the same conclusion about the extreme leanness of the Dinka and Shilluk herdsmen of the Upper Nile marshes. This must be even more valid for stature, which is less sensitive to the environment. The Mbuti Pygmies, the shortest people in the world, certainly owe this characteristic to heredity: compared with their much taller neighbours in the Ituri forest, they are better nourished and less infested with parasitic diseases.

In the absence of quantified data on diet and disease in many of the populations studied anthropometrically (and we stand very far from achieving this!), a precise evaluation is impossible. However, we may surmise that a large part of the diversity in sub-Saharan Africa is due to genetic variation.

This variation results from a number of evolutionary mechanisms: selection, mutation, genetic drift and interbreeding. The part each played in producing the present picture is discussed later. In the meantime, let us consider a factor of phenotypic variation which is not directly influenced by the environment nor by the differential action of the mechanisms of change: the mating structure.

The Influence of the Mating Structure on Physical Development
On an average, the offspring of marriages between closely related individuals are backward in their physical development and show a higher incidence of hereditary anomalies. If its social or religious rules favour this type of marriage, a population will show a lower mean vigour than if it had attained panmixia, that is, when no consideration of kinship is taken into account in mating. By systematically avoiding consanguinous marriages, that is by practising heterogamy, vigour will be much greater.

The Fadidja, a Nubian population living in the Nile valley just north of the Sudan–Egyptian border, have a particularly high frequency of consanguinous marriages. Nearly half the members of this tribe are offspring of first cousin marriages and other types of matings between relations account for another 26 per cent. Compared with the children of unrelated parents, the offspring of first cousin marriages attain lower adult values in stature, weight, trunk dimensions, bone robusticity, muscular development and grip strength. Some Fadidja villages have fewer consanguinous marriages than others and their inhabitants show a stronger body build [198].

Social rules about kinship in mates vary in sub-Saharan Africa from a preference for closely related marriages, as in the Fadidja, to complete avoidance of consanguinous marriages. They therefore constitute a significant factor of variation in the expression of genetic potentialities.

Even when they avoid marriages between closely related individuals, small closed communities necessarily have a high degree of consanguinity. The breaking up of such isolates, even by enlarging the circle of matings only to near-by settlements, produces an increase in physical vigour in the next generation, an effect often called heterosis, or hybrid vigour. Population size, density and distribution, social rules, types of habitat and economy, all contribute to the extent to which an ethnic group is fragmented into smaller mating circles. By bringing peoples from distant places together, the urbanization, industrialization and multiplication of traffic ways now developing in many parts of sub-Saharan Africa are likely to produce the effect of heterosis.

Mechanisms of Genetic Change

1. SELECTION Selection, whether natural or not, implies choice. It takes place in a genetic system initially presenting several alleles when one of these contributes more to the next generation than the other, or others. With time, the frequency of this allele will increase at the expense of the others, which will possibly disappear from the population's gene pool.

The contributors, however, are not genes but individuals, who possess two alleles, identical or different, at each place or *locus* occupied by a gene on a pair of chromosomes. Suppose that, at a given locus, a population has two alleles, *A* and *B*. Three genetic types of individuals, or *genotypes*, will be present in it: *AA*, *BB*, and *AB*. *AA* and *BB* individuals, who possess one allele at double dose, are called *homozygotes*; *AB* individuals, who possess two different alleles, are called *heterozygotes*. If, in each generation, *AA* individuals contribute more to the next one (either because they are more fertile, or because their children die less often before the age of reproduction), the frequency of *A* will progressively increase with the passing of generations; whatever its initial frequency, *B* will finally disappear from the population, in which *A* becomes fixed. The reverse will occur if *BB* is the fittest genotype, that is the one which has the more numerous offspring.

If the genotype which contributes more is the *AB* heterozygote there will be no choice: the two alleles – hence genetic diversity or polymorphism – will be maintained in the population. Their frequency will tend towards an equilibrium value which depends only on the relative fitness of the three genotypes. If *AA* and *BB* contribute equally, at equilibrium *A* and *B* alleles will have both a frequency of 0.5 (50 per cent); if *AA* is fitter than *BB*, the frequency of *A* at equilibrium will be higher than that of *B*. Geneticists call this state 'balanced polymorphism'. It is a stable equilibrium: if drift or interbreeding happen to change the allele frequencies, these will tend to return to their initial values after a number of generations, the only requirement for stability being that relative fitnesses keep constant.

If the relative fitnesses change, with the heterozygote remaining the fittest genotype, the allele frequencies will shift towards a new equilibrium.

This equilibrium corresponds to a minimum of waste in the reproduction of the population; so also does the result of selection, the fixation of the fittest allele. If relative fitnesses depend on the environment, selection and heterozygote advantage tend to lead each population to the most economical genetic state that it can attain in its particular environment: they tend towards genetic adaptation. Since they work on the existing alleles, two populations may attain different genetic adaptive states in the same environment if their initial sets of alleles were not identical.

These notions have been based on the simplest model of genetic diversity: one gene, two alleles. They are also valid for genes with more than two alleles, and for variables which are determined by a number of genes, as the anthropometric characters are known to be. Interaction between genes, however, complicates the picture: a change in a system may induce change in other ones; this is internal adaptation.

To most modern biologists, strict neutrality in a polymorphic system (that is, equal fitness of all genotypes) is hard to imagine, as well as independence of relative fitnesses from environmental variation. They therefore surmise that selective pressures (toward fixation of an allele or toward balanced polymorphism) are a factor of the genetical diversity of populations for most biological characters.

As we now see, environment influences biological characters in two ways: at each generation, it may influence the expression of the genotype in the individuals; along generations, it may make allele frequencies change in the populations.

The most clearly elucidated case of genetic adaptation in Africa is that of the abnormal haemoglobins; it will therefore be presented first.

Abnormal haemoglobins Haemoglobin, the pigment of the blood red cells, presents a number of hereditary variants in the human species. Somewhat simplified, the genetic system underlying most of them may be seen as a locus displaying many alleles. One of these determines haemoglobin A, or normal haemoglobin. It is the most frequent allele in any population; in many, it is the only one present at notable frequency. Let us designate it by *A*. Two abnormal haemoglobins, *S* and *C*, attain relatively high frequencies in Africa: in terms of allele frequencies, up to 20 per cent for *S*, 14 per cent for *C*. In sub-Saharan Africa, a majority of populations possess *S*; *C* is restricted to a minority; some populations possess both, other ones have only the normal *A*.

Where A and S are the existing alleles, there are three genotypes: AA, AS, and SS. A simple laboratory test detects the presence of S at single or double dose. Red cells are normally discoidal; when deprived of oxygen for some time, the red cells of AA individuals remain discoidal while those of owners of the S allele take the shape of a sickle. More refined laboratory procedures based on electrophoresis – electrical separation – differentiate AS from SS individuals. In the poor medical conditions which prevail in rural Africa, being born an SS means death in childhood from sickle-cell anaemia, with a near to 100 per cent probability. AS individuals suffer only very slightly, if at all, from possessing the S allele: they just carry the sickle-cell trait.

How can such a deleterious allele have attained notable frequencies in so many populations? There is only one possible answer: heterozygote advantage. The advantage of AS individuals over 'normal' AA ones has been elucidated; they die less frequently from malaria. This disease is a terrible killer in most of Africa. The more severe it is, the higher is the relative fitness of the AS genotype, hence the higher is the frequency of S at equilibrium. Assuming that the viability of the SS individuals is naught, the highest frequency of S recorded, 20 per cent, results from the fitness of AS individuals being one-third higher than that of AAs.

With such extremely high selective pressures in action, equilibrium is attained in a relatively short time: for the fitness values just cited, in about twenty generations when the initial frequency of S is as low as one per cent. If genetic drift or mixture happen to change the S frequency, this will quickly return to its equilibrium value. Shift towards a new equilibrium frequency will also be quick. It will occur when the population migrates to a region where the death toll of malaria is different, or when this toll changes locally. This last case may result from a change in medical practices, or from whatever change in the way of life which influences the populations of *Anopheles* mosquitoes, the transmitters of malaria. Migration to a malaria-free habitat, or eradication of malaria, will induce the gradual elimination of S, henceforth selected against.

We may therefore expect a strong correlation between the frequency of the S allele and the severity of malaria, with only little dependence on the relatedness of the populations. This

73

has been verified in East Africa; in particular, S frequency is independent of language in this area of large linguistic diversity [2].

However, the populations which show the highest S frequencies, above 18 per cent, all speak Bantu languages. They live in small distant pockets: the Simbiti on the east shore of Lake Victoria, the Makonde and Makua astride the Tanzania-Mozambique border, and the Humu-Amba and Mvuba at the foot of the Ruwenzori mountain astride the Zaïre-Uganda border.

From a study of abnormal haemoglobins in a part of forested West Africa where the introduction of agriculture is relatively recent, F. Livingstone [139] concludes that the frequency of S increases with the time that the population has practised agriculture; as an explanation, he suggests that the slash-and-burn method used for clearing the fields favours the breeding of mosquitoes, and that the severity of malaria is enhanced by the rise in human population density provoked by passing from hunting-gathering to agriculture. Hunter-gatherers in the equatorial forest indeed show a lower S frequency than the surrounding agriculturalists. The fact that the highest frequencies of S in Central and East Africa all belong to Bantu-speaking populations possibly reflects a similar situation. Archaeology strongly suggests that Bantu-speakers were the introducers of a forest-adapted agriculture in the areas, formerly occupied by hunter-gatherers, where the highest S frequencies are observed.

In accordance with expectations, the absence of S in Africa closely coincides with the absence of endemic malaria. S is absent from all the populations tested in the high regions of Ethiopia, among them the Tigre, Falasha, Amhara and Galla; it is very rare in the Dinka, Shilluk and Nuer of the High Nile Valley. In Kenya and Tanzania, no S has been found in the area peopled by the Masai, Kamba and Chaga. S is also missing in large parts of southern Africa, not only in the Bushmen and Hottentots, but also in Bantu-speaking groups like the Shona of Rhodesia. All the populations cited live outside the areas of endemic malaria. These are not entirely devoid of S, but where it occurs (as in the Ronga of southern Mozambique), its frequency is low, and it may be presumed to be on the way to disappearance.

S frequencies are not high in all malarious areas. They are particularly low on the Atlantic coast, in Portuguese Guinea and

Liberia. Livingstone [139] suggests that both the S allele and agriculture have been introduced recently in these regions.

To the geneticists, it is clear that S originated as a mutation of A. Did this mutation occur once or several times? We do not know, nor are we able to locate its source or sources: the tendency of S frequency to adapt quickly to the environment, however low its initial value, hinders tracing the origin and diffusion routes of the allele. S is found not only in Africa, but also in southern Europe, in Arabia, and in India. All imaginable hypotheses of origin and diffusion that this distribution permits have been proposed, but we have no basis on which to choose from them.

However, Africa west of the longitude of Greenwich may almost certainly be ruled out as a possible source of S, while it is the most probable area of origin of C, another mutant of A.

The highest frequencies of C are concentrated in a restricted area, on the Voltaic plateau, in the Haute–Volta and neighbouring countries. There C attains frequencies above 10 per cent in such populations as the Sembla, the Bobo Diula, the Mossi and the Senufo. Away from this nucleus, the frequency of C falls off sharply. C occurs only sporadically outside West Africa, except in an extension across the Sahara as far as North Africa and Sicily.

Like those of S, the frequencies of C represent different levels of a balanced polymorphism. The CC genotype entails death before the age of reproduction in about one child out of two; only hetero-zygote advantage could maintain the allele at the observed frequencies. Since the main area of C lies within the malarious belt, it has been suggested that, like S, it confers a relative protection against malaria to its carriers. The arguments in favour of this view are, however, less impressive than in the S case.

In a number of populations, S and C co-exist (together with A, of course). Where this is the case, S frequency tends to be low when C frequency is high, and vice-versa.

The relative fitnesses of the six genotypes of the system might be such that S tends to eliminate C with time in any population in which the two alleles are brought into contact. If this is true, C could have had a wider distribution in the past. The present picture would speak for a relatively recent introduction of S in the most western part of sub-Saharan Africa; the populations of the Voltaic plateau would owe their position at the top of the scale of C frequencies not only to the selective advantage of the AC genotype over the *AA* and *CC* homozygotes, but also to a strong genetic isolation which would have kept them free of *S* until very recently. An alternative explanation is that *C* would protect against *Plasmodium malariae*, one of the agents of malaria which is very frequent in Haute-Volta, while *S* would protect against *Plasmodium falciparum*, the agent of malignant malaria [139].

Disease as a selective agent. Besides haemoglobins S and C, another abnormal haemoglobin, which causes a genetic disorder called thalassemia, attains notable frequencies in some African populations, mostly in malarious areas. So also does an hereditary deficiency in an enzyme of the red blood cells, glucose-6 phosphate dehydrogenase (G-6 PD). Hence the hypothesis that malaria is the selective agent, or at least one of the selective agents, which act on their frequency. Whatever the true selective agents, thalassemia and G-6 PD deficiency are maintained by the mechanism of balanced polymorphism.

A number of observations suggest other infectious diseases as selective agents. Haemoblogin S might protect against leprosy as well as against malaria [6]; smallpox and plague might exert a selective action on ABO blood groups [222]. Genetic resistance factors seem to play a role in a number of other frequent diseases whose incidence varies in Africa, e.g. tuberculosis, measles, and poliomyelitis, though the genotypes conferring increased or decreased susceptibility to such diseases have not been identified [152]. It has also been suggested that the raising of the general level of life and of the efficiency of medicine induced a rise in the frequency of Rh-negative individuals and a fall in the frequency of B blood group in Western Europe, through a decrease in the selection by mother–child incompatibility; this mechanism could be at work in Africa also [204].

Whether disease is the selective agent or not, some systems of blood groups react when Africans go and settle elsewhere. This is clear in the North American Black communities. To a variable extent, all of them have incorporated genes from White communities. However, a number of their allele frequencies converge towards the Whites' values more than interbreeding accounts for. This is the case for the alleles which cause haemoglobin S, G-6 PD deficiency, the capacity to taste PTC (phenyl-thio-carbamide), and the variant Hp^1 of the system of haptoglobins [235]; perhaps also for the *r* (Rh-negative) allele [89]. We may assume that this convergence represents genetic adaptation of the African gene pools to new conditions of life. It implies that, in Africa, many gene frequencies tend towards adaptation to local factors, the nature of which remains to be unveiled in most cases.

Nutrition as a selective agent. As stated previously, food quantity and quality influences growth and adult physique. Conceivably it could also act as a selective agent: where food consumption is permanently low, a lean physique or a short stature – two character-istics which are partly controlled by heredity – would reduce food requirements by reducing the body mass.

There is no firm evidence for such a genetic adaptation as a factor of human diversity in Africa. Professor Stanley Garn thinks that the genetically shorter stature of the Pygmies represents an adaptation to a low food supply. However, there is no evidence for scarcity of food in the communities of the Mbuti of the Ituri forest, the shortest Pygmies. These exhibit a better state of nutrition than the surrounding agriculturalists of average stature, and a much better one than the Twa of the Kuba kingdom, a taller Pygmoid group.

Neither does it seem that the reduction of stature in the Khoisan ancestral line resulted from a diminished food intake. Hunting-gathering societies usually maintain an equilibrium between popu-lation density and food resources. Even in the inhospitable Kalahari Desert, where the Bushmen have recently been driven by invaders, food is not scarce everywhere. For example, the Bushmen of the Dobe area in Botswana find a source of calories in mongongo nuts, which rot on the ground each year for want of picking [130].

As stated in the next section, genetical shortness and leanness in Africa seem to represent adaptations to climate, not to food intake.

Climate as a selective agent. On a world basis, the clearest case of genetical adaptation to climate in man is displayed by skin colour. The selective agent seems to be the dose of ultra violet rays in the sunlight received by the skin. Too high a dose is harmful, too low an intake entails the risk of rickets, a disease caused by a deficiency in vitamin D. This vitamin is synthesized in the deep layers of the skin, a chemical process which needs to be activated by ultra violet rays. Melanin, the main pigment causing differences in skin colour,

77

filters the ultra violet rays in proportion to its quantity. This quantity is mostly controlled by heredity. Where ultra violet rays are superabundant, as in the tropics, the adaptive equilibrium results in a dark skin; a light skin is adaptive where solar irradiation is scanty.

Since it seems probable that man lost most of his body hair quite early in his evolution [160], emergent mankind in the African tropics was probably dark-skinned. The 'Whites' faded after their ancestors migrated far away from the tropics.

Up till now, strictly objective measurements of skin colour by the reflectometer have been taken in only a dozen African populations. They confirm what had been observed by cruder methods. The skin of most Khoisan groups is considerably lighter than that of any other population of sub-Saharan Africa. It is not possible now to say how close it is to the adaptive optimum in the present bio-tope. In the rest of the sub-continent, skin colour tends to be darker in the savanna than in the forest, in which much less sun-light actually reaches the ground. The Pygmies have not yet been tested with the reflectometer, but the observations made on them with crude colour scales are accurate enough for assessing that their skin is lighter than that of their agriculturalist neighbours, who have been in the forest for far fewer generations and spend more time in the sunny clearings opened up by their agricultural activities. If we admit, as will be argued later, a remote common origin outside the forests for the Pygmies and non-Pygmies now living in this biotope, the lighter skin colour of the Pygmies results from a shift in adaptive equilibrium induced by migration into the forest.

Even in the darkest-skinned African populations, genetic divers-ity for skin colour is preserved. Nowhere apparently does the adaptive optimum correspond to the darkest skin genetically possible.

Another sector of the gene pool shows a variety of adaptations to climate: the one that can be explored by external measurements. Human body build shows clear associations with climate in sub-Saharan Africa. Put in mathematical terms, many anthropometric means are significantly correlated with one or several aspects of climate. Of course this is only a statistical statement. There are – and could be – no strict associations between biological character-istics and environmental factors similar to the causal relations found in the domain of physics. What have been called 'ecological laws' in biology have many exceptions and should rather be called 'tendencies'. This is particularly true in the case of our species, whose populations display a general biological adaptability much more than particular adaptations. Human populations are repeatedly modified in their genetic constitution by interbreeding. Many of them have migrated for long distances several times in the past, successively occupying a variety of habitats (or biotopes), and local climate has fluctuated everywhere in Africa during human times. A characteristic of our species is that human populations adapt to new conditions more by changing their behaviour than by modifying the gene pool.

Genetic adaptation takes a great many generations to reach a new equilibrium, while cultural adaptation (that of the behaviour of the society) may bring much quicker responses to the challenge of a changing environment, despite the tendency to inertia of any cultural system. Moreover, cultural change by itself may deeply modify the selective forces.

Take the case of haemoglobin S, whose frequency tends to rise in conditions of increasing mortality from malaria. Besides moving to a non-malarial or less malarial area, mankind now has many means of reducing or suppressing this mortality: by antimalarial treatment and prophylaxis, by battles against the *Anopheles* mosquito by insecticides, by destruction of the resting places of this transmitter's grubs. More recently, other biological means of exterminating mosquitoes have been developed without using insecticides, which themselves represent a danger to man's health. If successful, such measures suppress in less than one generation the selective pressure towards a higher frequency of haemoglobin S, which takes a number of generations before reaching an adaptive optimum.

The relatively strong biological adaptations to climate shown by man in Africa can probably be explained in this way: in the absence of advanced technical means, human culture provides but little alleviation to the physiological burden of exertion in the heat – the physical activity needed for obtaining food. This challenge is different in dry and wet heat, which would account for closer correlations of human physique with air moisture than with temperature. For example, in the extremely wet equatorial forest, where air movement is at a minimum, cooling by sweating is not very

79

efficient, whereas this mechanism is paramount in the dry, sunny steppe country.

Not only do average air temperature and moisture vary in sub-Saharan Africa, but also their degree of uniformity over the year. Seasonal contrast is minimal in the equatorial zone, increasing as one moves away from the equator. For similar annual values of temperature and humidity, the biological challenge will differ with the intensity of this contrast. Selection – the basis of genetic adaption – is a matter of different death rates in different genetic make-ups; it therefore works more strongly in the most exhausting conditions of the environment. On the basis of the preceding considerations, correlations have been computed between a number of measurements in populations of sub-Saharan Africa and five climatic variables, some of which are annual means, the others monthly extremes [98].

The closest correlation of stature (body height) is with the seasonal contrast in air moisture, the next is with air temperature of the hottest month. Stature tends to be shorter where air moisture is more uniform over the year (a condition at an extreme in the equatorial forest), and taller where the summer is hotter and the seasonal contrast more marked (conditions which culminate in the dry steppes and savannas). The correlation of stature with air temperature is opposite to that postulated by Bergmann's rule, the most often cited ecological tendency: according to this rule, body size tends to be lower in a warmer habitat. Weight does not follow Bergmann's rule either: it is independent of both temperature and humidity. For the same stature, it remains independent of air temperature, but tends to be heavier in a moister climate.

Why does human physique in sub-Saharan Africa not follow the ecological tendency which has been found to be valid on a world basis? The answer ought to be in terms of the physiological needs which underlie Bergmann's rule. For keeping alive, man must maintain his internal temperature within a narrow range of values. His physical activities produce heat, the amount of which is a function of the active mass of the body. Heat dissipation occurs mainly through the skin. Therefore, in a hot climate, a low body mass-to-surface ratio is advantageous for survival. Now, if you reduce the size of a ball, its mass diminishes more than its surface: the former is proportional to the cube of the diameter, the latter to its square. Hence the adaptive value of a general diminution of body dimensions for survival in a hot climate. This is the basis of Bergmann's rule. The analysis of the African data shows that it has been produced by natural selection, not by an hypothetical shortage of food or bad health in the zone of short size: peoples of this zone are not underweight for their stature, and weight is known to be more sensitive than body height to adverse conditions. But the analysis of African data also shows that the trend to genetical reduction of body size is restricted to the damp variety of hot climates. It has attained its maximum in the Pygmies, whose ancestors have lived in the equatorial forest for the greatest number of generations.

In the hot and dry zones of sub-Saharan Africa, selection has favoured a different body build, which also displays a low mass-to-surface ratio: a gracile, elongated physique, with long legs and narrow shoulders. Weight is relatively very low in such people of medium or tall stature, but not especially so in absolute value. This tendency of the human physique toward tallness in the hot and dry zone explains the failure of Bergmann's rule in sub-Saharan Africa. Like size reduction, it represents an adaptation to heat, but this time in a dry climate in which cooling by sweating is the easiest.

The genetic nature of the contrast between the two types of adaptation to heat is demonstrated in Rwanda, where the Tutsi are of the elongated type, while the Hutu are much shorter and bulkier. Though living amongst the Hutu for centuries, the relative weight of the Tutsi is much lower than that of the Hutu. Food intake and hygiene do not account for the difference, they would rather favour the opposite [94]. As far as it can be reconstructed, the history of the two groups agrees in seeing the ancestors of the Tutsi having developed their characteristics in dry steppe country, and those of the Hutu having evolved in a much moister habitat. A similar contrast can be found in Kenya between the elongated Masai herders of the dry plains and the Kikuyu farmers of the well-watered mountainous areas near by.

Head and face shape also are significantly correlated with air temperature and moisture in sub-Saharan Africa. The more extreme are heat and dryness, the narrower tends to be the head. Face width tends to increase with air moisture and climatic uniformity. Nose height tends to be lower in wetter regions. Of all measurements, nose width shows the closest correlations with climate: it tends to increase with the annual rainfall and to decrease with the temperature of the hottest month.

Like those of body dimensions, these correlations probably also reflect genetic adaptation. The major physiological role of the nose is to warm up and humidify the inspired air. This must become saturated with the water provided by the nasal mucosa, constantly moistened by secretions, otherwise it would damage the lungs. In a dry climate, it is therefore advantageous to have a high and narrow nose, a shape which maximizes the contact of the inspired air with the nasal mucosa. Nose shape being determined by heredity, natural selection will be at work until this characteristic reaches its adaptive equilibrium [227].

In the equatorial forest, the adaptive optimum apparently corresponds to a very short and wide nose, one of the most conspicuous features of the Pygmies' face. The surrounding air is usually saturated and probably a short and wide nasal passage facilitates the ventilation of the lungs. Perhaps the tendency of the face to be wider in the uniform dampness of the equatorial forest is just an anatomical necessity linked with the wide nose favoured by selection in this biotope: obviously a narrow face could not accommodate a very wide nose.

The only indication about the possible adaptive value of a narrow head in a hot, sunny climate comes from an observation made on skulls. When a heating lamp is held vertically above a selection of human skulls, the temperature inside the cranial box rises more slowly in the case of the narrower and higher skulls [223].

From the foregoing it is clear that where the size and shape of the human body are concerned, climate has played an important role in the genetic differentiation of the populations of sub-Saharan Africa. In the light of this knowledge, we are now in a position to explain, in terms of genetic adaptation, the external characteristics of the populations labelled 'elongated Africans' in Chapter 3, such as the Masai of Kenya, the Tutsi of Rwanda and Burundi, and the Ful (or Fulani) of West Africa where they are not too strongly mixed. It has been stated that they owe much of their constitution to a peculiar evolution in the semi-arid or arid crescent which caps sub-Saharan Africa to the north and north-east. We may now say that their most conspicuous features – the elongated body, the especially long legs (which are very efficient cooling radiators owing to their short diameter), the narrow shoulders and thorax, the leanness, the narrow head and face, and the high and narrow nose – all represent genetic adaptations to dry heat. There is no need to postulate an extra-African 'Caucasoid' element in their gene pool for explaining such a characteristic as the narrow nose. Only genetic traits that appear to be insensitive to air moisture can indicate how important an extra-African component might have been incorporated in their gene pool. As previously pointed out on the basis of several genetic traits of the blood, such an exotic influence has been detected only in restricted peripheral areas.

We are now also in a position to explain how and why genetic differentiation produced such strikingly different physiques as those of the 'elongated Africans' and the Pygmies. These two opposite poles of morphological differentiation correspond to the two climatic opposites of tropical Africa: the hot and dry, with well-marked seasons, and the uniformly hot and wet.

Of course all intermediates are present between the two climatic extremes. Selection by itself, without mixture between contrasted populations, has been able to produce a continuum of adaptive states ranging from one morphological extreme to the other.

However, it would be an oversimplification to reduce the climatic diversity of environments in sub-Saharan Africa to scales of air moisture, air temperature, and seasonal uniformity. We may be sure that a number of other factors (including air movement) have intervened in determining the climatic biotope of many regions. In response to this diversity, selection has acted to produce a variety of adaptive states of human morphology on both sides of the line joining the two opposite poles of morphological differentiation.

Moreover, it must be stressed again that different adaptive equilibria may be attained in a similar environment by populations whose genetic make-up differed at the start.

Social and sexual selection. Let us repeat that selection is based on unequal reproduction of the various genotypes. Selection through disease, climate, and possibly nutrition, is adaptive; it induces a shift of the gene pool towards an equilibrium in which reproductive waste is minimal in the given environmental conditions. This list of factors of 'natural' selection is not exhaustive; perhaps some aspects of culture induce adaptive selection.

Let us leave aside the debatable question of whether selection towards a better intellectual and emotional endowment is still operative in mankind today. Alice Brues [22] suggested an example of culture as a possible factor of genetic differentiation in proposing that the short stature of the Bushman and Pygmy bowmen, and the tallness of the Tutsi and other spearmen, are each adaptive to their ways of hunting.

Whatever its importance as a factor of adaptive selection, culture certainly plays an important role in selective processes which are not directed towards adaptation. Polygamy is the basis of such a process. In a society which practises polygyny (that is, in which a man may have several wives, as is the case with most African populations), when a family attains a higher social or economic status, its males will marry more wives and beget more children. Whatever the adaptive value of their genome, they will contribute more to the next generation.

Traditions of many African ethnic groups assign a foreign origin to the ancestors of their chiefs or kings. If these ancestors and their descendants have reproduced more than the other members of the group, the gene pool of the population will have shifted towards that of the ruling family. Judging by the number of wives of some African kings in the recent past, this process may have gone far in transforming the anthropological picture of some areas in a few generations. In this case social selection contrasts with adaptive selection, a slow process even when selective pressure is high.

Sexual selection acts in a way similar to social selection. Suppose that, whatever its adaptive value, a feature is considered sexually attractive; it is probable that its bearers will marry younger, or stay widowed for a shorter time, or have more opportunity for extra-marital intercourse. If the favoured features are – even partly – hereditary, sexual selection will increase their frequency from one generation to the next.

Very little is known about the importance of this factor of genetic change. On the evidence of interviews, Tobias [205] suggested that steatopygia, an accumulation of fat on the buttocks, is especially frequent in Bushwomen and Hottentot women because the males find it sexually attractive. Perhaps also the *tablier* or macro-nymphia, an elongation of the labia minora, owes its frequency of nearly 100 per cent in Bushwomen to a similar mechanism. This feature seems to be genetical in the Bushmen [220]. This is not so, however, in some populations of sub-Saharan Africa where it is also frequent; in these cases the girls encourage it by mutual repeated elongation of the labia minora. They certainly do so in order to become more sexually attractive. This reinforces the belief that hereditary macronymphia – which, like steatopygia, has no known adaptive value – has increased in frequency among the Bushmen through sexual selection.

Why is this feature of genetical origin only in this one group? Probably because it arose by mutation in some ancestors of the Bushmen and attained a fairly high frequency by the hazards of drift. Only then was there a basis on which sexual selection could act.

Possibly in some cases sexual selection is 'aimed' at genetic adaptation. Whatever the level of consciousness of the process, a society may consider as sexually attractive those phenotypes which have proved more viable in their environment. For example, the pastoral Ful, or Bororo, who live in the arid Sahel just south of the Sahara, attach much importance to physique. They consider an aesthetic ideal to be that morphology which has been described here as being adaptive to a hot and dry climate: gracile body build, long legs, a long and narrow nose. Girls who conform to this ideal are courted more than others. From time to time the *gereol* dance is held, in which young men, watched by the girls and married women, try to display their beauty, grace and sexual attractiveness. The dance temporarily brings together people from far and wide and leads to casual intercourse, adultery and marriages [54]. Such behaviour, practised by a polygamous society, undoubtedly has a strong selective effect.

So far, social selection has been presented under its positive aspect: promoting the reproduction of certain individuals. A society may also exert a negative selection by preventing the reproduction of the bearers of certain characteristics. If these traits are determined by heredity, or partly so, selection will be at work. African societies practise this kind of selection, which is called eugenics by some scientists when it aims at eliminating those genes which the society considers to be undesirable. In the Luba of Zaire, a large number of traits are believed to bring bad luck to the community. They include some which may be partly inheritable, like club foot, hare lip, and hydrocephaly. Until recently (and even today to some extent), their bearers were suppressed soon after birth or, if this did not happen, were unlikely to find a mate [221].

Social behaviour had therefore a strong selective action against the genetic background of such anomalies.

Social selection will differentiate the gene pools if its rules differ between various populations. The frequency of albinism varies in Central Africa up to values which are astonishingly high in areas where plentiful ultra violet rays strongly handicap albino individuals. The explanation of such high frequencies seems to be social selection, perhaps combined with genetic drift in some cases; in sub-Saharan Africa, albinos are both feared and revered. Social behaviour towards them may hesitate between suppression in childhood and preservation; the balance differs between cultural areas.

2. GENETIC DRIFT. Contrary to selection, genetic drift differentiates the populations randomly. The part it has played in sub-Saharan Africa cannot be quantified from the biological data: we have no means of discriminating between the results of selection, genetic drift and interbreeding. We may however presume that genetic drift has been an important factor. We know that the probability and magnitude of drift over the generations is a function of the size of the mating circles. We also know that the period of hunting-gathering economy was by far the longest in the history of any population in the subcontinent (for a number of populations like the Pygmies and Bushmen, this period is not yet over). Throughout this time, men could live only in small groups, each occupying a rather large territory, as otherwise the food resources would have been quickly exhausted and famine would have reduced the community size down to the carrying capacity of the biotope. In this man does not differ from other animals; but to the animal, the carrying capacity of a biotope depends only on the characteristics of the environment, whereas to man it depends also to a large extent on culture. All techniques and habits relating to food gathering or production and to disease control greatly influence the upper limit to population density. We may therefore presume that during the millennia of hunting-gathering, the mating circles kept small.

In view of the genetic drift known to have occurred in some European rural communities [27], we may also suspect that it has acted, and still acts, to modify the gene pool of those many African populations who practise a rural way of life, whether based on agriculture or stock-raising, or both.

The size of the mating circles, however, depends also on the habits of the various groups: if their members customarily marry into other communities, the mating circles will obviously be larger. If such exogamy is important enough, genetic drift will be negligible even if each of the communities is small. Detailed demographic and genetic studies of the remaining hunting-gathering communities, and of a number of other African populations, will have to be made before it is possible to make meaningful extrapolations about genetic drift into the past.

Other circumstances favourable to drift have certainly occurred again and again in sub-Saharan Africa. The traditions of nearly all communities tell of their foundation by a very small group, which parted from a larger population and settled in new territory. The founder effect must therefore have produced instantaneous drift thousands of times in the biological history of man in Africa.

This process must have been especially frequent during recent times, when the hazards of the discovery or acquisition of more efficient means of exploiting the environment (most of all, those of agriculture and stock-breeding) gave to some groups the opportunity to increase quickly in number. As soon as the raised carrying capacity of the environment was saturated, such groups were forced to branch off, and their offspring gradually expanded over large areas by repeated parting of small founder groups. The only limits to such expansion were set by the suitability of the new habitats for the cultural equipment of the immigrants, and by the power of resistance of the local communities. However combative the latter, they could only be absorbed, exterminated or forced to leave if the carrying capacity of the biotope for their way of life was considerably lower than for the newcomers.

In many cases the founder effect would have been reinforced by the fact that the founders of the groups were relatives. This circumstance, attested by many traditions, increases the probability of a noticeable biological difference between the migrants and the remaining population.

The bottleneck effect, resulting from decimation by disease or war, must also have played a considerable part in the biological history of African communities. This kind of drift also probably found more favourable circumstances more frequently after the discovery of food production. In dense and settled populations, a number of communicable illnesses, like malaria and many epidemic diseases, strike much more severely than they do in the scattered, semi-nomad communities of hunter-gatherers. The owning of cultivated land and cattle also made people more warlike, encouraged by the urge to expand.

3. MUTATIONS As stated in the Introduction, mutations are rare events. Although some local conditions possibly increase mutation rates – like the presence of γ rays emitted from uranium deposits in an area of Shaba, formerly Katanga, in south-eastern Zaire – recurrent mutations cannot by themselves be an important factor of genetic differentiation in sub-Saharan Africa. The mutant alleles can attain relatively high frequencies only if backed by selection, as in the case of haemoglobin S in malarial areas, or through the hazards of genetic drift.

As a matter of fact, there is no proof that mutants like the ones responsible for haemoglobins S and C arose more than once in Africa. It has even been claimed that haemogoblin S was introduced to Africa from India, together with short-horned Zebu cattle [19]. If it arose only in one population, or were introduced through a narrow coastal strip, a mutant could tell much about migrations and admixture within Africa by its geographical distribution.

4. INTERBREEDING The incorporation of reproducers from a foreign source makes the gene pool of the population shift in the direction of the foreign one, in proportion to the ratio between the numbers of introduced and locally born reproducers. This is arithmetically obvious.

However, if this process has moved a gene frequency away from adaptive equilibrium, selection will tend to bring it back to the initial value. If interbreeding has introduced a mutant allele which was absent from the receiving gene pool, the adaptive equilibrium towards which selection will tend may be quite different from the initial one. For example, as already mentioned, haemoglobin S is perhaps in the process of replacing haemoglobin C on the Volta plateau, whose population was closed to gene flow until recently. Genetic drift may also disturb the intermediate position resulting from interbreeding.

This complexity and interaction of the processes of genetic change makes it a hazardous task to evaluate the relative importance of the contributing populations in the genesis of a gene pool. The greater the number of generations since the mixing, the harder does the task become. It degenerates into pure speculation when the contributing populations and their characteristics are postulated on the basis of racial typology. For example, Czekanowski [47] recognized in Rwanda's Twa population 51 per cent of Negritic, 19 per cent Austro-African, 15 per cent Mediterranoid, 3 per cent Oriental, and 12 per cent of Australoid components. His method is such that any set of anthropological means considered to represent a 'racial type' is given a percentage in the composition of a population. It does not tell anything about the biological history of the population concerned.

In many cases it is hard to evaluate the relative importance of selection and admixture in the building up of the biological characters of a population. One example is provided by the many Twa communities living in the equatorial forest of Zaire in symbiosis with agriculturalists. They are said to have lived in the forest for much longer than the agriculturalists, who were brought into contact with them relatively recently by the Bantu expansion (a process described in Chapter 12).

One such Twa population has been studied in some detail: those people living south of the Sankuru in Zaire, as a sub-tribe of the Kuba. In their morphology they roughly occupy a middle position between the Bushong, the agriculturalist sub-tribe to which the king of the Kuba belongs, and the Mbuti Pygmies, showing an extreme of genetic adaptation to the equatorial forest. In size, and much more so in shape, they stand nearer to the Bushong than to the Mbuti [97]. Judging from this anthropometric evidence, and from the assumption that the symbiosis has produced some gene flow from the agriculturalists to the Twa, one is tempted to conclude that the Twa of the Kuba represent a recent mixture between the agriculturalist newcomers and a Mbuti-like Pygmy community. However, the evidence from the ABO blood groups contradicts this view. For this system, the Bushong stand far apart from the Mbuti, from whom the Twa, instead of occupying an intermediate position, are still more different. The most likely explanation of this contrast in the evidence from different systems of hereditary traits is in terms of adaptive convergence. The Twa would represent the present state of a process of genetic adaptation to the equatorial forest, which would not have gone so far as in the Mbuti, who came from a different initial stock.

All this shows that, as elsewhere, the study of admixture in sub-Saharan Africa involves adding to the biological data all the historical, archaeological, cultural and linguistic evidence available. The effects of admixture from exotic populations have been considered in Chapter 5; biological evidence shows that it has been moderate. On the other hand, interbreeding between the populations of the sub-continent has certainly been highly active. Sub-Saharan Africa, as we saw in Chapter 2, presents strong barriers to penetration, but few obstacles to internal wandering.

The traditions of all African populations tell of the incorporation of foreign individuals or groups. In many cases such a process has been so frequent and important that the biological identity of a population in the course of time becomes a matter of convention. Our units of biological study represent only temporary groupings of peoples defined by their tendency to endogamy (breeding between themselves). Ethnologists also are today acutely aware of the frequent rearranging of the units called 'tribes', a term which tends to be abandoned because of its ambiguity [219].

Besides countless processes of regional admixture, the history of Africa, as reconstructed by archaeologists, cultural anthropologists, linguists and historians working on written documents, tells of large-scale migrations and expansions. Such events will have profoundly modified the anthropological map of the continent. They have produced population replacements and admixture between largely different stocks, favoured genetic drift, and released selection afresh.

7

Classifications: Biological, Cultural and Linguistic

Biological Classifications

A description of the biological features of populations requires factual knowledge only. Whatever the wording accompanying it, it consists of a list of anthropological means and frequencies by units. In the case of sub-Saharan Africa, such a catalogue already comprises more than one hundred pages of tables [98]. This information is the basis for reconstructing the biological history of the present peoples of the subcontinent, in terms of biological diversity (reviewed in the last chapter) and of historical data of a non-biological nature.

It would be cumbersome to present this reconstruction unit by unit. As stated in Chapter 5, there are approximately one thousand populations in sub-Saharan Africa; and the number of human populations in the world is, of course, several times this figure. Confronted with such large numbers, the human mind tends to reduce them to a lower number of classes. If attainable, the resulting classification would make the presentation and memorization of the characteristics of the populations much easier. By itself, however, it would not bring any understanding of the observed diversity. In particular, it would not necessarily reflect phylogeny (relationship by descent).

The logic of a classificatory procedure consists of grouping together those objects which most resemble one another. It fails when it groups in different classes those objects which resemble one another more than they resemble other objects of their own class.

Statisticians have elaborated measurements of the overall

differences between populations for a number of traits. A table of all
such anthropological distances between one hundred populations of
sub-Saharan Africa has been computed. A glance at it makes it clear
that all proposed anthropological (or racial) classifications of Africa
abound in cases of failure as just defined. Moreover, the analysis of
this table reveals that any other exhaustive classification of its units
would contain many contradictions to the logical basis of the classificatory procedure. Only a minority of the units can be grouped;
the highest number of populations in the taxons so delimited is
three. Reducing the computed multidimensional distances to a two-
dimensional drawing would show a fairly homogeneous cluster of
points with only a few units or groups of two units isolated at the
periphery of the figure [98].

The data used in this analysis concern only one-tenth of the
populations of sub-Saharan Africa. Adding the other units to the
picture would most probably reduce or suppress the isolation in
which some of the peripheral units stand. A satisfactory racial
classification of the populations of sub-Saharan Africa seems therefore impossible.

This failure implies that the differentiation of *Homo sapiens* in
sub-Saharan Africa cannot be reconstructed simply in terms of the
diverging evolution of a few genetically isolated groups of related
populations. One can easily appreciate why the genesis of the
present picture is much more complex: genetic drift – a factor of
random differentiation – has occurred in many circumstances
and places, mixture has shuffled the cards in countless ways,
and genetic adaptation to gradually distributed aspects of the
environment like air moisture has tended to generate smooth
clines.

The lack of any acceptable classification of the populations of
sub-Saharan Africa does not prevent us from presenting their
biological history by chapters, as is done here. In two cases, that of
the Khoisan peoples and that of the Pygmies, we are concerned
with groups of related populations which have undergone a
marked genetic differentiation and have kept their resulting origin-
ality through a relatively strong genetic isolation. Next to be considered are the Twa populations of the equatorial forest and
neighbouring areas, whose case has already been partly discussed.
They do not form a taxon, but their history looks similar: they
probably represent a wave of migration into the equatorial forest

later than that of the Pygmies. As opposed to the latter, who display an extreme morphological adaptation to a wet environment, there are a number of populations showing a marked morphological adaptation to dry conditions; their origins and spread will be discussed next. These are the populations (much too diverse to form a taxon) called 'elongated Africans' in this book, as well as a group of interrelated populations of the Upper Nile valley: the Dinka, Nuer and Shilluk. Chapter 11 is concerned with a tentative reconstruction of the biological history of a vast area: sub-Saharan Africa west of the Nile and north of the equatorial forest. Among the many factors of the present human diversity in this area, stress is laid on those which seem to have had a widespread influence: biological adaptation to climate along the north–south cline induced by the gradual desiccation of the Sahara, and vast expansions resulting from the invention or acquisition of new ways of subsistence. Chapter 12 deals with a relatively recent explosive expansion: that of the Bantu-speaking populations, who now occupy approximately one-third of the African continent, south of the area covered by the preceding chapter.

Cultural Classifications

This way of presenting the current biological diversity of man in Africa shows analogies with that used by Professor George Murdock [157] in presenting the cultural history of the peoples of the continent. Essentially he describes cultural states, like that of the African hunters, and processes, like the cultural impact of Indonesia. He groups forty-eight classes, defined as groups of tribes of essentially the same language and culture. These are treated as follows: African hunters; the Sudanic agricultural civilization; the North African agricultural civilization (including Saharan Negroes and Negroes of the Sudan fringe); synthesis in the Nile corridor; southward expansion of the Cushites; cultural impact of Indonesia (in which the Cameroun highland Bantu are considered); expansion of the Bantu; and North and West African pastoralism. This can hardly be called a classification.

Apparently, the African communities cannot be classified any more satisfactorily from the cultural aspect than from the biological one. As Professor Jacques Maquet [142] points out, the *Ethnographic Survey of Africa* classifies the populations, or groups of related populations, on a purely geographical basis, by first

Figure 16. Linguistic map of Africa

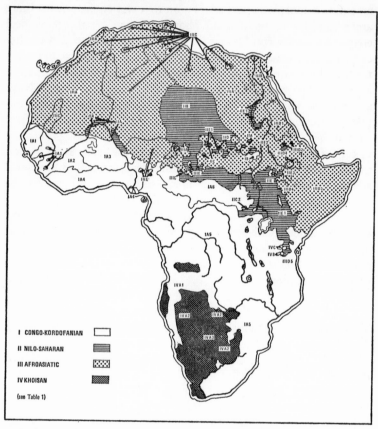

I CONGO-KORDOFANIAN

II NILO-SAHARAN

III AFROASIATIC

IV KHOISAN

(see Table 1)

sub-dividing Africa into large areas which are far from culturally homogeneous. Similar cultures are allotted to different primary classes, a contradiction to the logic of classification. Maquet also raises valid objections to Baumann and Westerman's [14] classification of African societies into twenty-six culture circles, derived from nine fundamental African civilizations which would have been 'purer' originally, though still recognizable as components of the present cultures. This view is reminiscent of the typological concept of race still adhered to by a few physical anthropologists, a concept which looks untenable in the light of current population genetics.

TABLE 1

Summary of classification of the languages of Africa (*after J. H. Greenberg* [74])

I Congo-Kordofanian	I A Niger-Congo	I A 1 West-Atlantic
		I A 2 Mande
		I A 3 Voltaic
		I A 4 Kwa
		I A 5 Benue-Congo
		I A 6 Adamawa-Eastern
	I B Kordofanian	
II Nilo-Saharan	II A Songhai	
	II B Saharan	
	II C Maban	
	II D Fur	
	II E Chari-Nile	II E 1 Eastern Sudanic
		II E 2 Central Sudanic
		II E 3 Berta
		II E 4 Kunama
	II F Koman	
III Afroasiatic	III A Semitic	
	III B Egyptian	
	III C Berber	
	III D Cushitic	III D 1 Northern Cushitic
		III D 2 Central Cushitic
		III D 3 Eastern Cushitic
		III D 4 Western Cushitic
		III D 5 Southern Cushitic
	III E Chad	
IV Khoisan	IV A South African	IV A 1 Northern
		IV A 2 Central
		IV A 3 Southern
	IV B Sandawe	
	IV C Hadza	

Maquet's own classification avoids historical considerations. He classifies the societies of sub-Saharan Africa into six civilizations: (1) the civilization of the bow, to which the Pygmies, Twa and Bushmen belong; (2) the civilization of the spear, which includes, among others, the Tutsi of Rwanda and Burundi, and the Dinka of the Nile valley; (3) the civilization of the granaries, which he restricts to the savanna south of the equatorial forest; (4) the civilization of the clearings, displayed by the agriculturalists of the moist forest; (5) the civilization of the cities, which is dominant in a wide strip from the Sahel southwards to the limit of the moist forest; (6) the industrial civilization. Most probably this classification of cultures is as objectionable as those of biological populations for similar reasons: it cuts a quasi-continuum into discrete classes.

Linguistic Classifications

Though an aspect of culture, language is such a paramount and diversified characteristic of man that its study constitutes an autonomous discipline: linguistics. Several classifications of the African languages have been proposed. The one adhered to in this book is that advocated by Professor John Greenberg [74]. It is widely used today and is based on purely linguistic evidence (a necessity which has been commonly disregarded in the past). It leans upon a mass comparison of the languages, a procedure similar to the computation of a matrix of all the biological distances between pairs of populations which is basic to the synthesis presented here. This classification is reproduced in Table 1.

The patterns of diversity of the African communities in the biological, the linguistic and the cultural fields do not coincide. For example, the Tutsi, Hutu and Twa of Rwanda, who differ largely from one another in culture and physical traits, all speak the same language, Kinyarwanda. Biologically, the Bantu-speaking Bushong are much nearer to the Zande, who speak an Adamawa-Eastern language, than to the Bembe of their own linguistic group. The Mande-speaking Gio and the Kwa-speaking Kran form a biological cluster. In their physique, the Luo of the Lake Victoria area, who speak an Eastern Sudanic language like the Dinka, Nuer and Shilluk of the Sudanic Nile, differ greatly from these groups and resemble much more closely a number of Bantu-speaking populations. There is no 'Hamitic' entity which could be defined as speaking languages of the same class, leading a pastoral mode of life, and displaying 'elongated' physical traits: the Ful herdsmen do not speak an Afroasiatic language any more than the Tutsi, and many Afroasiatic-speaking populations of the Chad do not raise cattle.

Even reference to common ancestors does not imply a close biological affinity, because the contribution of common ancestors to the gene pool, if not mythical, may vary largely between the populations. For example, those few Ful communities on which comparable anthropo-biological data have been collected differ greatly from one another; the Ful of southern Cameroun resemble the Haya of Tanzania more than they resemble any other Ful population studied.

It is as misleading to pool biological, cultural and linguistic data in a list of criteria for a biological classification as it is rewarding to confront these categories for the purpose of an historical reconstruction.

8

The Khoisan Peoples

If immigration from Europe and Asia is not considered, two main stocks have contributed to the present population of southern Africa: the Bantu and the Khoisan. These are linguistic terms, but with relatively few exceptions this linguistic distinction coincides with a clear-cut biological one. That is, most Bantu-speaking groups of the area differ from each other much less in biological traits than they do from Khoisan-speaking groups, and vice versa.

The Bantu populations of southern Africa owe their biological proximity to their sharing of a common history. Their ancestors, who belonged to related groups, started entering this part of the continent from the north during the first five centuries AD. They expanded over most of the arable land, introducing Bantu languages, iron-working and agriculture (perhaps also cattle-breeding) into an immense area populated by essentially hunting-gathering populations, the ancestors of the present Khoisan. This major population movement is only a part of the much larger process of Bantu expansion (Chapter 12).

The term Khoisan covers two groups of populations: the Bushmen and the Hottentots. The word is a compound of the Hottentots' name for themselves, Khoikhoi, and their name for the Bushmen, San. There is no basis for a linguistic distinction between the two groups: the language of the Hottentots is just one of the central South African Khoisan languages, close to that spoken by the Naron Bushmen. In particular, as Greenberg [74] has pointed out, there is no justification for classifying the Hottentot language as 'Hamitic', as once advocated by Carl Meinhof [148], nor even for assuming Hamitic (or Afroasiatic) influences on it, a view voiced by I. Schapera [183].

The Khoisan languages, which form a family of the highest rank in Greenberg's classification, are quite diverse. They have long been noted for their peculiar suction sounds called 'clicks'. To the linguist, this is only one of their characteristics. Clicks also occur in the speech of several Bantu tribes of southern Africa, like the Koba of Botswana, the Sotho of Lesotho, and the Nguni of Natal. Since they are absent from Bantu languages farther north, this is best explained on the hypothesis that the invading Bantu married Bushwomen and that these, in learning the speech of their husbands, substituted their own implosive consonants for some of the normal consonants of the latter. They then transmitted this pronunciation to their children, thus initiating a phonetic innovation which was perpetuated by their offspring [157]. This hypothesis, we shall see, is fully supported by biology.

Two populations of East Africa also use clicks in their speech: the Sandawe and the Hadza, who live some eighty miles apart on the plains of northern Tanzania. The Sandawe number about 28,000, the Hadza only about 800. Until 1964–5, most of the Hadza were nomadic hunter-gatherers, and some of them resumed this way of life after the group had been persuaded to settle. The Sandawe also were essentially hunter-gatherers until the relatively recent past, when they gradually became settled husbandmen practising shifting hoe cultivation and they also began to keep domesticated livestock. On the basis of rather scanty material, Greenberg [74] classified Hadza and Sandawe as Khoisan languages, each at the same taxonomic level as the whole set of South African Khoisan languages. With more detailed evidence, there is now some dispute as to whether the Hadza language should be classified as Khoisan or Afroasiatic.

Physically, the Sandawe and Hadza resemble each other closely. Are they the remnants of a once more widespread East African population of hunters which spoke Khoisan languages and shared at least some of the biological characteristics of the Khoisan of South Africa? If so, it would fit with Brothwell's [20] view that the source of the Khoisan people was in East Africa (see page 40). However, although the occurrence of subsidiary Bushmanoid characteristics has been alleged for the Sandawe and Hadza, these two populations closely resemble the neighbouring Bantu-speaking tribes (the Nyaturu and Sukuma respectively). If there was a Bushman-like element in their ancestry, its contribution to their present gene pool is small. In what concerns the physical anthropology of the living populations, the term Khoisan must be restricted to the Bushmen and Hottentots of southern Africa.

These two groups differ in their mode of life. Nomadism in migratory bands subsisting on hunting and gathering (and fishing among the marsh-dwelling Tanikwe) characterizes the Bushmen. Of an estimated total number of 55,000, some 35,000 confine themselves exclusively to hunting-gathering pursuits, like their Later Stone Age ancestors until a recent past. Some thousands more spend part of the year in this way and part in a more settled state on farms. Probably about 15,000 of those recognized as Bushmen have permanently lost their nomadic food-gathering habits [206].

The Hottentots, who today number about 30,000, are pastoral people, keeping large herds of long-horned cattle and fat-tailed sheep as well as a fair number of goats. The milk of these animals constitutes a staple element in their diet. In their culture as in their speech, many scholars once saw a clear, even predominant 'Hamitic' influence [205]. This view, together with a corresponding one in the field of physical anthropology, derived from the belief in a Hamitic entity characterized by a linguistic class, cattle breeding, and 'elongated' physical traits whose ultimate origin was ascribed to a 'Caucasoid' component. Murdock [157], who does not share this belief, states that apart from pastoralism, all other aspects of Hottentot culture show such striking affinities with that of the Bushmen that we are left with no reasonable alternative except to regard them as a Bushman group, who adopted cattle from the south-western Bantu and made modest readjustments to their culture in adaptation to the new and more stable mode of life.

Those Bushmen who maintain their ancient way of life are now confined to a few relatively inhospitable areas. Most are distributed in the hot and dry semi-desertic Kalahari, with small groups living in the Okavango Swamp region and others in more heavily wooded areas such as southern Angola. The main Bushman groups, of which bands of hunter-gatherers constitute a part, and on which a body of anthropo-biological data have been collected, are the Kung of northern South West Africa (together with a few bands who live in southern Angola), and the Naron and Auen of the central Kalahari. Only two groups of Hottentots still keep their ethnic individuality: the Nama and the Korana, although the latter are nearly extinct.

As mentioned in Chapter 3, a stock ancestral to the living

Khoisan was present from Zambia southwards thousands of years ago. It occupied the region now embraced by the Republic of South Africa, South West Africa, Botswana, Lesotho, Swaziland, Rhodesia, and portions of Angola and Zambia. The shrinkage of this vast territory down to the present habitat of the Khoisan results from a very recent sequence of events: they were squashed between the expanding Bantu waves, the first of whom entered the area from the north nearly two millennia ago, and the northward progressive expansion of the Europeans, who first settled at Table Bay, near the Cape, in 1652, and ultimately occupied large tracts of desirable land in Orange Free State and the Transvaal.

The Khoisan could not compete successfully with the invaders. The latter were equipped with iron weapons and tools (and firearms in the case of Europeans), far more effective than the Later Stone Age implements of the former. Still more striking was the contrast in the population density that the modes of life of the Khoisan and of the invaders permitted. Hunting-gathering allows only low densities: the equilibrium between the food that the human community levies off the environment and the capacity of the latter to restore itself necessarily fixes human density at a lower level in a hunting-gathering economy than a food-producing one.

In the long run, the Khoisan, who could not flee anywhere, could only face more or less total extermination, assimilation, serfdom, or withdrawal into inhospitable refuge areas. A combination of several of these events marked the recent history of most groups. The Heikum Bushmen are to a considerable extent culturally attached to the Ambo and Herero tribes of the south-western Bantu. The Hiechware, Nusan, Ohekwe and Tanikwe are largely serfs or dependants of the Tswana and other Bantu tribes of Botswana. The Xam, or Cape Bushmen, including remnants of unnamed groups farther east in Lesotho and the Transvaal, are extinct or nearly so. Extinct also are the Cape Hottentots, together with the Eastern Hottentots, who might have numbered about 50,000 by the time of the arrival of the first European settlers. In the late seventeenth century, a group of Hottentots, the Korana, split off from the Kora tribe, withdrawing north-eastward to escape the Dutch. Around 1850 their number was estimated at 20,000; it soon decreased sharply as a result of disastrous wars against the Sotho, who finally assimilated them; today they have disappeared as an ethnic entity. The Nama of South West Africa, who still number about 25,000,

Figure 17. Localities of the ethnic groups of Southern Africa cited in the text

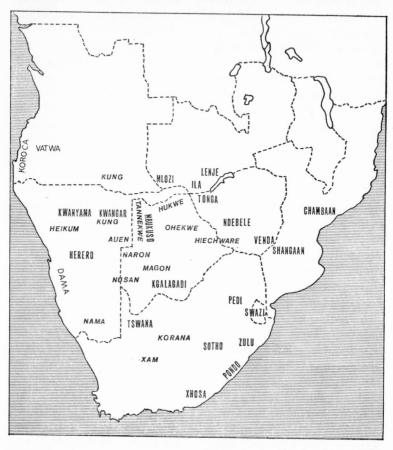

are the only Hottentot group whose aboriginal culture survived long enough to be studied by ethnologists. The Korana, who numbered 20,000 only a little more than a century ago, have now lost their ancestral culture; Professor C. S. Grobbelaar counted them as 377 in 1956 [77].

As a result of this dramatic fate of the Bushmen and Hottentots, the number of relatively unmixed Khoisan populations that anthropology can study today is very low; they are only a small proportion of the ones who lived until recently. Professor Sherwood Washburn

[225] estimates that there were perhaps three to five times as many Bushmen as there were Europeans only 15,000 years ago, when the ice sheets of the last glaciation reduced the habitable area of Europe to half that available to the Khoisan in eastern and southern Africa. Even restricting our attention to the distribution of Khoisan in southern Africa by the beginning of the Christian era, this immense area was surely peopled by several dozen distinct Khoisan populations. Living in small communities in an area which provided a variety of habitats, they most probably showed a relatively large biological diversity, as a result of genetic drift, differentiating selection, and isolation.

The available skeletal material is too scarce to permit an evaluation of this diversity (which in any case would concern oesteological differentiation only). Even by using refined mathematical methods like multiple discriminant analysis, nearly all subfossil crania from Zambia, Rhodesia, Botswana and South Africa fall within the range of variation of one of the modern groups of the area: Bushman, Hottentot, and Bantu [175]. Computed on measurements of the skull, the biological distance between recent Bushmen and Hottentots is small relative to the Bushman – South African Bantu and Hottentot – South African Bantu separations. However, the Hottentots depart from the Bushmen in the direction of the Bantu (Sotho, Xhosa and Zulu, who are close to each other) [176].

Little mixed groups of living Bushmen on which detailed data have been collected are mainly the Kung of South West Africa and Angola, and the Naron and Auen of Botswana. The Nama and Korana, who have also been studied in some detail by anthropobiologists, are the only groups which could represent relatively little-mixed Hottentots (although their recent history makes it clear that there were European and Bantu contributions to their gene pool).

These groups exhibit a number of features which, according to their frequencies, makes them markedly distinct from the South African Bantu, and still more so from Africans of other areas. The most striking anatomical feature to attain a high frequency in the Khoisan is steatopygia, which consists of an accumulation of fat over the buttocks and thighs, without general obesity. It has a skeletal basis, with an extreme curvature in the small of the back due to strong lumbar lordosis. In females, fat accumulates on this shelf especially at puberty and with ensuing pregnancies. Males have an approximately equal lordosis, but they accumulate relatively little fat.

It has long been suggested that steatopygia represents a reserve food and water store like the camel's hump or the sheep's fat tail, as a genetic adaptation to the desertic habitat of the Khoisan. However, their withdrawal into the Kalahari is very recent, leaving much too short a time for natural selection to have developed this feature; moreover, steatopygia appears in rock paintings made by ancestral Bushmen in well-watered regions [206]. Unless steatopygia was an adaptive trait associated with a hunter-gatherer economy in the ancestral homeland, a purely hypothetical supposition, the only mechanism favouring its high frequency in the Khoisan would seem to be sexual selection; as mentioned on p. 84, large buttocks are considered by Bushman males as highly attractive [206].

Sexual selection possibly also played a prominent role in the development of another striking anatomical feature: macronymphia, also known as the *tablier* or Hottentot apron, which is nearly general in Khoisan females. This elongation of the labia minora is apparently genetic in the Khoisan, though it might be acquired in most of the sporadic cases observed in Africa north of Southern Africa [220].

A high proportion of Bushman males also have a distinctive genital feature: a semi-erect, horizontal position of the penis.

Another morphological distinction of the Khoisan is the usual presence of eye folds. Together with narrow palpebral fissures (slit-like lids), a depressed nasal bridge and prominent cheek bones, eye folds in the Khoisan were once considered to be 'Mongoloid' features, introduced by Asians in more or less ancient times [50]. The evidence now available on gene markers makes this view untenable. Instead, Tobias [206] considers such features to be the result of tendencies towards infantilization; such tendencies also appear in the skeleton and arose in Africa long before there is any evidence of Asiatic contacts. For him, Mongoloid peoples and the Khoisan independently developed trends towards infantilization, with end results which necessarily show some similarity. He enumerates a list of other Khoisan features which recall the morphology of the infant. They include a number of cranial characters like a low skull with marked parietal flattening on the mid line, a vertical or even bulging forehead, smooth brows, strong bossing of the parietal and occipital regions, a very small face, and small teeth.

Another characteristic which distinguishes the Khoisan from the other populations of sub-Saharan Africa is their relatively light, yellow-brown skin colour. Skin reflectance at the 685 mu wavelength, which has a high negative correlation with the amount of melanin (black pigment) in the skin, is over 40 per cent in the Hottentots and Central Kalahari Bushmen groups measured by Weiner and co-workers [229], whereas the Okavango Bantu tribes (the Mbukuso and Kwangar) register in the low twenties.

Why are the Khoisan relatively light skinned? Surely not because of an Asiatic component in their gene pool. They are as genuinely African as any other group; the distinction between 'black' and 'yellow' Africans must be explained in terms of differentiation. As stated on page 78, the amount of melanin in the skin is currently considered to be adaptive to the dose of ultra violet rays in the sunlight. If the lighter skin of the Khoisan is to be explained on this basis, it means that it developed, over thousands of years of genetic adaptation, in an area where sun rays were less intense than in the original homelands of other African populations. The Hottentots and Central Kalahari Bushmen were indeed forced quite recently into their present habitat. Most of them came from the most southern part of the continent, the farthest away from the equator, where on a yearly average the dose of ultra violet rays is relatively moderate. It has been noted that in the Kalahari, where solar radiation is intense, the yellowish skin of the Bushmen is a positive handicap, for they are prone to sunburn. Probably there was quite a wide range of skin colours in the Khoisan populations when this group covered the whole of southern Africa.

Although not of pygmy stature, the Khoisan are small. Listing Bushman groups from north to south – no clear geographical trend is evident – average stature recorded is between 157 and 160 cm in four samples of Kung, 158 cm in the Auen, 159 cm in the Naron, and 158 cm in the Magon. The Hottentots are a little taller: the figures are 162 cm in the Nama and 160 cm in the Korana.

As stated in Chapter 3, the living Khoisan peoples are probably descended from a Large Khoisan (taller and large-headed) stock; the reduction in size occurred only a few thousand years ago in South Africa. What in the environment could have favoured this process in the communities of hunter-gatherers? There is no clear answer to this question, apart from the suggestion put forward by Brues [22] that hunting with a bow would favour short stature, contrary to hunting with a spear. An officer in charge of the Bushman Survey of Bechuanaland Protectorate (now Botswana) gained the impression that the taller members of Bushman groups are almost invariably poor hunters, are clumsy, and enjoy little prestige [208]. If this is the case, tall stature might be selected against in the Bushmen by a combination of natural and socio-sexual selection.

The hair on the Khoisan scalp is usually of the 'peppercorn' or tufted type. This is an extreme form of African hair, diametrically opposed to the straight hair of the yellow Asians. Why it developed remains unexplained.

Up to now, the accent has been laid on the distinctive features of the Khoisan. However, when compared to the rest of mankind, they show clear morphological affinities with the other populations of sub-Saharan Africa. This speaks for a common origin of Khoisan and non-Khoisan African groups, allowing enough time and isolation for the development of the present differences.

The set of purely genetic traits, like blood groups, depicts a similar picture and calls for the same interpretation. In these features also the Khoisan are clearly African, but display a number of peculiarities. Several alleles in which African populations differ sharply from the rest of mankind, or at least from Europeans and Arabs, even have 'ultra-African' frequencies in the Khoisan. This is the case for two alleles of the Rh system of blood groups: nearly all Khoisan groups have a very high R_0 frequency, the highest ever recorded occurring in a group of Bushmen; the r allele is almost completely absent in them. A number of genetic factors of the blood which are peculiarly African, namely V, Js and Henshaw, all occur in the Khoisan. Like other African populations, the Khoisan lack the Di^a allele of the Diego system of blood groups, a common variant in the Far East.

When the differences between Bushmen, Hottentots and Southern African Bantu for a number of genetic traits of the blood are pooled, the table of genetic distances so obtained makes it clear that Bushmen and Hottentots cluster together, the distance between them being closer than that between each of them and the Bantu [119]. This is what Rightmire [176] arrived at by computing general distances from measurements on the skull; and this is also what emerges from a description of the anatomical features. It justifies the use of the term 'Khoisan' in a biological sense, with the important reservation that this cluster has been defined from a very small number of populations out of a probably much greater diversity in the past; and that the analysis presented here has so far excluded a number of peripheral Khoisan-speaking groups whose consideration would make the picture appear more complex.

In two systems of genetic traits of the blood, the Khoisan possess alleles which seemingly arose through mutation in their ancestral line, attained a notable frequency, and migrated only to those Bantu tribes who recently came in contact with Bushmen or Hottentots. This, at least, is the picture suggested by the still scarce data on their distribution in Africa. One is the Gm system of genetic variants of gammaglobulins in the blood plasma. This system shows a large number of alleles in Man, some of which have a restricted distribution. Jenkins, Zoutendyk and Steinberg [118] have studied it in detail in Southern Africa. The Bushmen possess two alleles, $Gm^{1,13}$ and Gm^1, which have never been found in Africa north of southern Africa. In the Bushmen tested so far (a sample of nearly 200 Bushmen of Botswana), $Gm^{1,13}$ attains a frequency of 42 per cent. The corresponding figure in 57 Nama Hottentots is 28 per cent. The second case is offered by the red cell acid phosphatase, an enzyme: besides ubiquitous variants, the Khoisan possess a P^r allele which so far has been found only exceptionally outside southern Africa, except in American Negroes at a frequency of one per cent. It attains a frequency of 22 per cent in a sample of 271 Bushmen, and also in a sample of 149 Nama Hottentots.

The frequencies of such gene markers may be used to assess the proportion of Khoisan admixture in the Bantu-speaking populations of southern Africa [118]. The computed values should, however, be considered as indicative only, for they are based on a set of assumptions which are certainly not fully satisfied: that the allele frequencies in small samples of a few remnant groups of Khoisan represent their past values in the entire group, that the latter was homogeneous for these frequencies, and that mixture has been the only mechanism of change involved. However, the values for the two systems give roughly similar indications, which strengthens their credibility.

For both $Gm^{1,13}$ and p_r, the Tswana show a predominant Khoisan component in their gene pool: 53 and 54 per cent respectively. Were we interested in classification rather than in processes of genetic change, we should classify the Tswana as Khoisan on the basis of this evidence.

Next to the Tswana in proportion of Khoisan admixture come the Xhosa, with values of 60 and 36 per cent for $Gm^{1,13}$ and p_r respectively. These high figures are consistent with other evidence. Linguistically, the Xhosa tribe is a member of the Cape Nguni group, whose languages show a marked Khoisan influence. From a very detailed study of many hundreds of skulls from South Africa, Hertha de Villiers [220] concluded that the Khoisan admixture is especially strong in the Cape Nguni. Data on skin colour give a similar indication: average skin reflectance in Xhosa males is 32 per cent [226], the highest value ever recorded in sub-Saharan Africa in a non-Khoisan speaking group.

The other tribes of the Nguni cluster also show a considerable Khoisan admixture as estimated from $Gm^{1,13}$ and p_r frequencies: 45 and 13 per cent respectively in the Zulu, 25 and 13 in the Swazi, and computed from the $Gm^{1,13}$ frequency only, 45 per cent in the Pondo. The Khoisan admixture computed from the frequency of the same allele is much lower (5 per cent) in the Transvaal Ndebele, who are descended from the northern Nguni.

The Tswana, in whom the highest Khoisan admixture is detected when we consider the two gene markers simultaneously, are a branch of the Sotho peoples. They invaded the country now known as Botswana during the eighteenth and nineteenth centuries coming from the east where the Sotho still occupy Lesotho and a considerable area in the interior of the Republic of South Africa. Though lower than in the Tswana, the Khoisan admixture in the other Sotho tribes is strong: 29 and 13 per cent in the Sotho proper, 17 and 22 per cent in the Pedi, and, estimated from the $Gm^{1,13}$ frequency only 38 per cent in the Venda.

All these figures show a high Khoisan contribution to the gene pool of the Bantu-speaking tribes in southern and eastern South Africa, southern Botswana, and Lesotho. North of this area the figures fall sharply: as estimated from the $Gm^{1,13}$ frequency, 15 per cent in the Shangaan-Tonga of southern Mozambique who have received substantial Nguni increments, 13 per cent in the Mlozi who live along the Zambezi River in western Zambia, and constitute a nation founded in 1838 by a group of Sotho, 12 and 11 per cent in the Plateau and Valley Tonga of Zambia respectively, 6 per cent in the Shambaan of Mozambique and in the Lenje of Zambia, and no trace in a small sample of Ila of Zambia. At least part of the Khoisan genetic influence in Zambia is a recent introduction. In 1818 the famous warrior Shaka became the chief of the Zulu. In the following years he extended the influence of the Nguni tribes over enormous areas of South Africa by devastating military campaigns. Several Zulu chiefs and their followers fled northward, engaged in a career of cattle raiding and pillage, picking up on the way large elements of Sotho, Swazi, Thonga and other ethnic elements. They eventually conquered and settled their present territories in southern Tanzania, Malawi and Zambia, where they are known as the Ngoni. This major historical turmoil undoubtedly led to a considerable amount of genetic mixture, thus introducing or increasing the frequency of the $Gm^{1,13}$ allele in the area. Before the nineteenth century, the Khoisan people apparently did not contribute much to the gene pool of the Bantu-speaking tribes north of the Zambezi (either because Khoisan were absent from the area, or because they resisted assimilation). It might also be that the mutation giving rise to $Gm^{1,13}$ occurred only in South Africa. Moreover, we have no idea about the selective pressures that might act on this allele. More data are needed to make the picture unequivocal.

In striking contrast with the strong Khoisan impregnation in the Bantu of eastern South Africa, the $Gm^{1,13}$ allele is absent in a number of the Bantu tribes living in the northern regions of South West Africa and Botswana [118]. This is the case in the Kuambi, in the Mbukushu, and in a mixed sample of southern Angolans. Where detected in this area, it indicates only a moderate Khoisan admixture: 22 per cent in the Himba (a branch of the Herero), 13 per cent in the Kuangar (perhaps a branch of the Ambo), and 5 per cent in the Kuanyama. All these tribes are members of the south-western Bantu group whose languages form a distinct subdivision within the Bantu group as a whole and who likewise constitute a fairly homogeneous cultural province. Their economy rests upon agriculture and animal husbandry, the former assuming the first place in the north and the latter in the south, where the Herero pursue a life of independent pastoral nomadism which, according to Murdock [157], they transmitted to the Hottentots.

Why is Khoisan mixture so different in the western and eastern

Bantu food-producers of southern Africa? It can only be that in the east, where the land was richer, the Khoisan could only disappear as cultural entities once they were forced to compete with the Bantu invaders; whatever proportion of them did not flee and were not killed were finally assimilated. Judging from the $Gm^{1,13}$ and p_r frequencies, the Khoisan could largely resist assimilation in the dry habitat where they lived and also, until recently, they resisted conquest of their territory. Most probably their distribution did not extend far north in Angola when the Bantu arrived. Biologically non-Khoisan populations of hunter-gatherers were present in the area, and probably occupied all the country north of a line which was not far from the present Angola–South West Africa border.

In South West Africa, the Dama (or Bergdama, which means Mountain Dama) represent the mixed descendants of one of these populations of non-Khoisan hunter-gatherers.They number about 50,000 and speak the Nama Hottentot language. Most of them are herdsmen or servants to the Hottentots or Herero. A minority maintain their original way of life in the reserves. Rainer and Renate Knussmann [122] recently studied their anthropo-biological characters. They display clear signs of Khoisan and Herero admixture, but keep largely different from these groups. On the other hand, they resemble the Vatwa, a group of non-Bantu hunters of southern Angola. Despite Hottentot admixture, they are dark skinned and have relatively low R_0 and high r frequencies in the Rh system of blood groups.

The Koroca (or Kwadi), a group now reduced to about fifty people who live in the Mossamedes Desert and on the coast of southern Angola, are said to resemble the Dama. Their language, which has four clicks, is akin to neither Bantu nor Khoisan languages. They raise cattle and practise some agriculture, fishing and hunting [4].

On the borders of Angola, Botswana and South West Africa live the Hukwe, who are often described as 'Black Bushmen'. They number less than 1,500 and most of them are wandering hunter-gatherers. Measured with the reflectometer, their skin colour, though lighter than in the neighbouring Bantu, is much darker than in other Khoisan [229:]. In their morphology also they are closer to the neighbouring Bantu than to the 'Yellow Bushmen' [80]. Together with the Kanikwe, who subsist mainly by fishing in the swampy area around Lake Ngami like their Bantu masters, this mixed group has a predominant non-Khoisan component in its gene pool. To call the Hukwe 'Black Bushmen' is therefore misleading: their original supposedly Bushman gene pool has been overwhelmed by non-Khoisan accretions. An analogous but reverse situation is displayed by the Kgalagadi, a Bantu-speaking tribe who moved away from the Tswana into the Kalahari Desert and became strongly mixed with and acculturated to the Bushmen. As estimated from their $Gm^{1,13}$ frequency, the Khoisan component in their gene pool amounts to 66 per cent. In southern Africa, as elsewhere, there is no general coincidence between linguistic and biological affinities.

When compared to Africans living outside the area of southern Africa, Bushmen and Hottentots are biologically close enough to be grouped together, as has already been pointed out. Nevertheless, they are not identical. To be sure, those few Bushman groups who survive are themselves diverse, as are also the Nama and Korana Hottentots. When all Khoisan groups are compared, the pattern of their biological diversity is largely of the same type as the linguistic: a considerable diversity, but without a clear-cut subdivision into Bushman and Hottentot clusters.

In their measurements, however, the Hottentots as a whole tend to be slightly taller and narrower-headed than the Bushmen. This can be explained in terms of a slightly stronger Bantu admixture in them, a conclusion which also emerges from the multivariate comparison of skulls [176]. On the basis of this small differentiation, a clear 'Hamitic' component was once postulated in the Hottentots. Some Hottentots indeed do exhibit somewhat elongated' features; and it is known that Bantu and European admixture occured in all surviving Hottentot groups. Besides an European contribution, they could have picked up 'elongated' elements from the Bantu, particularly from the pastoral Herero in whom such features are marked.

Although Bushmen and Hottentots form a cluster for the genetic traits of the blood as well as for morphological features, as in the latter they show differences in some allele frequencies. The most striking one is in the frequency of the B allele of the ABO blood groups: this frequency attains one of the highest African values in the Hottentots, and one of the lowest in the Central Kalahari Bushmen. Bushmen are extreme for sub-Saharan Africa in their low Hp^1 allele frequency (of the system of haptoglobins), whereas the frequency of the Henshaw gene in the Hottentots is one of the highest known [193]. This serological differentiation between a few surviving out of the many Khoisan groups of the past does not look directional, but rather the result of random genetic drift in isolated breeding populations.

9

The Pygmies and Pygmoids

The Pygmies

As early as the second millennium BC, the Egyptian Pharaohs were sending military expeditions far away south along the Nile; one of their aims was to bring back dwarfs who would 'perform the dance of the gods to delight the king's heart'. This we are told in a letter that Neferkere, of the sixth Memphite Dynasty, wrote to his general Harkhouf, who had informed the Pharaoh that he would be returning to the court with one of these inhabitants of the 'land of legends'. In his *History of Animals*, Aristotle stated that these dwarfs, or Pygmies, were living in the region of the lakes in which the Nile has its source. There indeed still live today the most eastern bands of the Mbuti, the only true Pygmies in the anthropological sense (which restricts this term to populations whose average stature does not exceed 150 cm in the adult male).

The Mbuti inhabit the Ituri forest, the north-eastern corner of the equatorial forest of Central Africa. Their total number appears to be about 40,000. They live in semi-nomadic bands, who wander over recognized hunting territories owned collectively by the group. There are two economic divisions, as the intimate studies of Colin Turnbull [211] have revealed: the net-hunters, who live in large camps of seven to thirty families, based on communal or co-operative hunting; and the archers, who live in much smaller groups and hunt individually with the bow and arrow. The residential units of both net-hunters and archers change constantly in composition as individuals and families circulate between the territorially based bands.

Small animals are hunted, as well as wild pigs, antelopes, monkeys, apes and even elephants. The women collect wild fruits and roots, insects and larvae, lizards and shellfish, and they also fish. The Mbuti keep no domestic animals except the dog, which they use in hunting, and they practise no agriculture. This description makes it clear that, like the Bushmen, they perpetuate a mode of life that has been characteristic of man for by far the longest part of his history. However, whereas most Bushmen live as much reduced and displaced groups in semi-desertic refuge areas, the Mbuti have lived this way of life since immemorial times in their present habitat. Their close cultural adaptation to the forest is expressed conspicuously in their technology and subsistence, but is also deeply rooted in their ideology [212]. Their economy is far from precarious, and famine, or anything approaching it, is utterly unknown to the Mbuti. They have a maxim that 'the only hungry Mbuti is a lazy Mbuti'.

How long have the ancestors of the Mbuti been living in the forest? We do not know, for no fossil Pygmy has yet been discovered and, owing to the nature of the soil in the moist forests, it is doubtful if any ever will be found. As stated in Chapter 3, the first Stone Age culture known in the equatorial forest is the Sangoan, which seems to have developed in the forest-savanna mosaic; it produced the Lupemban, which in turn developed into the Tshitolian. The earliest archaeological remains from the primary forest are very late compared with other parts of Africa; it would seem that it is not until about twenty thousand years ago that men were living permanently within the forest [34]. Perhaps due to the lack of local research, no Stone Age industry has been described from the Ituri forest, although bored stones and movable grinding stones have occasionally been collected in the washouts of gold workings. We therefore have no direct evidence about the antiquity of the Pygmies in the forest, other than the earliest known possible date of about twenty thousand years.

All Mbuti are more or less closely associated with agriculturalist tribes who invaded their territory at least several hundred years ago. This association is a symbiotic relationship, the Mbuti exchanging game, forest products and ivory for agricultural produce and iron artifacts. Small bands of Pygmies are attached to particular agricultural headmen. The villagers regard them as vassals, but the Mbuti apparently manipulate this relationship to their advantage [211]. Faced with the higher population density that their protectors can attain owing to their economy, the continuation of their hunting life is possible to the Mbuti only because of the existence of the forest itself, which the villagers fear to penetrate.

The Mbuti have adopted the language of their protectors (the Bira to the south, the Lese in the east, the Mangbetu and Zande to the north-west, and the Mamvu-Mangutu to the north). The Bira speak a Bantu language, the Mangbetu, Lese and Mamvu-Mangutu speak an Eastern Sudanic one, and the Zande an Adamawa-Eastern one. However, some linguists believe it is possible to detect traces of their former language in the dialects spoken by the Mbuti; moreover, whatever the language, all Mbuti of the Ituri forest speak with an almost identical intonation.

There is no form of centralized authority among the Mbuti. Their subdivision into Aka, Efe and Sua is not a political one of their own, nor does it correspond with any clear biological differentiation. However, despite the apparent lack of cohesion, as a people the Mbuti are strongly united in opposition to their neighbours. From the viewpoint of physical anthropology also they may be described as one entity.

The most striking feature of the Mbuti is, of course, their short stature: on an average, 144 cm in the adult male and 137 cm in the adult female, as computed on large samples by Dr Martin Gusinde [78]. These are the lowest values ever recorded in any human group.

As compared with the other populations of sub-Saharan Africa, the Mbuti have relatively short legs, long arms and wide shoulders. These, however, do not necessarily represent distinctive characteristics of the Mbuti independently of their short stature, since in any human population the shorter individuals tend to have relatively shorter legs, longer arms and wider shoulders. (Table 15 gives a number of anthropological means for the Mbuti and the Bira).

The Pygmies have a big head relative to the body; it is only a little shorter in length than that of the other inhabitants of the moist forest and nearly equal in breadth, giving it a more rounded form. Two striking features of the Pygmies are the broad nose and wide mouth. The breadth of the nose generally exceeds its height; depressed at the root and often bulging only at the nostrils, it looks like an equilateral triangle laid on the face. The wide mouth has thin lips, and in profile the area between nose and mouth is often convex due to a very marked subnasal prognathism. Because of the protrusion of the jaws, the chin appears to recede.

Despite the differences, Dr Guy Thilmans [203], on the basis of biometric distances computed from ten characters of the head and face, finds the Mbuti near to groups of forest agriculturalists living in Gabon and Zaire. These groups are nearer to the Mbuti than they are to a number of populations living outside the forest, like the Teita of Kenya and the Zulu of South Africa. The distance between the Mbuti and the Bushmen, however, is large.

The Mbuti are lighter in skin colour than their agriculturalist neighbours, but how much in terms of reflectance remains to be investigated. Another distinctive external feature of the Pygmies which strikes observers is the strong development of pilosity, or hairiness, as compared with their agricultural neighbours and even more so when compared with the savanna Africans. The form of the head hair, however, is typically African, being spiralled or even peppercorn.

For a number of genetic traits of the blood, the Mbuti show 'ultra-African' frequencies: they stand at or near to the end of the African range of variation, at the opposite pole to the European or Arab values. This is the case for the Rh system of blood groups. The Mbuti have an extremely high frequency of R_0^u (23 per cent), a very high frequency of R_0 (71 per cent), and no Rh-negative alleles. In the MNS system, the Mbuti show an extremely high frequency (35 per cent) of individuals whose red cells are not agglutinated by the anti-U antibody. Another case is the Js^a allele of the Sutter blood groups, whose frequency in the Mbuti is extremely low [60]. Like most populations of sub-Saharan Africa, all 120 Mbuti tested for the Gm system lack the $Gm(x)$ factor [196]. For the ABO blood groups, the Mbuti stand near to the upper limit of both A and B alleles frequencies in sub-Saharan Africa, as also do the Binga Pygmoids, the Korana Hottentots, and the Ngbaka of north-western Zaire.

The Mbuti are also extreme in their fingerprints: their total ridge count, a highly heritable variable, is the lowest ever found anywhere in the world, due to a very high frequency of arches (16 per cent) [70].

The frequency of the transferrin D_1 allele in the Mbuti (3 per cent) is within the range of values for this gene marker in sub-Saharan Africa.

The allele frequencies given here are only indicative, since they have been computed on a very small sample (a few more than one hundred individuals), except in the case of the ABO frequencies, for which samples of over one thousand subjects are available. Whatever the error around the estimated frequencies, the evidence from genetic traits of the blood makes it clear that the Mbuti are related to other sub-Saharan Africans. Within this frame, they are rather markedly distinct when all systems of blood traits are considered together. This implies a genetic isolation long enough for the Mbuti's ancestral line to have developed its differentiation (through drift, selection, or both), and strong enough until recently for this differentiation to have been preserved.

The same conclusion emerges from a comparison of the physique of the Mbuti and other sub-Saharan Africans; but in this field, contrary to that of blood traits, the analysis of the data suggests a very likely hypothesis about the selective pressures which have modelled the gene pool of the Mbuti.

There is no doubt that their shortness is genetical. They have a better standard of nutrition than their agriculturalist, taller-statured neighbours; they are stronger in muscular development; and their weight is greater when allowance is made for stature. As already discussed in Chapter 5, their extremely short stature (and related proportions), the extremely low and wide nose, and the relatively light skin colour apparently represent the result of long selection by climatic factors. These include high average rainfall and air moisture, only slight seasonal contrast in temperature and humidity, and relatively low ultra-violet irradiation under the tree cover. The Mbuti represent an extreme biological adaptation to the equatorial forest.

As already mentioned, palaeontology gives no clue as to when the ancestors of the Mbuti started their particular evolution in the forest. The possible antiquity of twenty thousand years indicated by prehistory would be quite long enough for selection to have modelled the Mbuti's gene pool into its present state. Judging by their affinities with other forest Africans and their relatively long biological distance from the Khoisan, they presumably emerged from a West Central African stock which had already differentiated from the Khoisan line. The populations from whom their ancestors parted most likely lived near to the rain forest, in a savanna-forest mosaic environment.

In its new biotope, the Mbuti line was submitted to strong selective pressures favouring short stature. How these worked is indicated by observations on the Binga Pygmoids of the Central African Republic, described in the next section. A team of endo-crinologists studied their growth hormone and found that in the Binga adult there is no deficiency in its secretion, but a tissue resistance to its action [149, 177]. We may therefore suppose that selection in the Pygmies and Pygmoids favoured alleles which stop growth by blocking the receptivity of the cells to the human growth hormone at a certain stage of development.

This does not necessarily mean that growth ceases early in the Pygmies. From small samples of Mbuti children of estimated age (the Mbuti do not know their age), two studies suggest an early cessation of growth [141], while another points to very low yearly increments producing the mechanism of short adult stature [184]. A study of yearly increments by dental age, an objective parameter, supports this second view [115].

In this context, it is easy to understand why the head escapes reduction in the Pygmies. Growth of the brain reaches its peak soon after birth and its nerve cells cease to multiply after the age of twenty months. The brain and brain case approach their adult size very early, before the blocking mechanism described above stops body growth. At a later but still relatively early stage, permanent teeth eruption conditions the full development of the jaws.

As a consequence the head, and to a lesser extent the face, of the Pygmies is similar to that of the Africans with whom they share a common ancestry, those who live near to the rain forest fringe or who invaded the forest recently. Selection in the Pygmies reduced body size but left the head nearly unchanged, and the face was little modified except in those features, like nose shape, which are adaptive to air moisture.

The Pygmoids

The territory of the Mbuti in the north-eastern corner of the equatorial rain forest is sharply defined. In other parts of this forest live populations who have cultural affinities with the Mbuti; their mode of life is based on hunting, gathering and association with

Figure 18. Localities of the Pygmy and Pygmoid populations and neighbouring agriculturalist ethnic groups

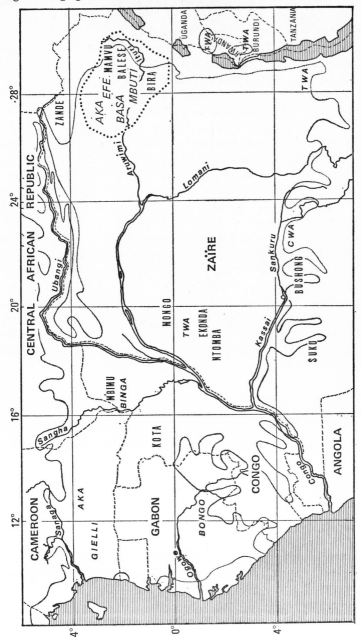

agriculturalist Bantu-speaking tribes whose language they adopted. The tightness of this association, and the degree of dependence of the hunters on the agriculturalists, varies between a situation much like that of the Mbuti, as in many Binga bands in the Central African Republic, and a close association of the two communities. These live side by side in permanent villages and their means of subsistence differ only moderately, as with the Twa who live with the Ntomba and the Ekonda east of lake Tumba in Zaire. (Ntomba and Ekonda societies may be described as a caste system [154].) Figure 18 shows the distribution of these populations, who are estimated to total more than 100,000 individuals.

Most Bantu tribes who are known to have penetrated the forest only recently admit that their dependants were occupying the forest before them. The name they give to them varies from tribe to tribe, but most are based on the same radical (-Ka, -Koa, -Twa or -Cwa), as are also the names of two Mbuti sub-groups (-Ka and -Sua). These groups do not occupy the whole of the equatorial forest; on the contrary, they are absent in large parts of it where only Bantu-speaking agriculturalists live today. Was there a continuous distribution of hunter-gatherers all over the forest in the past, possibly followed by elimination or complete assimilation by the agriculturalist invaders in some areas, and elsewhere withdrawal into their present discrete territories? There is no clear evidence on which to base an answer.

A few Twa groups live outside the forest, such as a community inhabiting a compact area south of the Sankuru which ranks as a tribe within the Kuba kingdom or federation of tribes. This population lived in the forest until recently, when the Belgian administration forced it to settle in open country along a road. Far from their former hunting territory, they now practise a poor form of agriculture and are severely undernourished. Due to a deficiency of protein in their diet, a high proportion of children suffer from kwashiorkor, a disease which, when not fatal, permanently impairs physical and mental development [90]. A number of Twa bands live in open country in Rwanda and Burundi; they earn a living by making pottery, dancing on social occasions, and serving the chiefs in various ways. Deforestation is quite recent in these two countries, but these open-country Twa do not live in the eastern savanna, which is well stocked with game. It is far from the forest which still persists on the slopes of mountains of the Congo–Nile watershed

Figure 19. Biometric map derived from a table of ten-dimensional distances

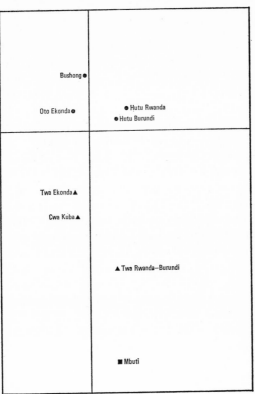

■ Pygmies
▲ Pygmoids
● agriculturalist neighbours of the Pygmoids

and on the volcanoes of northern Rwanda, and perhaps these Twa have remained in their formerly forested territories. Culturally they keep quite distinct from the surrounding Tutsi and Hutu, particularly in their food habits.

In physique, all the non-Pygmy hunter-gatherers and related groups are roughly intermediate between the Mbuti and their agriculturalist protectors, but their relative distance to each varies (Figure 19 and Table 15). In all these groups, average stature in the adult male exceeds 150 cm, justifying the term 'Pygmoid', but it varies from 152 cm to 160 cm as follows:

Binga, Lobaye forest, Central African Republic   152 [42] –
153 [28] cm

Ka, Cameroun	153 cm [217]
Binga, Lower Ubangi	155 cm [125]
Twa, northern Rwanda (volcano forest)	155 cm [79]
Twa of the Ekonda, Zaire	157 cm [108]
Twa, Rwanda (open country)	159 cm [91]
Cwa of the Kuba	160 cm [97]

Stature by itself does not distinguish the forest hunter-gatherers and related populations as a distinctive group: a number of African agriculturalist populations have an average male stature lower than that of the Cwa of the Kuba. This is the case not only for forest agriculturalists who live in contact with Pygmies or Pygmoids, like the Bira of the Ituri forest [195] and the Kota of Gabon [131], both having a male average stature of 158 cm. It applies also to savanna agriculturists who, at least today, have no Pygmoids in the neighbourhood, like the Suku of Kasai in southern Zaire; in a sample of two thousand of them, the mean stature was 157 cm [218].

Even when considering a set of ten measurements of the head and body by means of multivariate analysis, we find that the Cwa of the Kuba are near to the Humu-Amba agriculturalists, who live at the foot of the Ruwenzori Mountains across the Zaire-Uganda border, in contact with the most eastern Mbuti. The Twa of the Ekonda appear to be nearly identical with the Mvuba, neighbours of the Humu in the Semliki Valley, and are near to the Bira of the Ituri forest (see Figure 20).

In morphology, therefore, there seems to be no discontinuity between forest hunter-gatherers and agriculturalists who live in or around the equatorial forest. On these grounds, there is no justification for grouping the hunter-gatherers into a separate class, even when the Mbuti are excluded. The evidence clearly shows a morphological cline running from populations like the Bushong, the ruling Kuba tribe, to the Mbuti Pygmies (Figure 20). Savanna agriculturalists cluster near to the upper end of the cline, while forest hunter-gatherers stand near to the lower end; in the middle there is a mixture of forest hunter-gatherers and agriculturalists, as well as savanna populations whose ancestors are known to have been forest hunter-gatherers in the recent past.

Figure 20. Biometric map derived from the same table of distances as in Figure 19. To the Pygmy and Pygmoid populations plotted on Figure 19 are added a number of ethnic groups of Zaire, Rwanda and Burundi, living either in the forest (F) or in the savanna (S):

In the forest: 1 Humu-Amba, 2 Mvuba, 3 forest Bira, 4 Nyanga, 5 Tembo, 6 Lega, 7 Oto Ekonda. In the savanna: 8 Swaga, 9 Shu, 10 Havu, 11 Hunde, 12 Shi, 13 Hutu of Burundi, 14 Hutu of Rwanda, 15 Bushong, 16 savanna Bira. The Pygmy and Pygmoid populations (P) are: 17 Mbuti, 18 Twa of Rwanda and Burundi, 19 Twa Kuba, 20 Twa Ekonda.

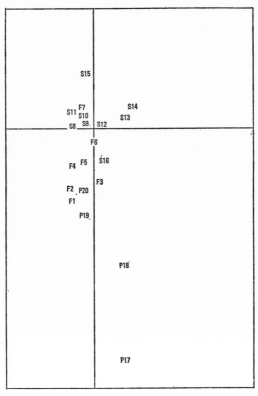

Excluding only the Mbuti if the anthropological definition of the term 'Pygmy' is applied, the populations who occupy the lower part of the cline are usually called Pygmoids. The upper limit of this class can be defined only arbitrarily. 'Pygmoid' is considered here as a cultural term, designating the forest hunter-gatherers and the few derived savanna populations but excluding the Mbuti Pygmies.

Two processes could have produced the intermediary position of

the Pygmoids between the Mbuti and their agriculturalist protectors, a position observed not only for stature but also approximately
for the measurements used in Figure 19. The first is a mixing of
Pygmies and agriculturalists. The second would imply origins from
a stock similar to that which was ancestral to the Mbuti and the
agriculturalists, followed by a less extreme dwarfing evolution in
the Mbuti under similar selective pressures owing to a shorter time
of occupation of the forest. The two processes are not mutually
exclusive; probably in most cases both are involved.

For example, some genetic admixture with the agriculturalists is
acknowledged by the Cwa of the Kuba: about one per cent of the
parents of the present adult population is of agriculturalist origin
[97]. However, the data on the ABO blood groups contradict the
hypothesis that the present gene pool of these Cwa results from the
mixture of Mbuti-like and agriculturalist Kuba contributions; for
this system, the Cwa differ significantly from the Bushong, but in
a direction opposite to the Mbuti. Such is also the case for the Twa
of the Bolia and the Twa of the Mongo in the Equator Province of
Zaire [93]. For the ABO system at least, the ancestral Twa-Cwa
contribution to the present Pygmoids of western and southern
Zaire differs greatly from the present Mbuti gene pool.

In their body and head proportions also, the Cwa of the Kuba
clearly depart from what would be expected in a Mbuti-Bushong
mixture. The Mbuti differ twice as much in shape from the
Bushong as do the Cwa [97]. The case is similar in a comparison
between the Twa and the Oto of the Ekonda [108].

All this favours seeing the ancestral Twa-Cwa populations,
before their admixture with agriculturalists, as clearly different
from the Mbuti, and less differentiated than the latter from the
ancestral stock common to hunters and agriculturalists in and
around the African rain forest. Since no difference in the selective
pressures imposed on hunter-gatherers is apparent between the
habitat of the Mbuti and that of the Twa of Zaire (including that of
the Cwa of the Kuba until very recently), it seems reasonable to
explain the lesser size reduction of the Twa by postulating fewer
generations spent in the forest.

The same probably holds true for the Binga (a European deform-
ation of the name Mpenga given by the agriculturalists to the forest
hunter-gatherers in an area on the boundaries between the Central
African Republic, Zaire and Cameroun). This group, which may

number something of the order of fifteen to thirty thousand, is physically intermediate between their agriculturalist protectors and the Mbuti. They stand about half way in skull measurements, as computed by multivariate distances [203], but are nearer to the Mbuti in body size.

When six blood group systems (ABO, Rh, MN, haptoglobins, transferins and Gm) are considered together, the Mbuti, the Binga, and a pool of agriculturalist ethnic groups of Central Africa are almost equidistant [28]. This does not favour a mixture of Mbuti and agriculturalists as the main determinant of the Binga's gene pool: mixture alone would make Mbuti-Binga and Binga-agriculturalist distances much closer than the Mbuti-agriculturalist distance.

The Binga are not intermediate for several genetic systems. In strong contrast with the Mbuti, their B allele frequency of the ABO system is low, as in the Twa-Cwa populations of central and southern Zaire. In the Duffy system, they are 'ultra-African' in their complete lack of the Fy^a and Fy^b alleles [28]. The Mbuti, who have not been tested for this system, could not be more 'ultra-African'. They are 'ultra-African' in the lack of the Rh-negative alleles, which the Binga possess at low frequencies. For two other systems which have not yet been tested in the Mbuti, the Binga are also 'ultra-African': the Kidd system, for which 162 out of the 163 Binga tested were Jk(a+); and the acid phosphateses, of which the P^b allele has a frequency of 95 per cent in 92 Binga [28].

In fingerprint frequencies, the Binga differ greatly from the Mbuti (13, 49); they occupy the highest whorl and lowest loop extremity of the African range.

The picture obtained from the large set of genetic data collected on the Binga is clear: their gene pool differs greatly from that of the Mbuti, and this difference is not accounted for merely by the degree of admixture with agriculturalists. The common ancestors of the two seem to be remote, as remote as the common ancestors of the Binga and Mbuti and of the agriculturalists who now live in contact with them. To explain the intermediate body size of the Binga, we are left only with the hypothesis already put forward in connection with the Twa of central and southern Zaire: that, in comparison with the Mbuti Pygmies, the Pygmoids underwent a less extreme differentiation, probably owing to the lower number of generations submitted to the selective pressures inherent in a hunting-gathering life in the rain forest.

10

The Elongated Africans
and the Nilotes

The Elongated Africans

As already discussed in Chapters 5 and 6, a number of African populations have an elongated body build, with narrow head, face and nose. Their skin is dark (in varying degree), their hair is spiralled, and they have thick but not everted lips. In many of these people, such as the Tutsi of Rwanda and Burundi and related Hima of Uganda, the Masai of the East African steppes and the Ful communities of the Western Sudanic savanna, there is no evidence of an exotic (Arabic or North African) element in their gene pool. Their physical features can best be explained in terms of genetic adaptation to dry heat. Apparently they represent the result of a peculiar evolution in the semi-arid crescent which caps sub-Saharan Africa to the north and north-east.

At the northern periphery of this crescent, a mixture of Elongated Africans and Arabs or North Africans is evident in the Somali and the Moors. The Galla of southern Ethiopia are intermediate between the Tutsi and the Somali. In northern Ethiopia and Eastern Sudan, biological affinities with the Somali and Galla fade away as one moves north within the Beja ethnic group. The most southern Beja subgroups, the Beni Amer and the Hadendoa, differ only moderately from a northern community of Somali, the Warsingali.

These populations speak a great variety of languages. The Tutsi and Hima speak Bantu languages, the Masai an Eastern Sudanic one. Fulfulde, spoken by the Ful, is related to the languages of the Serer and Wolof, which belong to the West Atlantic class. The Somali and Galla speak Eastern Cushitic languages, the Beja a Northern Cushitic one. The Moors speak a Berber language.

Besides having similar physical characteristics, the Elongated Africans share a major cultural trait: they are essentially pastoral, except for a few communities who abandoned this way of life recently. Many of them are nomadic or transhumant, a necessity in keeping large herds in a dry environment. Certain features are basic to African herding cultures in whatever part of the continent they are found. For example, in their subsistence modes and in their beliefs about livestock, the pastoral Ful show many close parallels with the Somali. The role of dairy foods and animal products in the diet is almost the same, although the Ful, unlike many East African pastoralists, do not consume the blood of their cattle [66].

The nomad pastoral mode of life is considered to derive from a mixed economy in which agriculture and animal husbandry are the main sources of subsistence. The shift occurs where the biotope is unfavourable to extensive cultivation. According to Murdock [157], independent pastoralism did not appear amongst the Somali and Galla until near the end of the first millennium AD, whereas apparently it was already practised by the Beja when they first appear in Egyptian history around 2700 BC. Nor does it seem to have been adopted early by the ancestors of the Masai.

The ancestral Ful may have been pastoralists for much longer. The very wide present scattering of the Ful nomad communities over Western Sudan appears to have started about the eleventh century in the Senegal, most probably from the Fouta Toro area. This can be inferred from historical and linguistic arguments. Only archaeology can tell about the more remote history of the ancestors of the Ful. It shows that neolithic pastoralism appeared in the Sahara in the fifth millennium BC, perhaps earlier, when it was still a relatively well-watered country where large lakes were numerous. The skull of a domestic ox has been found in a layer of neolithic deposits in a Saharan rock-shelter at the eastern end of the Tassili range dated about 4000 BC, and domestic cattle may also be present in the lowest layers dating to about 5500 BC [151]. The life of the Sahara pastoralists is depicted in the countless paintings and engravings they made wherever suitable canvases were to be found, on flat rocks in shelters and caves, or in the open. Neolithic rock art abounds in the mountains of the Tassili, the Tibesti, the

Hoggar and the Adrar of Mauretania. There and in the surrounding plains the pastoralists drove large herds of long and short-horned cattle and goats and flocks of sheep. There is no convincing evidence that they cultivated crops until quite late times [34]. Techniques of tool-making in the neolithic Sahara did not differ much from those of the local hunters of the preceding period. Archaeology does not suggest a population replacement, but the adoption of a new mode of subsistence – pastoralism – by the pre-neolithic hunters of the Sahara, in addition to hunting and collecting wild grasses.

African sheep and goats are of West Asiatic origin, whereas it is possible that African domestic cattle include in their ancestry the indigenous wild species of North Africa, as well as Asiatic domestic strains. The cultural innovations which initiated the 'neolithic revolution' in the Sahara seem to have had their main source in Western Asia.

Techniques and equipment circulated very widely across the southern Sahara in neolithic times and even before. The Meso-lithic Khartoum wavy line pottery tradition was spread from the Nile valley as far west as Tibesti, the Hoggar and Mauretania; and amazon stone was traded extensively from Tibesti right across the Sahara from the west coast to the Nile [34].

The increasing desiccation which followed the last climatic optimum in the Sahara seems to have resulted from overgrazing by the huge herds of cattle as well as from climatic deterioration. By the end of the second millennium BC it had become so severe that a large proportion of the population had been forced to move to the south. The pastoral scenes painted on the rocks cease during the fourth millennium BC [173]. It is reasonable to regard the neolithic pastoralists of the Sahara as ancestors of the Ful. The ethnologists Amadou Hampate Ba and Germaine Dieterlein [83] have found evidence to support this view in the details of an initiation cere-mony painted by the Tassili pastoralists and similar to the rites of the present Ful of Senegal.

Quite possibly the migration of the Sahara pastoralists reached the Horn and East Africa. Settlements of village farmers, basically neolithic but also using some copper, are known from the plateau of north-western Ethiopia; their material culture shows affinities with that of the C-group peoples who moved into Nubia from the western desert about 2500 BC. Rock paintings in the eastern parts of

THE ELONGATED AFRICANS AND THE NILOTES

Ethiopia and Somalia are reminiscent of those of the eastern Sahara; they depict herdsmen and long-horned, humpless cattle [34].

Herdsmen owning sheep and cattle were present in the East African Rift Valley by the end of the first millennium BC [34], though it has not been proved that they practised cultivation. Thick stone platters and bowls are characteristic of their cultures, but these do not necessarily imply agriculture: they may have been used for cooking meat and wild vegetable food, grinding wild roots and grain, and crushing red ochre [36]. These stone bowls suggest links with the southern Sudan and the eastern Sahara, but the associated obsidian industry of long blades and microliths shows a continuation of the local tradition of the Upper Kenya Capsian hunters and the subsequent Elmenteitan culture of the Kenya Rift Valley. Here too, therefore, archaeology does not suggest population replacement. Stone bowl culture peoples continued to occupy the Kenya highlands until the middle of the sixteenth century AD, when they were replaced by Bantu-speaking populations, whose ancestors had introduced iron metallurgy in other parts of East Africa more than a thousand years earlier.

All this is cultural evidence; what has the study of ancient skeletons to tell about the possible ancestors of the present Elongated Africans? Marie-Claude Chamla [31] has studied the very fragmentary remains of fifty-eight individuals from about thirty neolithic sites located within a band between 21° and 15°N, in the southern Sahara. Most of the sites were on river banks or lake shores, or in shallow depressions. The skeletons are usually associated with shells (a number of sites are shell mounds) and bones of fish, crocodile, hippo and other mammals. Among the implements are arrowheads, spear points and bone harpoons. This suggests a mode of subsistence based on shellfish gathering, fishing and hunting – that is, a mesolithic way of life. We therefore cannot presume that the associated remains represent pastoralist populations, unless pastoralism was part of an otherwise essentially mesolithic culture. Perhaps by that time the Sahara was inhabited by communities living different ways of life; if so, they might have lived independently, or have had bonds of economic interdependence, such as those which bind so many present pastoralist communities with agriculturalists.

The neolithic skeletons of the southern Sahara share a number

Figure 21. Prehistoric sites and areas mentioned in Chapter 10

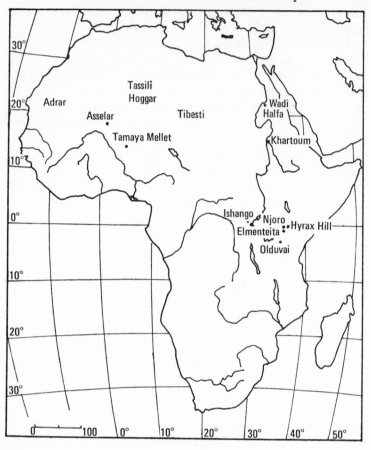

of characteristics: a massive skull with thick walls, a very thick lower jaw, very large teeth which generally do not show the usual decrease in size from the first to the third molar and which often possess supernumerary cusps compared with the present norm, and sturdy lower limbs. A number of these and other characteristics of the group are considered by Chamla [31] to be archaic. In most cases the remains are too fragmentary to allow an estimate of stature to be made; however, it is clear that several individuals at the Tamaya Mellot site, a large shell mound in the Niger Sahara, were very tall. Only eight faces could be reconstructed and their measurements show a wide range of values. The nose is usually wide, but in several instances it is narrow; prognathism, although present in all faces, varies between slight and extremely marked.

Three skeletons from Mali show affinities with a skeleton from Asselar, in the Saharan part of Mali, which was described by Professors Boule and Vallois in 1932 [16]. A recent carbon 14 date of 4400 BC for this skeleton by Professor Cheik Anta Diop falls within the range for the Sahara neolithic. All four skeletons have a more gracile build than the rest of the group from the southern Sahara. Judging by their features as a whole, this group of neolithic skeletons from the southern Sahara may be considered to belong to populations ancestral to the present peoples of West Africa [31]. Evolution from one to the other would require mainly a gracilization or fining down of the skeleton and the disappearance of archaic features.

That such a process actually took place locally is strongly suggested by a study which Chamla made of a series of protohistoric skeletons from the central and southern Sahara, most of them probably dating from the first millennium BC. Compared with the neolithic remains, they are more gracile and a number of archaic features have disappeared, though the shape of the skull has not changed. This speaks for a local evolution without any important population replacements.

The neolithic Sahara skeletons, particularly those from Tamaya Mellet, show affinities with the very fragmentary human remains found at the Early Khartoum site on the Upper Nile. These were associated with a mesolithic industry which has many similarities with the Tamaya Mellet assemblage [7]. Mesolithic Khartoum is dated to about 4000 BC, well within the time range for the physically and culturally related populations of neolithic Sahara.

Older mesolithic sites in the Sudan have provided rather plentiful skeletal material. One is the cemetery at Wadi Halfa, near to the Egyptian border, which has been called 6B36 by the University of Colorado Nubian expedition. The associated remains indicate hunting, fishing and shellfish gathering as the mode of subsistence. The industry, characterized by microliths and bone points, is similar to the Quadan industry of the area, for which reliable carbon 14 dates range from about 10,000 to 4500 BC [230].

David Greene and George Armelagos [76] have analysed the human remains from 6B36, which include thirty-six skeletons, many of them fragmentary. They were quite robust, muscular, long-legged individuals, with a long and narrow head, showing a complex of bony and dental features indicating a heavy chewing musculature. The face is prognathous, with a low and wide nose. The teeth, which are strongly abraded, are exceptionally large for *Homo sapiens* and show a high frequency of supernumary cusps. Their size and morphology suggests an adaptation to a diet which includes much grit [75].

The skulls from 6B36 are very similar to those unearthed from a near-by cemetery of the same period, site 117 of the Southern Methodist University's expedition, which have been studied by James E. Anderson [5]. The Wadi Halfa mesolithic skeletons show clear affinities with the more massive ones of the Sahara neolithic group, especially with some of the ones from Tamaya Mellet, but no quantified general comparison has yet been published.

Anderson, from the site 117 material, and Greene and Armelagos from that of site 6B36, have compared the Wadi Halfa mesolithic population with a number of other African skeletal series. They agree that, in terms of gross morphology, there is considerable overlap of these samples and a series of people from Mechta-Afalou in north-west Africa. As stated in Chapter 3, they lived about 12,000 years ago, at a time when the Quadan mesolithic industry, which resembles their own industry, the Mouillan, was being made by the people of Wadi Halfa.

Greene and Armelagos also point out a possible relationship of the Wadi Halfa mesolithic population with another African mesolithic one, the people who lived at Ishango, on the north-western shore of Lake Edward, probably in the seventh millennium BC or perhaps earlier. Fishing was a major activity, as testified by the large number of bone harpoons found in the Ishangian layers [873]. The human remains, particularly the skulls, are very fragmentary, but the very thick skull bones, the large teeth and the morphology of the mandible of the Ishango people [214] compare with the Wadi Halfa material. The limb bones of the Ishango people, however, are rather slender. In addition, Greene and Armelagos draw attention to similarities between the Wadi Halfa skulls and the 'Boskop type' from South Africa, as described by Professor Alexander Galloway. However, it has not been proved that this 'type' represents a biological population; in it are grouped a selection of individuals, the more massive ones selected out of the Large

Figure 22. Localities of the Elongated Africans and Nilotes mentioned in the text. Nine major concentrations of Ful (F) are figured:

1 Senegal Valley, 2 Futa Toro, 3 Futa Jalon, 4 Kita, 5 Masina, 6 Liptako, 7 Sokoto, 8 Bauchi, 9 Adamawa.

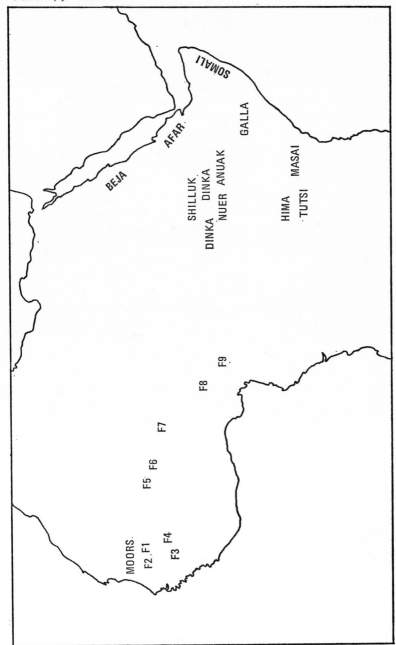

Khoisan stock. Similarities between Ishango Man and the ancestral Khoisan have also been suggested [87].

All this casts no particular light on the origin and differentiation of the Elongated Africans. It does, however, suggest an evolutionary line leading to the other present inhabitants of the Western Sudan from a population like that of mesolithic Wadi Halfa through those of the southern Sahara in neolithic and protohistoric times. Are the Ful so distinctive that they could not have evolved from the same line? In particular, how much do the Ful differ from the non-Ful populations of West Africa, from where they recently spread?

As a whole, the Ful and the non-Ful of West Africa are very similar in their allele frequencies for blood trait systems. The R_0 allele of the Rh system, which has a generally high frequency in sub-Saharan Africa, has a frequency of 61 per cent in a sample of Ful from Senegal; this value lies between those for the Wolof and Serer (71 and 56 respectively) and is near to that of the Tukulor (64 per cent). Like the Serer, this sample of Ful has no $Gm(x)$ factor (in this it shows no trace of an admixture from North Africa or Arabia), whereas the Wolof and Tukulor possess it at low frequencies [121]. Like the three non-Ful populations, it has the abnormal haemoglobins S, C and K [25]. The A allele of the ABO blood groups has a higher frequency in this sample of Ful (22 per cent) than in those of the Wolof, Serer and Tukulor (14, 15 and 14 respectively); but the Ful of Portuguese Guinea have a frequency of 16 per cent [133], the pastoral Ful of Nigeria a frequency of 14 per cent [15], and the Ful of Upper Volta a frequency of 11 per cent [231].

The $Gm(x)$ factor is also absent in the sample of Ful from Upper Volta, as well as in one of the neighbouring Marka, a sub-group of the Soninke. The two samples do not differ significantly in their ABO, Hp, Gc and Gm allele frequencies; they differ only in the frequencies for the still rarely investigated Lp system [231], for which the Ful are nearer to European values.

In the frequencies of their fingerprints also, the Ful and non-Ful of West Africa do not depart systematically from each other. For example, the percentage of whorls is 38 in the Ful of Senegambia, 38 in the Tukulor, 37 in the Serer, and 36 in the Wolof [134]. In Mali, the Ful and the Dogon have the same total ridge count [69]. The Ful samples differ between each other; in a sample

of Ful from Portuguese Guinea, the percentage of whorls is 34
[167], and in another sample 41 [145]; in a sample of Ful from
Futa-Jalon it is 30 [134].

Metrically, the pastoral Ful differ systematically from the
neighbouring populations in having a narrower head, face and nose.
In the four comparisons cited in the literature, there are no exceptions: in four out of five of these comparisons, the Ful have longer
legs. The other metrical differences between the Ful and non-Ful
are not systematic.

In West Africa, the mean stature of the Ful is near to that of
their neighbours; the Ful of Senegal (172 cm) are 1 cm taller than
the Serer and Tukulor; in the Badyar region of Guinea, the Ful are
shorter than the Badyaranke (168 cm against 170 cm); in Portuguese Guinea also the Ful are shorter than the Manding (166 cm
against 168 cm); in the Futa-Jalon area, the Ful have the same
mean stature as the Landuma (167 cm).

Farther east, a sample of Ful of Upper Volta and Mali has the
same average stature as both their Fulse neighbours and the Ful of
Senegal, whereas a small sample of Ful of Niger is insignificantly
taller than the former, but significantly taller than the neighbouring
Bellah.

At the southern limit of the Ful expansion, the metrical differences between the Ful and non-Ful are more marked, mostly
because the latter are distinctively different from West Africans.
The pattern of the differences is roughly similar in those two areas
where detailed anthropometric surveys have been made, central
Cameroun and north-western Central African Republic (see Table
2, which gives the means for these two pairs of populations and for
the only other pair of Ful and non-Ful groups on which detailed
anthropometry has been made). In the two regions, the Ful are
much taller than the non-Ful; they have a longer and narrower
head, a narrower face, and a higher and narrower nose. The two
samples of Ful differ from the corresponding non-Ful in the
opposite direction for face height and relative trunk length (hence
also for relative leg length).

Skin reflectance has not yet been measured in the Ful. However,
the anthropologists who estimated skin colour by eye, or matched
it with colour scales, have been struck by the lighter and more
reddish skin colour of the Ful when compared to other Africans of
Western Sudan [140, 216].

TABLE 2

Anthropometric means in three samples of Ful and three samples of non-Ful neighbouring communities

| Area | Badyar | | North-western C.A.R. (Cresta 1965) | | Central Cameroun | |
Character	100 Ful [135]	100 Badyaranke	72 Ful	164 Baya	59 Ful	352 Bamileke [163]
Stature (cm)	168	170	172	164	173	168
Head length (mm)	188	192	191	187	194	190
Head breadth (mm)	141	143	140	144	145	153
Face height (mm)	114	116	115	113	116	119
Face breadth (mm)	132	136	131	134	136	141
Nose height (mm)	48	48	49	45	50	49
Nose breadth (mm)	40	43	39	43	43	45
Relative trunk length	48·8	49·2	50·1	49·2	49·8	51·0
Cephalic index	74·9	74·1	73·3	76·8	74·7	80·4
Facial index	86·6	85·3	87·4	83·7	85·1	84·4
Nasal index	82·2	89·1	79·7	94·1	85·2	91·8

The data from both blood genetics and anthropometry clearly indicate that the Ful are a variety of West Africans. On these grounds, we may suppose that they descend from the same evolutionary line as the other inhabitants of West Africa, that is from populations like those of neolithic Sahara. As already shown, there are ethnological arguments for considering the neolithic pastoralists of the Sahara as the ancestors of the Ful and this ties in with the biological data.

What caused the Ful to develop their biological distinctions, their narrower head, face and nose, and lighter skin? As stated in Chapter 6, their morphological distinctive features seem to be adaptive to a hot and dry environment like that of the Sahara. Their colour also conforms to that considered to be adaptive to the Sahara by Professor Paul Baker [11]. Owing to their pastoral mode of subsistence, the ancestral Ful could remain in the desiccating Sahara a longer time than the agriculturalists, and diverged from the latter through adaptation to a drier environment. Moreover, the neolithic populations of the sub-Saharan Western Sudan, which most probably were akin to those of the Sahara, surely contributed for a large part to the ancestry of the present agriculturalist populations of the same area. Since they lived nearer to the Equator in a moister environment, we may suppose that genetic adaptation caused them to have a darker skin colour and a wider head, face and nose than the ancestral Ful.

Is there an alternative to such an ecological explanation of the distinctive features of the Ful? Were we to explain them on the basis of interbreeding between the West African line and a hypothetical population, this population should have typically African allele frequencies in the field of blood genetics, and a lighter skin, narrower head, face and nose, and longer legs than the present Ful. Perhaps such a population has featured in the ancestry of the Ful; if so, its features would call for the same explanation as those of the Ful.

The only alternative explanation is in terms of sexual selection. As stated in Chapter 6, this process is active in the present pastoral Ful, whose aesthetic ideal is that morphology which has been described here as being adaptive to a hot and dry climate. Girls who conform to this ideal are courted more than others, and boys who conform to it are likely to have a higher rate of reproduction. The pastoral Ful attach a special importance to nose morphology. A

Ful proverb runs 'See the nose, understand the character' [197]. Most probably, sexual selection acts particularly strongly on this feature, which is the most distinctive of all characters measured in the Ful.

If such sexual selection already operated in neolithic times, it was probably subsidiary to climatic selection. Although it is not inconceivable that it might have been the main cause of the morphological divergence of the ancestral Ful, it seems much more probable that it started only after some differentiation through climatic selection had occurred. Continuing sexual selection tends to preserve the distinctiveness of the Ful. It acts against two processes: climatic adaptation, which tends to make the Ful more similar to the surrounding populations, and interbreeding with these surrounding populations. The action of the first process is inferred from our knowledge of ecology, whereas that of interbreeding can be assessed by the study of matings. In a study of the pastoral Ful of northern Nigeria, Dr Derrick Stenning [197] mentions the union between a Ful man and a non-Ful woman as an accepted, although rare, type of marriage. The rate of genetic admixture produced by this type of union varies between Ful communities; a paramount factor of this variation is the tightness of the relations with non-Ful populations.

Today the Ful, who number over six million, are scattered in the savanna belt from Senegambia in the west to parts of the Central African Republic in the east, and they have even penetrated into Sudan. The most important concentrations are found in the Senegal valley and the Futa Toro in Senegambia, the Futa Jalon in the Guinea highlands, on the upper and middle Niger, in the Northern Region of Nigeria (Sokoto, Katsina, Kano, Bornu, Bauchi and Jos Plateau), and in the Adamawa highlands.

The pastoral Ful, often described as the Bororo, are found in those areas of the savanna belt where the population density is lowest, and also in well-favoured highland areas. Their wealth derives from their herds of cattle, although they also own sheep and goats. They live mainly, but not exclusively, on dairy produce, exchanging surpluses for cereal and root foods in the markets. Looking after their cattle keeps them aloof from the life of village and town, but it does involve special relations with sedentary populations for rights of access to water and pasture. They follow a consistent pattern of transhumance, governed by seasonal changes. Associated with changes in temperature, humidity and vegetation cover are changes in the availability of pasture and water and in the activities of those species of tsetse fly which carry human sleeping sickness and bovine trypanosomiasis. Cattle move southward in the dry season in response to shortages of pasture and water, and northward in the wet season to avoid the tsetse [197].

Stenning describes three other modes of life and social organization in the Ful: semi-sedentary communities, sedentary communities, and states. The semi-sedentary communities have a dual mode of subsistence, in which farming and stockraising complement each other; they arise mainly as the result of loss of cattle. In highland areas, some of these communities depend on wealth in cattle and the availability of non-Ful labour to work on the farms and help in tending the large herds.

Sedentary Ful communities merge into the major ethnic groups in which they are formed and have strong communal and kinship ties with them. Sometimes they represent the final stage of sedentariness of semi-sedentary Ful communities. Others are communities of ex-slaves established by Ful pastoralists in the nineteenth century, whose masters may have moved on to new pastures or who, in the twentieth century, relaxed control on them as a result of legislation. In the nineteenth century in this geographical zone, a number of empires arose which were built up by the Ful under the leadership of their Muslim holy men. In this way the empires of Futa Jalon, Futa Toro, Masina and Sokoto were founded.

The semi-sedentary and, still more, the sedentary mode of life puts the Ful in closer contact with the non-Ful and increases the opportunities and motivations for mixed unions. Ex-slaves are likely to have been influenced by their masters more in language and culture than in their gene pool. We may therefore expect the sedentary Ful to be less distinctive than the pastoral Ful; as a matter of fact the only sedentary Ful community that has been studied in some detail by anthropo-biologists is indistinguishable from the non-Ful population of the area. The sedentary Ful of northern Nigeria have the same stature (167 cm), head length (192 mm), head breadth (145 mm), face breadth (138 mm) and nose breadth (42 mm) as the Hausa [202].

The degree of mixture with local populations, and the differences between them and the Ful, are not the only known factors of the rather wide morphological variety in Ful communities. First marriages are usually made between close kin, and members of some Ful groups, in which this has produced a high degree of endogamy, take pride in their often distinctive facial likeness [197].

As already mentioned, the archaeological evidence suggests that pastoralism, together with grain cultivation, may have diffused to the Ethiopian highlands and the Horn of Africa in the second, if not the third, millennium BC, and that it was established in the highlands an dRift Valley region of Kenya and northern Tanzania in the last millennium BC or earlier. There are reasons to believe that this early expansion of food production in Kenya and northern Tanzania can be attributed to Cushitic-speaking peoples from Ethiopia. The plains of northern Kenya, despite their aridity, would have been suitable for herds and would have provided a link with the Horn; the well-watered Kenya highlands would have been suitable for a mixed agricultural and pastoral way of life [200].

However, the Kenyan and Tanzanian populations who practised pastoralism long before the coming of iron were themselves akin to the ancestors of the present Cushitic-speaking Galla and Somali, whose nucleus of expansion lies in southern Ethiopia [136]. The skeletons of hunter-fisher-gatherers of the Stone Age all belong to populations characterized by tall stature, generally with a long and narrow head, high and narrow face and nose, and frequently showing subnasal prognathism – features which are all displayed by the living Elongated Africans (see Table 3). Such skeletons include those associated with the Upper Kenya Capsian of Gamble's Cave, Naivasha and Olduvai, who may date to about 4,000 BC; the makers of the ensuing mesolithic Elmenteitan culture of Bromhead's Site; the remains associated with the neolithic stone bowl culture at Hyrax Hill and Njoro River Cave (dated by carbon 14 to 960 BC), and with the more recent stone bowl culture at Willey's Kopje, Makalia and Nakuru, which almost certainly date from the Iron Age.

This East African skeletal material is not closely related to the mesolithic Wadi Halfa remains [5]. However, these people may have evolved from the stock represented by the Wadi Halfa population, in the same way as the Ful may be descended from the related populations of Tamaya Mellet and other neolithic Sahara sites. The marked similarity of the Ful and the present Elongated Africans of East Africa indicates their descent from not very dissimilar ancestral populations. However, the earliest material from East Africa, if correctly dated, shows that the modern Elongated Africans there differentiated at a time when the peoples of the Sahara were still relatively archaic. According to archaeology, the centre of this differentiation might be in the Horn. The extremely hot and dry climate of this area might be expected to cause, through climatic selection, the most rapid evolution towards the Elongated African morphology from a still little differentiated stock.

It does seem as though the early Elongated Africans of East Africa might possibly have contributed to the ancestral Ful line. If interbreeding ever played an important part in Ful genesis, the hypothetical Sahara population which mixed with ancestors of the non-Ful inhabitants of western Sudan should have had metrical features like the Masai, and still more like the Tutsi (see Table 3). Compared with the Ful, the Tutsi have a higher facial index (face width expressed as a percentage of face height) and a lower nasal index (breadth as a percentage of height). The Tutsi are darker in skin colour, but this is to be expected as their habitat is nearer to the equator. The study of the living can do no more than indicate possibilities; only the discovery of new sites in the Sahara could throw further light on this question.

The Tutsi are often classified as Nilotes in the literature [53]. However, they differ strikingly from the Dinka, Nuer, Shilluk and Anuak, closely related populations of the Upper Nile region to whom the term Nilotes should be restricted if it is to have any biological meaning. In comparing Tables 3 and 4 it is clear that the Tutsi's affinities link them much more closely with the Galla, Somali and Masai, although these four ethnic groups (or even sections of them) differ rather markedly between each other.

The first Tutsi kingdom was founded in Rwanda in the fifteenth century. The Tutsi, or their Hima kinsmen, were already present in southern Uganda and in parts of their present area (Rwanda, Burundi, and small regions in the adjacent parts of Zaire) some time before this political event. Their more remote home is hypothetical; it may have been in southern Ethiopia, from where the Galla and Somali expanded in historical times, or in the Kenya-Tanzania area where pastoralism was established long ago. The Tutsi abandoned the transhumant way of life, which is still practised by the Hima herdsmen of north-eastern Rwanda, and settled as an

TABLE 3

Anthropometric means in five Elongated African populations of East Africa

Population Character	177 Tutsi of Rwanda [91]	149 Masai [57]	49 Galla [164]	42 Sab Somali [174]	80 Warsingali Somali [164]
Stature (cm)	176	173	171	173	168
Head length (mm)	198	194	190	194	192
Head breadth (mm)	147	140	147	145	143
Face height (mm)	125	121	122	119	123
Face breadth (mm)	134	137	133	134	131
Nose height (mm)	56	54	53	49	52
Nose breadth (mm)	39	39	37	36	34
Relative trunk length	49·7	47·7	50·3	49·7	50·7
Cephalic index	74·5	72·8	77·6	74·7	74·5
Facial index	92·8	89·0	91·5	88·5	94·1
Nasal index	69·5	72·0	69·0	72·8	66·0

hegemonous pastoralist caste ruling over a large majority of Hutu agriculturalists (whose Bantu language they adopted) and a tiny minority of Twa Pygmies. They number about 60,000. In Rwanda, a Hutu revolution in 1960–1 put the monarchy and the Tutsi's privileges to an end.

The Tutsi have the reputation of being very tall, and indeed they are the tallest East Africans, though not the tallest Africans. The Nuer and the Dinka, with mean male statures of 185 and 183 cm respectively, are much taller than the Tutsi, who average 176 cm.

The pastoral Masai, who number more than 100,000, subsist exclusively by animal husbandry in the steppe country of southern Kenya and northern Tanzania. Like that of the Nilotes, their language belongs to the Eastern Sudanic class in Greenberg's classification. However, both their language and their culture show a strong Cushitic influence, which makes Murdock [157] describe them as 'Kushitized Nilotes'. In particular, like the Tutsi, they have some characteristically Cushitic food habits, notably the drinking of fresh blood drawn from the neck of their cattle by means of an arrow, and a taboo against eating flesh.

Physically, the Masai differ from the Tutsi, Galla and Somali mainly by their considerably narrower head. Since the head of the Nilotes is extremely narrow, this might indicate some Nilotic admixture in the Masai, which would support the linguistic data. However, the Masai do not share the other main distinctive feature of the Nilotes, their extremely tall stature. Their mean stature is only 173 cm. In nose shape they are much nearer to the Tutsi, Galla and Somali than to the Nilotes. Anthropometry does not therefore suggest a strong Nilotic element in the Masai gene pool.

The recent history of the Galla is closely connected with that of the Somali. By the tenth century AD, Arab and Persian Muslim settlers had founded very active trade centres in the ports of Zeila and Berbera in the Gulf of Aden and at Merca, Brava and Mogadishu on the Indian Ocean in the south of the present Somali Republic. Probably by that time the country inland from the Gulf of Aden was occupied first by Somali nomads and, to their south and west, by pastoral Galla who, apparently, had expanded from their traditional homelands of Borana in south-west Ethiopia. To the south of these Somali and Galla, the fertile lands between the Shebeli and Juba rivers were occupied by Bantu agriculturalists [137].

The ancestors of the scattered bands of hunters in Kenya and Jubaland known as the Boni were probably also present in the region. Perhaps they had affinities with the Khoisan, as is often stated, but their present features do not make this evident; on the contrary, they differ only moderately from the upper Somali castes, mainly in having a wider nose.

During the first centuries of the present millennium, two sheikhs who migrated from Arabia to settle in northern Somaliland founded the Darod and Isaq Somali clans. The growth in numbers and territory of these clans caused a general thrust of Somali and Galla groups towards the south and west.

In the sixteenth century, the Muslim state of Adal, whose port was Zeila, took the lead in the holy war against the Christian Amhara of Ethiopia. The Somali armies harried the country almost to the point of collapse, but Abyssinia, with Portuguese support, won in 1542. This victory increased the pressure of the Somali and Galla thrust southwards. With this stimulus, the main mass of the Galla swept into Ethiopia from the south and south-west and streamed in conquering hordes as far north as the ancient city of Harar. The Somali thrust southwards continued – largely at the expense of the Galla and Bantu – until the beginning of the twentieth century, when it was halted at the Tana River by the establishment of administrative posts [137].

History and ecology have divided the Somali into a northern and a southern group. The northern Somali, who are dedicated to a mainly nomadic existence, extend northward from the Shibeli river in the south to the southern part of the French Territory of Afars and Issas in the north. They also occur again south of the Juba river in the Somali Republic and reach into northern Kenya, where they form the dominant Somali element. The southern Somali, who practise agriculture besides animal husbandry, form an enclave between the Juba and Shebeli rivers. The northern Somali, whose main divisions are the Dir, Isaq, Darod and Hawiye, descend from the founder Amale, whereas the Digil and Rahanwiin, who form the southern Somali, descend from Sab [138]. A descent from Arabia is claimed for Amele and Sab, and therefore for all the Somali.

The Somali number well over three million: some 2,250,000 in the Somali Republic, about 750,000 in Ethiopia, over 240,000 in the North-Eastern Region of Kenya, and 37,000 in the French

Territory of Afars and Issas. Northern Somali pastoralism is based on the husbandry of sheep and goats, camels, cattle, donkeys and horses. The milk of sheep, goats, camels, or cattle forms their staple diet [138].

The Galla now occupy much of western and south-eastern Ethiopia, stretching into northern Kenya with a detached group in the Tana area of eastern Kenya. They number about 2,500,000 and are pastoral people, owning large herds of cattle, together with sheep, goats, donkeys, and horses. In the highlands, they also cultivate barley.

Physically, the Galla resemble the Tutsi in face and nose shape but they are shorter in stature and head length. Their skin is dark brown or black. Their hair form falls most often in the curly to kinky class; a few individuals show the peppercorn type, but nearly 9 per cent of them have hair with long, broad waves, which speaks for a moderate Arab influence in their gene pool. The high frequency of the M allele (64 per cent) and the relatively low frequency of the R_0 allele (54 per cent) in a small sample of them give a similar indication[1].

The two samples of Somali on which detailed anthropometric data are available show significant differences (see Table 3). The small sample of southern Somali soldiers, mostly of Sab descent, measured by Puccioni [174] resemble the Tutsi rather closely. The larger sample of northern Somali belonging to various groups, the best represented being the Warsingali, are much shorter (169 cm) and have a relatively narrower face and nose; apparently they are strongly Arabicized. As a whole, however, the northern Somali do not tend to have an especially important Arab component in their gene pool. In the Dir and Darod, average stature is 172 cm [185]. M allele frequency, which is over 70 per cent in southern Arabia, is only 51 per cent in the Dir [71] and in the Somali of the French Territory [59]. R_0 allele frequency in the latter is around 65 per cent, a high value even for Africa as a whole. Arab influence in the French Territory is much more marked in the Afar (or Danakil), another pastoralist Eastern Cushitic-speaking population; their allele frequencies are 62 per cent for M and 51 per cent for R_0 [58].

R_0 frequency has relatively low values also in northern and central Ethiopia, which has a long history of contacts with southern Arabia: it is 48 per cent in the Tigre. The typically African D^1

variant of transferrins is absent in a small sample of the Tigre, as well as in a small sample of the Amhara, the dominant group in modern Ethiopia who number at least three million and speak a Semitic language like the Tigre. The Gurage, another Semitic-speaking group who occupy an enclave in Galla country, have an R_0 frequency of 35 per cent. The Falasha, who are of Jewish religion and have divided into two groups, one in Tigre country and the other in Amhara country, are close to the Tigre in allele frequencies. All these populations have high M frequencies of between 63 and 68 per cent[1]. Their gene pools clearly result from interbreeding between African and southern Arabic populations.

Farther north, in the Beja pastoral nomads, an African component, probably similar to that which is present in the Somali, has mixed with exotic elements whose origin may be partly Egyptian, partly Arabic.

The Nilotes

In southern Sudan, three ethnic groups, the Nuer, Dinka and Shilluk, show a marked similarity in their biological features, and a common relatively strong differentiation from the other African populations. A fourth group, the Anuak, who live east of the Nuer across the Sudan-Ethiopia border, shows clear affinities with the three others. All groups speak languages of the Nilotic branch of the Eastern Sudanic subfamily.

These populations are largely riverain. The Shilluk villages, which contain over 100,000 people, are strung out along the banks of the White Nile and the lower Sobat River. The Dinka, who number about 900,000, occupy two distinct territories: to the south and west of the Shilluk, the western Dinka live in scattered homesteads a few miles inland from the swampy water courses of the Bahr el Ghazal and White Nile basins, whereas the eastern Dinka live east of the Shilluk up to thirty miles inland from the Nile. The Nuer, some 300,000 in number, live in the marshy and savanna country on both banks of the Nile south of the Shilluk and Dinka. The territory of the Anuak, who number about 40,000, is centred on the Sobat River.

The Nuer and Dinka are primarily cattle peoples, but they supplement milk and meat by the culture of millet and the spearing of fish (E. E. Evans–Pritchard [54A]). They lead a transhumant life, moving their herds to riverain pastures during the dry season and back to permanent settlements on the higher ground in the savanna during the rains. The Shilluk and Anuak are completely sedentary; they depend for subsistence more upon agriculture and fishing and less upon herding than the Nuer and Dinka.

TABLE 4

Anthropometric means in four Nilotic populations
The stature of the Dinka is from a sample of 279 individuals (Roberts and Bainbridge 1963)

Population Character	51 Nuer [215]	49 Dinka [179]	68–107 Shilluk [179]	64 Anuak [215]
Stature (cm)	185	181	179	177
Head length (mm)	196	196	196	192
Head breadth (mm)	137	140	139	138
Face height (mm)	114	—	—	110
Face breadth (mm)	134	137	135	135
Nose height (mm)	47	46	47	44
Nose breadth (mm)	41	42	42	41
Cephalic index	70·1	71·7	70·9	71·9
Facial index	85·4	—	—	81·7
Nasal index	86·9	90·6	87·9	92·0

Compared to the Elongated East Africans, the four Nilotic groups are taller and have a narrower head in both absolute and relative terms (their cephalic index is much lower), also a lower and wider nose resulting in a much higher nasal index (see Table 4). Their body is very slender, with extremely long legs and little fat [182]. This combination of features makes them distinct from all other African populations.

The four groups differ moderately from each other, the main difference being in stature, which attains the highest recorded value in the world (185 cm) in the small sample of Nuer. The Anuak are the shortest of the four groups and they also have the shortest head and lowest nose.

Small samples of Nuer, Dinka and Shilluk have been tested for a number of blood group systems and in none of these do they differ significantly from each other [178]. They differ strongly from all other African populations in the pattern of their *Rh* allele frequencies (see Table 5), having a high frequency of R_0, a notable one of $R_o{}^u$ and r_o, a very low frequency of R_1, and the absence of R^1. In particular, this pattern is quite different from that of the Galla and of those other Ethiopian populations which have been tested for this system. It stands in contrast with the European and Western Asian pattern, which shows a low R_0 and a high R_1 frequency. Contrary to Murdock's [157] statement, there is no ground on which to detect 'an unmistakable Caucasoid admixture in the Shilluk'.

TABLE 5

Allele frequencies of the Rh blood group systems in some African popula-tions (*Closely related populations have been pooled if not significantly different; the pooled frequencies are unweighted; they are given in percentages.*)

Populations	R_o (cDe)	$R_o{}^u$ (cD$_u$e)	R_1 (CDe)	R_2 (cDE)	r (cde)
Nuer + Shilluk (a)	70	6	0	1	20
Galla (b)	54	4	17	6	20
Falasha + Tigre + Billen (c) (Ethiopia)	48	1	19	4	27
Shi + Hunde + Swaga (d) (Kivu Province of Zaïre)	60	8	7	8	16
Ashanti (Ghana) (e)	56	7	12	3	23
Naron Bushmen (f)	84	0	14	2	0
Mbuti (g)	71	24	0	4	0

References to Table 5
a: Roberts, Ikin and Mourant [178]   e: Armattoe, Ikin and Mourant [9]
b and c: Adam et al. [1]   f: Weiner and Zoutendyck [228]
d: Hiernaux [92]   g: Fraser, Giblett and Motulsky [60]

Blood genetics and morphology coincide in seeing in the Nilotes the results of a peculiar African evolution, but the palaeontological record is silent about this process. The extreme slenderness of the Nilotes, which looks largely genetical, gives them a specially efficient thermo-regulation in their hot and dry environment [182]. Climatic selection has undoubtedly shaped their body build, but why they are so different in head, face and nose proportions from East African populations like the Galla and Tutsi remains to be elucidated. Their blood group genetics makes it clear that they have been very isolated in the past. This is demonstrated not only in the Rh system, but also by the haemoglobins; although they suffer from malaria, the Nilotes show only a very low frequency of haemoglobin S, which therefore seems to have been introduced recently by a few migrants.

In the fifteenth century, Nilotic-speaking peoples left the Bahr-el-Ghazal area and expanded to the south. This expansion led them into western Uganda, where they brought the Cwezi state to an abrupt end. Their rulers were perhaps akin to the Tutsi. Nilotic peoples then founded the Bito dynasty of Bunyoro. However, the inhabitants of this country, the Nyoro, speak a Bantu language and closely resemble those Bantu populations of the area which have not been reached by the expansion of Nilotic-speaking peoples. Their mean stature is 166 cm and their cephalic index 74.9 [164].

Nearer to the centre of the expansion, the Alur of northern Uganda and north-eastern Zaire, though Nilotic-speakers, are as different from the Nilotes as the Nyoro. They are a little taller than the Nyoro (168 cm) but their head is much broader (147 mm), resulting in a mean cephalic index of 78.5 [47].

The recent expansion of Nilotic-speaking people finally reached south-western Kenya, where they are represented by the Luo. The Luo differ only moderately from the surrounding Bantu populations. They are taller than the Nyoro (172 cm) and broader-headed, with a cephalic index of 75.5 [164].

In reconciling the historical and biological data, two hypotheses may be proposed: either the Nilotic-speaking migrants were different from the Nilotes originally, or their contribution to the gene pool of the Nyoro, Alur and Luo has been very modest. At present there is no evidence from which to choose between the two hypotheses, which are not mutually exclusive.

The Peoples of the Western Sudan and the Guinea Rain Forest

Western Sudan stretches from the Atlantic Ocean to the Nile Valley, between the Sahara in the north and the rain forest in the south. Its landscape is one of woodlands and savanna, merging into a forest-savanna mosaic in the south. It is crossed by big rivers, abounding in fish. The main one, the Niger, describes a vast bend through Guinea, Mali, Niger and Nigeria and finally traverses the moist forest and flows into the Gulf of Guinea through marshes and mangrove. Between the Niger and the Nile basins, the water is drained into Lake Chad by the Shari, Logone and smaller rivers.

The exclusively or predominantly pastoral Ful communities of Western Sudan have been described in Chapter 10. The other populations of the area base their subsistence mostly on agriculture, and those living along rivers or the sea supplement it by fishing.

Climatic changes, the development of agriculture, the adoption of iron working, and the opening up of large-scale trade, have undoubtedly been major factors of the biological history of the present populations of western Sudan and their distribution.

Unfortunately, the pre-neolithic fossil record of Western Sudan is almost a complete blank. The only clues are those provided by the remains of the Wadi Halfa mesolithic populations and of the related people who occupied the southern Sahara in neolithic times; and by the skeleton from Iwo Ileru in the Nigerian rain forest, which is earlier than the Sahara neolithic peoples by several millennia.

The characteristics of these human remains attest the presence of a stock ancestral to its present populations in the periphery of the Western Sudan in mesolithic times. This west-central stock undoubtedly occupied Western Sudan long before the neolithic stage. Most probably the men who made the Lupemban industry belonged to it; as stated in Chapter 3, this industry, which developed in a central African forest-mosaic environment, expanded northward as far as 22°N during a wetter climatic phase.

There is no reason to suppose that the cultural step from a mesolithic to a neolithic economy was accompanied by a significant influx of foreign populations into Western Sudan. This step consisted merely of experimentation in the domestication of wild species and subsequent adoption. Egypt adopted crops from western Asia, mainly wheat and barley, before 4000 BC (emmer wheat was cultivated in the Fayum by approximately 4400 BC), but in Western Sudan these crops are cultivated only to a very limited extent [157]. Instead, the main food crops derive from local species. This 'Sudanic complex' includes four genera of cereals: fonio (*Digitaria*), pearl millet or bullrush millet (*Pennisetum americanum*), sorghum (*Sorghum vulgare*), and the African rice (*Oryza glaberrima*). In addition, it includes such tuber and root crops as the Bambara groundnut and the Guinea yam (*Dioscorea cayenensis*); ground fruits, among which are the bottle gourd or calabash and the watermelon; three oil plants (oil palm, sesame and the shea-butter tree); and two textile plants (ambary and cotton) [157].

Some would have it that the idea of plant domestication came to Western Sudan from outside, whereas Murdock holds the view that agriculture was invented independently in Western Sudan some time between 5000 and 4000 BC. Most probably, he suggests, it was invented by the ancestors of the Mande peoples around the headwaters of the Niger, and quickly spread throughout the whole area, diffusing as far east as Ethiopia by about the end of the fourth millennium BC. If such an early date is hypothetical, the presence of crops of Sudanese origin in Ethiopia is a fact. This is the case also in India, where Murdock believes they were adopted very early. As yet, factual evidence to support this claim about the antiquity of the cultivation of Sudanese crops is lacking. In Western Sudan, the oldest layers in which the microlithic tradition becomes enriched by polished stone axes and pottery – which can reasonably be interpreted as indicating cultivation – are dated about 3,000 BC. This was revealed by excavations in Sierra Leone, Ghana and Nigeria [34].

Murdock's hypothesis depends on the kind of crops cultivated in the Sahara in early neolithic times, if indeed cultivation was practised there at all at that time. The abundance of saddle-querns in Saharan neolithic sites is no proof of agriculture: they might have been used for grinding wild grain and seeds. The fruits of the tree *Celtis australis* were gathered (two large neolithic pots found in the Ténéré still contained a number of them). Today, some fifty-six wild plants of the Sahara and its Sahelian southern fringe are capable of providing food; many of them are used in times of famine and prepared on grindstones similar to the neolithic ones [150]. Possibly the Saharan 'neolithic' communities based their subsistence on collecting, hunting, fishing and cattle-keeping, as the Hottentots still do; or perhaps there was a co-existence of two separate modes of life, one mesolithic and the other pastoral.

The only evidence for early agriculture in the Sahara was recorded by Henri Hugot [111]: analysis of pollen collected at Méniet, in the Hoggar, in neolithic layers dated to 3,450 BC, indicates the presence of a 'cultivated grass' presumed to be wheat. However, the earliest firm detailed evidence of cultivation in the Sahara is much later. It comes from the large neolithic villages of the Tichitt-Walata region in south-central Mauretania. Hundreds of villages, some of which are of stone masonry construction and cover one square kilometre, were built there in neolithic times beside lakes which have now disappeared. Radiocarbon dates run from 1,400 to 380 BC. The Tichitt pottery bears a large number of very clear grain impressions and several species were tentatively identified. They belong to five genera, some species of which are still collected as famine foods in West Africa, while species of two of these genera are now cultivated as minor crops in this area [155]. There is also some evidence that bullrush millet was cultivated at Tichitt Walata [34]. The identified grain crops that may have been cultivated in this major group of neolithic sites were therefore all of Sudanic origin, wherever the initial impetus to agriculture originated.

The development of neolithic agriculture in the Sudanic belt surely induced population growth. This, as the archaeological record seems to indicate, also affected the forest fringes in the south by the second millennium BC. The abundance of ground stone forms and the distribution pattern of some objects of known date seem to indicate that the population was filling out in the forest fringe areas by 1,500 BC [172]. The basis of such a growth must have been the cultivation of yams and of oil palm trees.

There are forest areas in West Africa, and also in the Congo basin, which seem to have been largely cleared in the neolithic [51].

Much later, new cultivated species were introduced which enriched the Sudanic complex. These include such plants of ultimate south-eastern Asian origin as the banana, the taro and the Asian yam, *Dioscorea.alata*, and also a number of species whose domestication was achieved in tropical America, among them maize, cassava and the sweet potato. There is some dispute about when these new crops reached West Africa. Murdock [157] believes that the south-eastern Asian crops crossed Africa from the east coast to the Atlantic around the beginning of the Christian era. He further believes that it was their introduction in the Guinean area which laid the foundation for a dense agricultural population and the rise of powerful states. Others consider that *Dioscorea alata* was introduced in West Africa by European seafarers after AD 1500 and that the impact of banana cultivation is moderate in West Africa.

Although it is generally believed that the tropical American crops were introduced by Europeans in the sixteenth century, after Christopher Columbus had opened the Atlantic route in 1492, it has been suggested, on the basis of still undated archaeological evidence, that maize might have reached Africa before Columbian times. Murdock has suggested the same for the sweet potato. The route from America might have been across the Pacific to South East Asia, and from there to Africa [51].

Another cultural innovation which increased the productivity of the populations of the Western Sudan and of the Guinean forest was iron metallurgy. The earliest radiocarbon dates for indisputable evidence of iron smelting in West Africa are 440, 300 and 280 BC [55]. All come from Taruga in Nigeria, one of the sites of the Nok culture. This culture could of course have started earlier than the dates obtained for the occupation of Taruga, and it continued at least until the second century AD. The cultural contents of the Taruga site are entirely Iron Age, with no neolithic elements [56]. The Nok culture occupied a hilly area east of the Niger from 10° to 7°N, crossed by the Benue valley. This area is now covered by savanna woodlands, with some rain forest timber species in the more densely wooded valleys. The abundance of palm nuts at some sites indicates that the region was more heavily forested during the period of the Nok culture, which possibly was also widespread in the forest area of Nigeria [234].

The Nok culture is famous for its human and animal figurines made of baked clay ('terracottas'). Some of them portray features of dress or hair style which can still be fairly closely matched among the small groups occupying much of the area of the Nok culture [234]. They are also clearly ancestral to the sculpture of the Yoruba, who live south-west of the Nok area in a partly forested territory.

By the end of the first millennium AD this ethnic group, which today includes about ten million people, had founded several kingdoms and built large towns. They probably spread from the Ife area, on the fringes of the rain forest. The Ife culture continued the manufacture of terracotta sculpture ultimately derived from the Nok tradition, but supplemented it by translation into bronze casting [234]. The technique of bronze casting seems to have been introduced from North Africa as a result of the intensification of trade through the trans-Saharan caravan routes which followed the Arab conquests from the beginning of the eighth century AD onwards [189].

Iron metallurgy, which almost certainly was not invented independently in Africa, probably also diffused to West Africa from the north through the Sahara. Iron was known to the Carthaginians and appears in their burials in the sixth century BC [746]. Another possible route is from the Meroe kingdom on the Nile, at the eastern end of the belt of steppe land which runs across Western Sudan. However, iron metallurgy seems to have started too late in Meroe for this to have been a probable source for iron working in West Africa; it seems that it was not carried out on a considerable scale at Meroe before the beginning of the fourth century BC [8].

Another metal which came to play a major role in the history of West Africa was gold. The control of the gold trade has been the paramount factor in the development, rivalries and sequence of three empires which flourished in Western Sudan from the eighth to the sixteenth century between the middle Senegal valley and the Nigerian plateau: Ghana, Mali and Songai. Soon after the conquest of North Africa by the Arabs, large cities developed along the southern fringe of the Sahara at the terminal point of the trans-Saharan caravan routes. Their prosperity was based on the trade of gold (and also of slaves, cola nuts and ivory) from the south. Gold was bartered for salt and natron from the Sahara, horses, and Mediterranean goods and products, among which copper was an important item. Such cities as Ghana, Tumbuctu and Gao, and others farther south in the Sudanic states at capitals or inter-mediary trade centres, contained several distinct quarters. Some were inhabited by the rich Arabo-Berber merchants, others by various groups of sub-Saharan Africans who were either local people or traders. The most dynamic group of these Sudanic traders was the Dyula, most of whom were of Manding or Sarakole origin.

Farther east, several states developed and fought for hegemony from the twelfth to the eighteenth century. Their prosperity was also based on trade with North Africa, mostly of slaves and alum. These were the Kanem-Bornu states in the Lake Chad basin and the Hausa states, whose main cities were Kano and Katsina.

Most of the gold mines were not on the territory of the Sudanic states, but farther south in the forest. They were much nearer to the Atlantic coast than to the Mediterranean, but the Atlantic was not navigated until the fifteenth century, so that the outlet to the gold-hungry European nations was through the Sudanic states and the Sahara. The development of sea-borne trade between Europe and the coast of the Gulf of Guinea from the sixteenth century reversed the flow of goods and influences in the Western Sudan. This caused the economic decline of the northern zone, to the benefit of developing southern states like the Kong empire and the Ashanti federation.

Colonization of Brazil and the Antilles by European nations had created a heavy demand for slaves. By the end of the seventeenth century, the slave trade had become the basis of European trade with the Guinea coast. In exchange, the Europeans offered firearms, alcohol, and various fabrics.

During the eighteenth and nineteenth centuries, before the European conquests, Western Sudan was once more the scene of important political events, resulting in the creation of the Ful states.

In shaping the biological history of man in the Western Sudan and the Guinea forest from neolithic times onwards, two processes have been paramount: gracilization and climatic adaptation. Gracilization has been referred to in Chapter 10; it consists of a fining down of the skeleton and the disappearance of archaic features. In Africa, as in other parts of the world, this process seems to result from major changes in living conditions associated with passing from food gathering to food production. It took place in the central and southern Sahara between neolithic and proto-historic times [31], and presumably it also occurred in the Western Sudan.

The cultural, economical and political events which have been sketched above induced vast expansions and migrations, many of which were northward or southward, crossing the climatic and vegetation zones. These zones themselves shifted northward or southward with time, the forest front advancing to the north during the climatic optimum in the Sahara, and retreating southward when the Sahara dried up. From what has been said about climatic adaptation in Chapter 6, it can be deduced that changes of climatic zone released selection afresh in the populations concerned. However, several tens of generations, or even a hundred, are needed to attain a new genetic equilibrium. Many populations of the Western Sudan have lived in their present environment for too short a time to have reached the equilibrium state of climatic adaptation. It is therefore all the more striking to see how clear is the statistical association between human morphology and vegetation zones in sub-Saharan Africa, even after excluding the Elongated Africans, Pygmies and Pygmoids (see Table 6). From the Sahelian arid zone

TABLE 6

Means of four anthropometric characters in the Sahelian, savanna and rain forest zones of sub-Saharan Africa.
(*Elongated Africans of the Western Sudan, Pygmies, Pygmoids and Khoisan are excluded.*) *The Mbuti Pygmies are added as showing an extreme of adaptation to the rain forest.*

	Stature	*Nasal index*	*Facial index*	*Cephalic index*
Sahelian zone	171	85	90	75
Savanna	169	86	86	75
Rain forest	164	94	82	76
Mbuti Pygmies	144	104	78	77

to the rain forest, stature gradually decreases, the nose and face become gradually broader in proportions, and the head becomes slightly rounder. As pointed out repeatedly, the factors of these morphological clines lay in the environment, not in a gene flow from North Africa or Arabia.

Clear-cut though they are, these clines concern anthropometric averages in the various zones, and within each zone there is a wide variety of populations. Each has its own biological history, which responded to many interacting factors. At present it is impossible to reconstruct the puzzle in the Western Sudan and Guinea forest, because too few populations have been studied by anthropo-biologists in adequate detail. Only a few pieces of the puzzle will be discussed here.

Some have already been investigated in the preceding chapter where the case of the Ful was mentioned. Long after the desiccation of the Sahara had pushed the Ful southward in the Senegal, they had expanded eastward and southward. This brought some of their communities into a considerably moister habitat, where two forces thrust their gene pool toward adaptive equilibrium: climatic selection, and gene admixture with local populations who had lived in the new biotope for longer. In turn, the Ful, as a potential source of gene admixture, affected these local populations.

Across the fourteenth parallel, two populations have been studied in some detail by Professor Johan Huizinga [114]: the Dogon of central Mali and the Fulse (or Kurumba) of Upper Volta. They have lived in their present territory for some twenty to thirty generations. Where they came from is not known with certainty, but possibly it was from Mande, a region west of Bamako at a slightly lower latitude. The Kurumba are significantly taller than the Dogon (171 cm against 168 cm), a difference which is accounted for by their longer legs; their head is narrower (141 mm against 144 mm), and their nose is shorter by 3 mm. The Dogon are lighter in skin colour. Both populations show a low weight/surface ratio, a feature which is adaptive to their hot biotope.

The high cliff of Bandiagara, along which a number of Dogon villages are grouped, is honeycombed with caves, many of which contain human remains. According to the Dogon, some of these belong to their ancestors, others to an ancient population which they call the Tellem, whose caves are usually distinct. The Tellem flourished in the eleventh, twelfth and thirteenth centuries, but the

Figure 23. Localities of the populations of the Western Sudan and the Guinea forest mentioned in the text

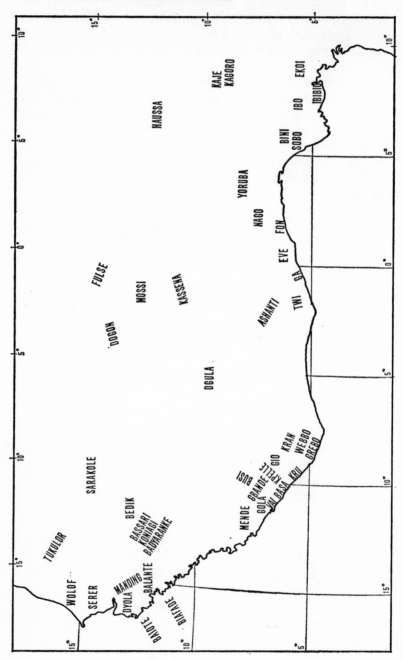

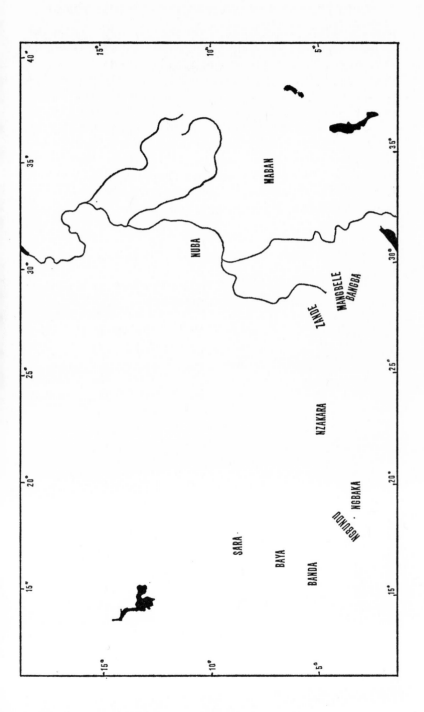

final part of their occupation of the site probably overlaps the Dogon occupation. The Tellem clearly differ from the Dogon by their rounder head and broader nose; in these and other features they are nearer to the populations of the Central African forest [112]. They also differ from the Kurumba [113]. The Tellem might be late representatives of a wave of forest-adapted populations who possibly occupied part of the Western Sudan during the last wetter climatic phase. Perhaps the neolithic site of Kurunkorokale, on the twelfth parallel near to the springs of the Niger in Mali, gives earlier evidence of such an occupation; according to Coon [37], the skeletons unearthed there show affinities with the present populations of the Congo basin.

TABLE 7

Anthropometric means in five populations of Gambia and Portuguese Guinea

	95 Dyola [165]	45–120 Baiote [143, 169, 199]	63–75 Balante [199]	220 Biafade [143, 144]	58 Kasanga [199]
Stature (cm)	168	169	169	166	163
Shoulder breadth (mm)	—	376	376	—	361
Head length (mm)	190	192	194	192	190
Head breadth (mm)	146	146	141	144	143
Face height (mm)	—	117	117	—	112
Face breadth (mm)	—	138	136	137	134
Nose height (mm)	52	52	51	—	49
Nose breadth (mm)	42	43	44	43	43
Lip thickness (mm)	—	24	23	—	26
Cephalic index	76·1	76·9	72·6	74·9	75·3
Facial index	—	84·9	85·6	—	83·5
Nasal index	81·9	82·7	86·5	—	86·5

At a latitude of 12° along the Atlantic coast, several populations have been studied by anthropo-biologists. In particular, these include the Dyola, who live in Gambia and in the extreme south of Senegal; and, in Portuguese Guinea, the Baiote (whom Greenberg considers to be a sub-group of the Dyola), the Balante, the Biafade and the Kasanga. Greenberg [74] classifies them all in a Senegambian group, together with the Tenda, who live inland farther east, and populations of western Senegal like the Wolof and Serer.

In Gambia and Portuguese Guinea, a strip of mangrove swamp forest borders part of the coast, and forest galleries stretch along the streams. Fishing assumes an importance second only to agriculture, while pigs hold a prominent place in animal husbandry [157].

A number of anthropometric means for the five populations are given in Table 7. The Dyola and Baiote resemble each other very closely, which agrees with their ethnic affinity. Between this Dyola-Baiote group and the Balante and the Biafade, the overall difference is moderate. The Biafade are distinguished mainly by their shorter stature, whereas a longer and narrower head is the main distinction of the Balante. The Kasanga are considerably shorter in stature and face dimensions, and they have thicker lips.

The Tenda, now a group of some 25,000 people, are the most ancient inhabitants of an area which covers part of Guinea, south-eastern Senegal and eastern Portuguese Guinea across the twelfth parallel north, at longitudes 12–13°W. They were occupying their present territory in the thirteenth century when the first waves of Malinke, expanding from the Mali empire, invaded the area. Later, the creation of Ful states north and south of the Tenda area in the eighteenth century was followed by a period of Ful invasions which further contracted the territory of the Tenda and reduced their number.

Monique de Lestrange [135], now Mrs Gessain, measured representative samples of three Tenda populations: the Koniagi, Badyaranke and Bassari. More recently, Professor Jacques Gomila [73] undertook the most searching anthropo-biological study yet made of an African population. He surveyed the total Bedik population, a Tenda group of some 1,500 people who are subdivided into two sub-groups, the Banapas and the Biwol. Only two Tenda groups have not been studied, the Tenda Boini ('Islamized' Tenda) and the Tenda Mayo ('stream' Tenda).

Table 8 gives the means of a number of anthropometric characters which have been measured in the four Tenda groups which have been investigated. They differ only moderately from each other. Gomila [73] computed all multidimensional distances between them and the Ful of the Badyar (who appear in Table 2) and a sample of a hundred Wolof, measured by Dr Léon Pales and Miss Tassin de Saint-Péreuse. (These anthropologists have studied a large number of populations of West Africa, but up till now have

TABLE 8
Anthropometric means in four Tenda populations

	200 Koniagi [135]	100 Badyaranke [135]	128 Bassari [135]	280 Bedik [73]
Stature (cm)	169	170	166	167
Head length (mm)	196	192	189	192
Head breadth (mm)	141	143	141	141
Face height (mm)	116	116	117	116
Face breadth (mm)	135	136	135	136
Nose height (mm)	49	48	50	47
Nose breadth (mm)	42	43	43	42
Lip thickness (mm)	26	25	26	23
Relative trunk length	48·5	49·2	49·7	49·6[1]
Cephalic index	73·9	74·1	74·5	73·5[1]
Facial index	85·3	85·3	86·8	85·6[1]
Nasal index	85·9	89·1	86·5	90·0[1]

[1] Computed from the means of the measurements

published only means of stature, cephalic index and relative trunk length). The shortest distance is between the two Bedik sub-groups. The four Tenda populations show moderate distances between each other and the Ful. The Tenda and Ful differ much more from the Wolof.

Except in cephalic index, the Tenda populations as a group are near to the anthropometric means for the savanna zone given in Table 6. Their morphology is apparently near to a state of adaptive equilibrium with climate.

A large number of blood polymorphisms were studied in nearly half the Bedik population [17]. Like the Bassari [65], the Hausa of Nigeria [12], and the Mossi of Haute-Volta [161], the Bedik are peripheral to the sub-Saharan African distribution of ABO allele frequencies in having high B and moderate A frequencies. Their R_o frequency (63 per cent) is usual for sub-Saharan Africa. They have a rather high frequency of the haemoglobin S allele (14 per cent), which is consistent with the prevalence of malaria in the area, but no haemoglobin C or G6PD deficiency. They possess the P^A, P^B and P^R alleles of the acid phosphatase polymorphism, but not the P^C allele. At the PGM^2 locus, only one out of 755 individuals possess the PGM^2 allele. The V^W antigen of the Rh system is present in all of them. The AK^2 allele of the adenylate kinase system and the Tf^{D2} variant of transferrin are absent. This set of frequencies suggests a relatively strong genetic isolation for a number of generations, and a loss of alleles which may have resulted from the reduction of the Bedik population probably caused by the wars against the Ful.

In the frequency of ABO and MN alleles and in that of finger-prints, the Bedik differ largely from the Wolof, as they do in morphology, whereas the Wolof resemble the Serer and Tukulor who live close to them in western Senegal (see Table 9). Although the Tenda and the set of three western populations all speak West Atlantic languages, they differ markedly genetically.

TABLE 9

ABO and MN allele frequencies and fingerprints in the Bedik, Wolof, Serer and Tukulor

	Bedik	Wolof	Serer	Tukulor
ABO system				
Number	771	1380	300	558
	(Bouloux et al. [17])	(Koerber et Linhard [123])	(Moullec et al., [153])	(Koerber et Linhard [123])
A	·20	·14	·15	·14
B	·23	·12	·13	·15
O	·57	·74	·72	·71
MN system	795	316	311	306
Number	(Bouloux et al. [17])	(Kane et Ruffié [121])	(Kane et Ruffié [121])	(Kane et Ruffié [121])
M	·51	·32	·37	·33
N	·49	·68	·63	·67
Fingerprints	128	1092	109	362
Number (♂)	(Gomila et al. [72])	(Leschi [134])	(Leschi [134])	(Leschi [134])
Arches	·07	·06	·05	·07
Loops	·62	·57	·58	·55
Whorls	·31	·36	·36	·38

A long way east of the Tenda, on the Haute-Volta-Ghana border, the Kasena have been measured by Dr Pales. Like the Dogon, they speak a Voltaic language. However, they show a closer morphological affinity to the Badyaranke, who speak a West Atlantic language. Their means are 169 cm for stature, 192 and 144 mm for head diameters, 137 mm for face breadth, and 47 and

43 mm for nose dimensions [35], all values which differ from those of the Badyaranke by no more than one unit.

Still farther east, in northern Nigeria, the Hausa form an ethnic entity of some five million people. Before European colonial occupation, they had achieved a degree of cultural unity comparable to that of the great nations of Europe [157]. Their language belongs to the Chad subdivision of the Afroasiatic class. The available data are not detailed enough to investigate how biologically homogeneous are the Hausa, whom C. K. Meek [147] considers to be a hotch-potch of peoples of various origins. Their vast territory stretches over the Sahelian and savanna zones, from 13° to 9°N. From what we know, their morphology does not differ greatly from the means for the Sahelian zone, except for their shorter stature (168 cm); their cephalic index is 75, their nasal index 85, and their facial index 90. The first two values concern a sample from both vegetation zones [202], whereas the last two concern a northern group of Hausa who live in an arid environment [124].

South of the Hausa territory, a large number of small tribes live on the Nigerian plateau. Two of them, the Kagoro and the Kaje, have been subjected to physical measurements. Both speak a Benue-Congo language and live close to each other at latitude 9°N. Dr A. J. Tremearne, who published their means in 1912, records some difficulty in measuring their stature accurately. On small samples, he obtained an average stature of 168 cm in the Kaje, but only 160 cm in the Kagoro. The two populations do not differ much in head and nose proportions, but the measurements on which these are based have higher means in the Kaje. Tremearne believes that the Kagoro came from the south, and the Kaje from the north. If this is correct, the shorter size of the Kagoro would suggest an explanation in terms of adaptation to a formerly moister climate.

At a similar latitude in southern Chad, the Sara group of tribes covers most of the Moyen-Chari Province. This group of some 400,000 people subsists mainly on agriculture and fishing; they have occupied their fairly homogeneous savanna biotope since time immemorial. Their language belong to the Central Sudanic subdivision of the Chari-Nile class. The group is nearly completely closed to genetic admixture; the ten tribes or so included in it intermarry at a rate of 2.5 per cent. This rate is low enough for stature and cephalic and facial indices to keep fairly heterogeneous between the tribes, but the nasal index is homogeneous over the whole area, probably owing to the higher sensitivity of this character to climatic adaptation [100].

Compared to twenty-eight other populations of sub-Saharan Africa by means of multidimensional analysis, the four main Sara tribes form a tight cluster. It lies at the periphery of the scatter, at a considerable distance from the nearest population, the Bushong of southern Zaire (in Figure 19, it stands north-west of the latter). The Sara cluster therefore appears as a highly distinct African group. Table 10 gives the means of a number of anthropometric

TABLE 10

Anthropometric means in urban and rural Sara Majingay

	308 urban Majingay [98]	348 rural Majingay [46]
Stature (cm)	176	174
Lower limb length (cm)	102	100
Shoulder breadth (mm)	377	384
Hip breadth (mm)	258	264
Head length (mm)	189	190
Head breadth (mm)	151	154
Face height (mm)	122	121
Face breadth (mm)	140	144
Nose height (mm)	53	52
Nose breadth (mm)	45	43
Lip thickness (mm)	31	26
Arm circumference (mm)	271	276
Skinfold (0·1 mm)	68	63
Cephalic index	80·3	81·1
Facial index	86·9	83·5
Nasal index	85·0	83·7

characters in two samples of the most numerous Sara tribe, the Majingay; these are a sample of young men from Fort-Archambault, the chief town of the Moyen-Chari Province, and a sample of young men from Ndila, a large village. The rural Majingay differ from the urban ones in being shorter and more developed in breadth, and in having more muscle and less fat [45]. Probably the heavier work-load of the rural Sara during growth is responsible for these differences. The urban Sara also have a narrower head and face and thicker lips, for which no explanation is offered. The Sara are outstanding in combining very high stature, a broad head (their cephalic index is over 80) and very thick lips. What evolutionary pressures and events have shaped their present morphology is unknown. With a mean reflectance of 23 in the males and 26 in the females, the Sara are among the darkest-skinned peoples of Africa [105]. This looks like a genetic adaptation to their intensely sunny biotope, in which they used to go naked until a few generations ago.

The only population in which there are indications of tight affinities with the Sara is an agricultural ethnic group of south-eastern Sudan, the Maban. This Eastern Sudanic speaking group of some 10,000 people lives at a latitude of 10°N, east of the Nilotes who speak languages of the same class. Ethnologists generally classify them as Prenilotes, and Murdock [157] considers that they are descended from the introducers of Sudanic agriculture into this part of Africa. Less than forty Maban have been measured. Their means are near to those of the Sara, and contrast strongly with those of the near-by Nilotes. Stature is 177 cm, head diameters 191 and 149 mm, resulting in a cephalic index of 78, face breadth 140 mm, and nose breadth 44 mm [179].

North-west of the Nilotes, a linguistically highly distinctive group of populations, the Nuba, live in the hills of Kordofan. Their languages form a subclass of Congo-Kordofanian, whose rank is equal to that of the whole Niger-Congo subfamily [74]. Protected by their mountain environment, they have remained relatively untouched by the movements of peoples and cultures in the Nile Valley and between the latter and the central Sudan. They practise agriculture and stock-breeding, and they keep genetically isolated. They are said to be very dark-skinned [157], undoubtedly an adaptive feature for people who, like the Sara until recently, go naked under an intense ultra-violet irradiation. Fifty of them have been measured [187]. With a stature of 172 cm, head diameters of 188 and 145 mm, a cephalic index of 76, a face breadth of 137 mm and a nose breadth of 44 mm, they do not resemble the Nilotes, the Maban or the Sara, but are intermediary between the Sara and the Tenda.

The populations of southern Nigeria have been extensively surveyed by P. Amaury Talbot for a number of anthropometric characters. His data were published in 1962 under his name and that of the statistician who elaborated them, H. Mulhall. They concern forty-one populations, twenty of which are sub-groups of the Ibo ethnic entity. The territory of the Ibo, who number nearly four million, is one of the most densely populated in sub-Saharan Africa. In the south, it is covered with moist forest, whereas its northern part is grassland. However, the northern Ibo area was originally forest; even here, the village settlements lie among palm trees and degenerate forest. The Ibo have no tradition of migration from elsewhere. They appear to have settled in northern parts of their present territory for a very long period and to have spread out from there, their main expansion being southward, south-eastward, and eastward to the Cross River. Intermarriage between them and other peoples has been a rare event [202].

West of the Ibo, the Yoruba rival the latter in total population. They inhabit south-western Nigeria from the coast to the river Niger, north of its junction with the Benue. Most of them have been notably urban for centuries. Their country is savanna-woodland in the north, forest in the south. Six Yoruba sub-groups have been studied by Talbot and Mulhall. Their survey also includes four Edo populations, who live in the forest south-east of the Yoruba. They form two sub-groups: the Bini, who live to the west of the lower Niger, and the Sobo who inhabit the western Niger Delta. Edo is the native name for Benin City, the capital of the Benin Kingdom whose present dynasty traces its descent from Oronmiyon, a great Yoruba warrior. In recognition of this, the head of the deceased King of Benin was sent to Ife, the sacred city of the Yoruba, for burial on the site from which Oronmiyon set out [234]. The Edo number about 500,000 people.

Ibo, Yoruba and Edo all speak languages of the Kwa branch of the Niger-Congo subfamily. East of the Ibo, southern Nigeria is inhabited by speakers of languages of another branch of Niger-Congo: the Benue-Congo branch, to which the group of Bantu languages also belongs. Talbot and Mulhall studied nine populations of so-called Semi-Bantu or Bantoid linguistic affiliation, the most important being the Ibibio, who number more than a million, and the Ekoi, a group of some 90,000 people.

Talbot and Mulhall computed the multidimensional D^2 distance for eight head and face measurements between all the populations studied. On the basis of the matrix of distances so obtained, they classify the latter into six clusters: the Yoruba, the Sobo, the northern Ibo, the central Ibo, the Ekoi and the Ibibio. The transition from Yoruba, through Sobo, northern Ibo and central Ibo to Ekoi is almost additional, and can be represented, roughly, as points on the circumference of a circle, with the Ibibio at the centre. This clustering does not coincide with the cultural and linguistic grouping: among the Edo, the Bini and the related Kukuruku belong to the Yoruba cluster. Indeed, this cluster groups the two most northerly-living Yoruba populations, the Oyo and Ekiti, together with the three most northerly-living Edo populations, the Bini, Esa and Kukuruku; four out of the six Yoruba populations belong to the Sobo cluster.

Table 11 reproduces anthropometric means from the study of Talbot and Mulhall; it is restricted to measurements whose technique is similar to that used in the other surveys referred to in the tables of this book. The values for the Sobo concern this population, and not the cluster bearing the same name. The Northern Ibo and the Yoruba clusters of populations, who live in grassland, are considerably taller in stature than the other ones, who live in the forest. The stature of the latter is near to the African average for their biotope, 164 cm, whereas that of the Northern Ibo is equal to the average for the African savanna, 169 cm, and that of the Yoruba cluster, at 167 cm, is intermediate. The Yoruba cluster also differs noticeably from the others by the relatively narrower head, whereas face and nose breadths do not vary much over the area. All multidimensional distances are moderate. Including stature in their computation would bring the Yoruba and Northern Ibo nearer together, and the other clusters nearer to each other, making the impact of sharing the same biotope on morphological resemblance clearer.

The zone of rain forest along the Guinea coast is interrupted for a stretch at the western border of southern Nigeria, which extends westward across Dahomey, Togo and Ghana to the eastern Ivory Coast. The populations who inhabit it all speak Kwa languages. In Dahomey, two of them have been studied in some detail: the Nago (a Yoruba sub-group), and the Fon, a population of nearly a million people [43]. Table 12 reproduces their anthropometric means. In their stature and in their head, face and nose proportions, the two populations are very similar. For these four characters they are intermediary between the general means for the African savanna and forest zones, in concordance with the characteristics of their biotope, a moist savanna.

In stature, cephalic index and face and nose breadths, the Nago are near to the Yoruba cluster of southern Nigeria, which occupies a similar biotope. This observation strengthens the distinction between the savanna- and the forest-dwelling Yoruba groups,

TABLE 11

Anthropometric means in four clusters and two populations of Southern Nigeria [202]

	Yoruba cluster	Central Ibo cluster	Northern Ibo cluster	Sobo	Ibibio	Ekoi cluster
Number	426	397	227	340	217	233
Stature (cm)	167	164	169	165	163	165
Shoulder breadth (mm)	395	380	387	382	380	387
Head length (mm)	195	189	193	193	190	190
Head breadth (mm)	144	146	147	145	143	146
Face breadth (mm)	139	137	140	140	138	138
Nose breadth (mm)	43	42	43	43	43	42
Cephalic index	74·1	77·2	76·4	75·4	75·2	76·9

which obeys the ecological associations of human morphology with climate and vegetation. This distinction has been noted also in culture: despite the considerable amount of population movement southward in the nineteenth century, the northern Yoruba of the savanna-woodlands have a rather different culture from the southern Yoruba of the forest. Only certain elements of the northern culture were absorbed into the pre-existing culture of the forest dwellers [234]. The biological data suggest that this relative cultural isolation of the two zones was genetical also: the two ecological Yoruba sub-groups were isolated enough for the southern one to develop and keep a biological adaptation to the forest, and the northern one a biological adaptation to a moist savanna. Admixture between northerly populations and the savanna-dwelling Yoruba groups may have played a role in the differentiation. Pygmy admixture in the forest-dwelling Yoruba populations looks highly improbable, since there is no trace of Pygmies or Pygmoids in the Nigerian forest.

The Yoruba and Ibo differ moderately but significantly. In particular, the Ibo have a shorter and broader head. The two ethnic groups also differ in their ABO blood groups; the Ibo have higher A and lower B allele frequencies [85, 63]. The haemoglobin C allele is much more frequent in the Yoruba (4 per cent) than in the eastern Ibo (0.4 per cent), whereas the haemoglobin S allele has the same frequency in the two populations (12 per cent) [224, 63, 132, 181]. H. Lehmann and C. Nwokolo conclude from this that the River Niger has been a barrier in the spread eastwards of haemoglobin C. The hereditary deficiency in the enzyme group G6PD is also much more frequent in the Yoruba (22 per cent) [169] than in the Ibo (6 per cent) [68]. Indeed, unless the selective pressures which act on these traits differ between Yorubaland and Iboland, the marked differences in frequencies observed for haemoglobin variants and G6PD deficiency bear witness to the strong genetic isolation of the Ibo. A similar indication is given by the very different frequency of G6PD deficiency (27 per cent) in the Ogoni of the Niger delta, probably a population of Ibibio descent [86].

The Nago and Fon are similar in stature and head shape, but the Nago have wider shoulders and hips. In southern Nigeria also, the Yoruba cluster has higher means of shoulder width than the other clusters. The Fon are noticeable by their relatively high frequency of the M allele, which they share with their western neighbours, the Eve of coastal Togo and Ghana: 57 per cent in the former [194], 54 per cent in the latter [9], whereas the M frequency stands below 50 per cent in the other populations of the Gulf of Guinea from the Yoruba westward to Liberia. The Fon also stand out by their high frequency of the haemoglobin S allele (16 per cent) which, combined with a high frequency of G6PD deficiency (19 per cent) [194], might represent a genetic adaptation to a particularly heavy malarial infestation.

In Ghana, an ethnic group of over 700,000 people, the Ashanti, inhabits a part of the rain forest inland of the narrow stretch of coastal savanna. They also speak a Kwa language. Anthropometrically, they resemble the central Ibo cluster (see Table 12), a resemblance which parallels that of the habitats of the two groups. Like the Yoruba and the Ibo, they have the haemoglobin S allele at a frequency of 12 per cent, and like the Yoruba the haemoglobin C allele at a frequency of 4 per cent [9]. Frequencies of S and C similar to those in the Ashanti have also been found in the Ga and Twi of Ghana [3].

Still farther west, the rain forest which lies in the south-western Ivory Coast and in Liberia and Sierra Leone is inhabited by populations who exhibit markedly less complex cultures than their neighbours [157]. They speak languages of three branches of

TABLE 12

Anthropometric means in two populations of Dahomey (Nago and Fon), in the Ashanti of Ghana and in the Kran of Liberia

	80 Nago [43]	176 Fon [43]	48 Ashanti [23]	105 Kran [109]
Stature (cm)	169	168	164	165
Shoulder breadth (mm)	373	365	—	—
Hip breadth (mm)	251	248	—	—
Head length (mm)	191	190	187	191
Head breadth (mm)	142	141	145	144
Face height (mm)	117	115	—	—
Face breadth (mm)	138	136	135	135
Nose height (mm)	48	48	—	—
Nose breadth (mm)	42	42	42	43
Relative trunk length	50·0	50·6	—	50·9
Cephalic index	74·2	73·3	77·5	75·3
Facial index	84·4	84·8	—	—
Nasal index	88·1	87·4	—	—

Niger-Congo: Kwa, Mande, and West Atlantic. Table 12 gives a few anthropometric means of the Kran, a Kwa-speaking population of Liberia. They are usual for forest people: stature and cephalic index are medium, the nose is wide, and the legs are relatively short. Like the linguistically related Kru, Grebo and Webbo of Liberia and the Mande-speaking Gio (or Dan) of the same country, the Kran possess the haemoglobin S allele at very low frequencies, less than one per cent, despite the presence of malaria. As an explanation, Livingstone [139] suggests that slash-and-burn agriculture, which favours the breeding of mosquitoes and enhanced the severity of malaria through the rise in human population density, has been introduced only recently in the area. This zone of very low haemoglobin S frequencies covers only a part of the forest. East of it, in the Ivory Coast, a mixed sample of Bete, Wobe, Gere and Godie – all populations linguistically related to the Kru of Liberia – has a haemoglobin S allele frequency of 4 per cent [24]. West of it, the Basa of the Liberian coast, who are also linguistically related to the Kru, the Mande-speaking Kpelle and Gbanda of the Liberian hinterland, and the West Atlantic-speaking Vai and Busi of Liberia and Sierra Leone, are similar in having a frequency of 5 to 7 per cent of the haemoglobin S allele. Farther west, in the Mende of Sierra Leone, the frequency rises to 14 per cent.

The Kpelle differ considerably from the Kran in stature and cephalic index [166]. For these features they have the same values as the savanna-dwelling Nago. It is clear that the biological history of the populations of eastern Liberia differs from that of their neighbours in the same forest. In all this area, however, the haemoglobin C allele, where present, keeps to very low frequencies, under one per cent. This has been found in the Kru-speaking populations of the Ivory Coast [24] and in the Kpelle of Liberia; haemoglobin C was absent in the sample of Basa tested for this variant [158], but it has a frequency of 2 per cent in the Mende [3].

The sixth branch of Niger-Congo languages, the Adamawa-Eastern, is spoken by a small cluster of tribes in Adamawa and by a larger body of populations in an area which lies astride the boundary of savanna and rain forest in the Central African Republic, northern Zaire, and south-western Sudan. In this eastern area, Dr Massimo Cresta [39, 40] has studied three populations of the Central African Republic: the Baya, Banda and Nzakara. Farther

TABLE 13

Anthropometric means in three savanna-dwelling populations speaking
Adamawa-Eastern languages

	215 Banda [40]	104 Nzakara [39]	217 Zande [47]
Stature (cm)	167	166	170
Shoulder breadth (mm)	363	376	—
Hip breadth (mm)	243	257	—
Head length (mm)	188	189	193
Head breadth (mm)	144	145	150
Face height (mm)	112	113	121
Face breadth (mm)	136	138	142
Nose height (mm)	45	46	53
Nose breadth (mm)	42	41	44
Relative trunk length	50·5	50·3	—
Cephalic index	76·3	76·3	78·2
Facial index	82·2	82·9	85·9
Nasal index	94·6	89·9	82·5

east, Professor Jan Czekanowski [47] studied 217 Zande. Table 13
concerns the Banda, Nzakara and Zande; the values for the Baya
are given in Table 2.

The Banda and the Nzakara are similar in stature, relative trunk
length, and cephalic and facial proportions. Compared to the
Banda, the Nzakara have a slightly higher and narrower nose, and
much broader shoulders and hips. Head, face and nose indices in
the Banda are equal to the African means for the rain forest, but
their stature is higher. The Baya are similar to the Banda in head
and nose proportions, but their face is slightly narrower; they are
shorter in body size, with relatively longer legs, narrower shoulders
but equally wide hips. As a whole, the features of this group of
three populations of the Central African Republic, living in the
savanna close to the equatorial forest, fit approximately in the
climatic cline of morphology.

The Zande are very different. They are much taller, and all their
head dimensions are larger; although the head is broader, the face
and nose are narrower. In all these features, the Zande deviate
from the three Adamawa Eastern-speaking populations of the
C.A.R. towards the Sara, the northern neighbours of the latter. As
a matter of fact the Zande, comprising some 750,000 individuals,

are an amalgam of ancient local populations and recent Ambomu conquerors who came from the north, perhaps from as far as the present Chad Republic where the bulk of the Sara live. The historical data are therefore consistent with the anthropological picture, which suggests that the Zande result from the mixture of a Sara-like population and local populations whose morphology has been better retained in the Baya-Banda-Nzakara group.

South-east of the Zande, in the forest, Czekanowski [47] also measured small samples of Mangbele and Bangba. According to Murdock [157], the Mangbele were originally a Bantu people who became largely acculturated by Mangbetu conquerors. The Mangbetu, who speak a Central Sudanic language like the Sara, are said to have infiltrated the area, which is the home of the Mbuti Pygmies, before Adamawa-Eastern and Bantu speaking peoples. The Bangba are a medley of peoples, partly Bantu but mainly Adamawa-Eastern in language, who have been shattered by Mangbetu and Zande expansions. The Mangbele and Bangba have head, face and nose proportions similar to those of the Zande, but their stature is lower by three centimetres. Their morphology could therefore be explained as a result of the size-reducing effect of the rain forest biotope on a population whose original constituents were similar to those of the Zande. This would be in accordance with the historical and linguistic data.

In north-western Zaire, large samples of two Adamawa-Eastern speaking populations, the Ngbundu and the Ngbaka, have been tested for the ABO blood groups. They are outstanding in their high frequencies of both A and B alleles [117]. This is not the case for the Nzakara, who occupy a central position in the African scatter for these frequencies [39].

South and west of the Adamawa-Eastern linguistic zone, the Benue-Congo branch of Niger-Congo stretches over an immense area. The next chapter is devoted to it.

12

The Bantu Expansion

Some seventy million people speak Bantu languages, south of a line stretching approximately from Duala on the Atlantic coast to the mouth of the Tana River on the Indian Ocean. Although there are nearly seven hundred Bantu languages [81], they merely form part of the Benue-Congo branch of Niger-Congo, according to the classification of African languages. The Bantu group has no higher rank than the other members of this branch, the individual Bantoid languages spoken in eastern Nigeria and central Cameroun. This implies that the speakers of Bantu languages must have expanded very rapidly and recently to have achieved such a wide geographic dispersion along with such a small degree of linguistic divergence [74]. To Greenberg, the location of the related Bantoid languages suggests the central Benue valley in eastern Nigeria as the ultimate source of Bantu origins. The historical inference from the linguistic data, he suggests, is as follows. At the time when the speakers of the Niger-Congo languages moved southwards to occupy also the forest belt, those who started from the eastern Nigerian end, and who were therefore not brought to a halt by the Atlantic coast like the ancestors of the Yoruba and Ibo, moved straight on southwards and eastwards into the Congo basin. From there they fanned out to occupy the whole of what is now Bantu Africa [162].

Greenberg's hypothesis has been modified in an important way by another linguist, Professor Malcolm Guthrie [82] who compared in detail some two hundred Bantu languages. He sees a first migration of a few dozen or hundred Bantu speakers from a region north of the forest (possibly the central Cameroun or Ubangi-Shari) to an elliptical area with its main axis running east and west, roughly from the mouth of the Congo on the Atlantic coast to the mouth of the Rovuma on the Indian Ocean. Its centre, in the Luba country

Figure 24. Guthrie's four stages of Bantu expansion

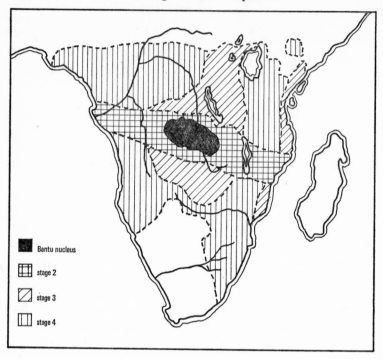

of northern Shaba (Katanga), would have been the Bantu nucleus. This is predominantly a light woodland area intersected by many rivers, neither very dry nor very humid. It is ecologically similar to the symmetrical belt of moist savanna which stretches north of the rain forest in central Nigeria, central Cameroun and the Ubangi-Shari watershed. According to Guthrie, expansion from this area first extended north to the Great Lakes area, where rainfall is higher and more evenly distributed throughout the year, and along the coast of the Indian Ocean. The last stage consisted of the colonization of the remainder of present Bantu Africa. This last expansion, as Guthrie sees it, includes the Gaboon-Cameroun Bantu-speaking area (see Figure 24).

The initial migration, from north to south of the equatorial forest, is seen today by most authors not as a clockwise move around the forest, but as a crossing of it. How long it took we do not know in the present absence of archaeological evidence. A motivation for a rapid migration of some two thousand kilometres is hard to imagine. It is easier to see this step as a steady trickle along the Congo river system by populations whose subsistence was based mainly on fishing and horticulture. According to Murdock [157], this pre-Bantu movement into the forest could take place as the result of the introduction of South-East Asian food plants. As he sees it, these entered Africa through the Ethiopian lowlands and travelled westwards along the Nile-Congo watershed, following the northern margin of the forest to the Guinea coast. As Professor Roland Oliver [162] points out, it is much more likely that the South-East Asian food plants reached Bantu Africa directly, at a time when Bantu cultivators were already on the east coast. To peoples of the northern forest fringe, Sudanic yams and oil palm trees were available as forest-adapted food crops before the time of the pre-Bantu migration (most probably during the first millennium BC).

Did the pre-Bantu know iron metallurgy, or were they still Stone Age people? A firm answer to this question must also wait for archaeological traces of their migration. On the other hand, archaeology provides ample evidence for the widespread expansion of iron metallurgy in the third and fourth centuries AD within the areas covered by Guthrie's stages two and three of Bantu expansion and in an area south of the Zambezi. At all the Early Iron Age sites of these areas, pottery belongs to the same industrial complex; its regional variants clearly derive from a common tradition [110]. Such sites have been found as follows:

Zambia: in a wide arc stretching from the north-east to the south, with an earliest carbon 14 date of AD 345 at Kalambo Falls, AD 300 at Kalundu, and AD 340 at Kangonga in the copperbelt.
Malawi: in the north, AD 295 at Phopho Hill, and on the western shore of Lake Malawi AD 360 from layer 3 at Nkope.
Rhodesia: in the eastern highlands and the central plateau, AD 320 for Zimbabwe Period I.
Rwanda: AD 250 and AD 300 for two iron-smelting furnaces.
Uganda: at Chobi on the Nile between Lakes Kyoga and Albert, AD 290.
Kenya: north-east of Lake Victoria at Urewe, AD 270, 320 and 390; in the hills behind Mombasa on the coast, AD 120, 160, 260, 270 and 300 at Kwale and related sites.
Tanzania: in the Pare Hills of the north-east, AD 220 at Bombo Kaburi; in the Uvinza area, AD 420 at the salt works of Pwaga. [55, 168, 201].

If the errors around the means are considered, all these dates are roughly contemporaneous and none is significantly earlier or later than the others. This also holds true for the date of AD 180 for Mabveni in Rhodesia; but significantly earlier dates (several centuries BC), which must be treated with caution for the time being, have been obtained for Rutare in Rwanda and Katuruka in the adjacent north-western part of Tanzania [201]. Even without these last dates, and although the data allow for some lapse of time, they imply a very rapid expansion over an immense area. Undated sites culturally related to the dated ones are known in the Kivu, Kasai and, possibly, lower Congo regions of Zaire; in Sandaweland in central Tanzania; and in southern Somalia.

The only possible antecedents of the pottery co-tradition of the subequatorial early Iron Age at present suggested by archaeology lie to the north-west. In particular, some parallels in decoration are found on the pottery of the Nok culture, which initiated the Iron Age on the fringe of the Nigerian forest, near to the area where Greenberg locates the pre-Bantu cradle in the middle of the last millennium BC [171].

The rapid expansion of the Bantu languages south and east of the equatorial forest, and the scattering of related Early Iron Age sites in an area and at a period largely compatible with the linguistic evidence, correspond so tightly that there is little doubt that they represent two aspects – language and material culture – of the same story: the radiation of Early Iron Age Bantu peoples from a common source area.

Such a wide and rapid expansion was necessarily based on a superiority in exploiting the environment over the local populations, resulting in a higher human density. These indigenous inhabitants were Late Stone Age communities who subsisted on hunting and gathering, to which some of them perhaps added tenuous vegeculture. Iron technology was undoubtedly one of the bases of success of the Bantu invaders; agriculture must have been another one. The food plants of the nuclear Bantu soon became enriched with the East African varieties of cereals, sorghums and millets, which were cultivated in Ethiopia and, possibly, by the peoples of the Stone Bowl cultures in Kenya. Indeed, Bantu expansion lapped around the area already occupied by these food-producing societies in the Highlands and Rift Valley of Kenya [171], from whom the Bantu also acquired cattle and pastoralism.

The area occupied by stage two of the Bantu expansion during the first centuries AD is the light-woodland southern belt. Stage three included areas of higher rainfall, in the region of the Great Lakes and the humid coastal belt of East Africa. There the South-East Asian food plants (mainly the banana, and the coconut on the coast) play a vital role in the economy of the present Bantu populations. Oliver [162] suggests that it was their introduction which provoked a population explosion leading to stage three of the Bantu expansion. During the first five centuries AD, Madagascar was colonized by sea-borne migrants from Indonesia. Possibly they temporarily colonized part of the East African coast as well, as many believe on the basis of similarities in a number of cultural elements in the Lake Victoria area and Indonesia, in particular certain boat types and musical instruments. Alternatively their food plants were transmitted through Indian-African contacts. (There is no recognized archaeological trace of an Indonesian occupation of the coast).

For Oliver [162], stage four of the Bantu expansion consisted of the colonization of the remainder of present Bantu Africa by the surplus populations generated within the area occupied during stage three: the drier regions of East, Central and South Africa, Angola and South West Africa; and also the equatorial forest. The large variety of domesticates, both animal and vegetable, possessed by the Bantu – as a whole, not necessarily in each area – during stage three allowed them to occupy the most varied environments. The Iron Age, presumably introduced by Bantu peoples, has been dated back to the fifth century AD as far south as Swaziland, and to the ninth century AD in the north of South West Africa [201].

Late Stone Age technology and mode of life did not disappear suddenly with the beginning of the Early Iron Age in Bantu Africa. Late Stone Age occupation of caves persisted until the present millennium in many areas, not only in southern Africa but also in Central and East Africa. The presence of Early Iron Age pottery in Late Stone Age layers, which date from long after the introduction of iron metallurgy in the vicinity, implies a relatively peaceful symbiosis of hunter-gatherers and food producers, such as that which today binds the Pygmies and Pygmoids to the agricultural-ists in the equatorial forest.

The history of Bantu Africa after the Early Iron Age is too complex to be summarized here beyond a few landmarks. Powerful

Figure 25. Localities of the Bantu populations mentioned in Chapter 12

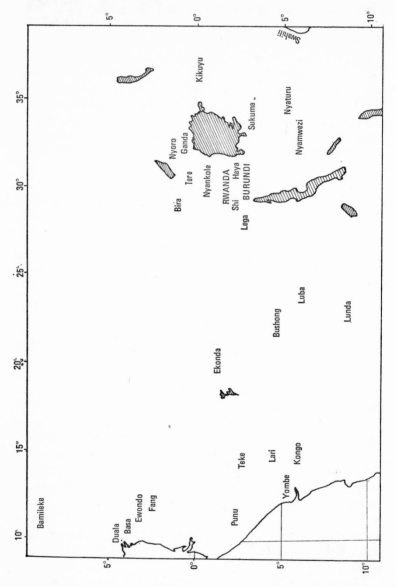

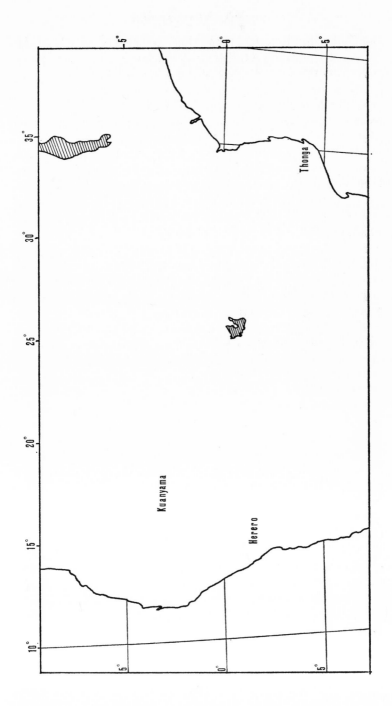

states arose in the second millennium, among others those of the Luba and Lunda in Guthrie's Bantu nuclear area; that of Mono-matapa south of the Zambezi with its famous stone buildings at Zimbabwe and other places, and that of Kongo in the lower Congo area. The wealth of their ruling class was based on trade with one or both coasts. Trade goods included copper from the copperbelt, which stretches over the Shaba (Katanga) area of Zaire and over northern Zambia, gold and copper from farther south, ivory, and slaves. On present evidence, the Luba area of Shaba seems to have been an explosive nucleus again and again [162]. Already in the last centuries of the first millennium AD the upper Lualaba valley, now inhabited by the Luba, was the home of a variety of cultures which attained a high degree of technical skill and elegance in pottery making and in the working of copper, iron and ivory [159, 103, 104]. During the present millennium, large migratory move-ments, like those of the Zulu, profoundly changed the ethnological map of Bantu Africa. In East Africa, the Galla and Somali invas-ions of Jubaland pushed the most northern groups of coastal Bantu inland, as the traditions of the Kikuyu, Kamba and Chagga tell [162]. The penetration of the Bantu deep into the equatorial forest seems to have been a late event everywhere, as told in the traditions of many peoples as well as by Guthrie's interpretation of the linguistic data.

Morphologically, the Bantu-speaking populations show quite a large diversity, even after removal of the Pygmies, Pygmoids and Elongated Africans who have adopted Bantu languages. On a biometrical map extending Figure 20 to multivariate analysis of other samples of Bantu populations, they would form a wide scatter of points. Nearest to the centre would be the Basa, Ewondo and northern Fang of Cameroun, the savanna Bira of north-eastern Zaire, the Nyamwezi of western Tanzania, and the Luba of Shaba (Katanga). Such populations, who live in areas at a considerable distance from one another, may be regarded as relatively little modified descendants of a common stock; this can only be the nuclear Bantu, wherever their source [99].

As shown in Table 14, these people differ in stature to some extent, but they strongly resemble one another in head, face and nose proportions. They live either in a forest-savanna mosaic (the Luba), or in the forest not far from its fringe (the Basa, Ewondo and northern Fang), or in the savanna bordering the forest (the

TABLE 14

Anthropometric means in four Bantu populations of the centre of Bantu morphological diversity

	112 Luba of Katanga [95]	200 savanna Bira [195]	76 Nyamwezi [47]	100 Ewondo [163]
Stature (cm)	164	161	166	169
Lower limb length (cm)	94	93	96	—
Head length (mm)	193	189	192	191
Head breadth (mm)	148	145	145	148
Face height (mm)	117	117	118	118
Face breadth (mm)	139	138	138	140
Nose height (mm)	51	50	51	52
Nose breadth (mm)	46	45	44	44
Relative lower limb length	57·0	57·4	57·6	—
Cephalic index	76·9	77·4	75·7	77·0
Facial index	84·0	84·5	85·8	83·9
Nasal index	90·5	89·1	86·3	86·0

Bira), or in the savanna not far east of the rain forest (the Nyam-wezi). Their pooled means are intermediate between the African means for the rain forest and the savanna. It may therefore be postulated that the nuclear Bantu lived near to the savanna-forest border, and that their descendants keep morphologically similar to them and to each other because their present home lies in a similar biotope. Most of the Bantu populations studied within a broken ring encircling the forest to the north, east and south, including the forest-savanna border, show moderate biometrical distances from the peoples cited above who also live in this ring, and their mor-phology may be explained in the above same terms. This applies also to the closely similar Swahili, who live far away from the ring on the coast of the Indian Ocean in a moist environment.

The Bantu populations living near to the forest-savanna border not only resemble each other, but also resemble a number of populations of Western Sudan and southern Nigeria who occupy a similar biotope. Talbot and Mulhall [202], who have extended their multidimensional analysis of the populations of southern Nigeria to a number of Bantu-speaking populations of Cameroun, group the Bantu Koko with some Bantoid-speaking populations and some Yoruba sub-groups in the Ibibio cluster. (Bantoid is used here for designating non-Bantu Bantoid-speakers; Talbot and Mulhall's

Bantu cluster, however, includes the Bantoid Bangangte). For the limited set of measurements from which a biometrical distance can be computed, the Onitsha, who belong to the northern Ibo cluster, are nearly identical with the Nyamwezi and near to the Swahili. The Ekiti, a sub-group of the Yoruba, are nearly identical with the Haya, who live in Tanzania west of Lake Victoria. Also on the basis of multidimensional analysis, the Bamileke, who form the most numerous Bantoid population of the Adamawa Highlands in central Cameroun, appear closely similar to the Bantu Duala of the coastal area of Cameroun. They differ moderately from the Basa [10]. Their main general distinction from the Bantu populations of the circum-forest ring lies in their broader head and face (see Table 2).

There is, in fact, no biological objection to locating the ultimate area of Bantu origins where Greenberg sees it on the basis of linguistics; that is, the present area of Bantoid languages in Nigeria and Cameroun, and more specifically in the central Benue valley. Anthropo-biology agrees with linguistics and, as Greenberg also points out, it agrees also with cultural anthropology in emphasizing the affinities between the populations of the Guinea Coast area and those of the Congo basin. A more eastern origin of the pre-Bantu, in the Chad area as Guthrie would have it, is not supported by the biological data; no population studied there is so biologically near to the Bantu as are a number of populations in Greenberg's area.

The scanty data available on hereditary blood traits agree with the biometric facts. Of all the groups listed in Table 5, the nearest to the Bamileke in their Rh frequencies are the Shi-Hunde-Swaga group of populations who live in Zaire in the circum-forest ring west of the Great Lakes – indeed, they do not differ significantly from the Bamileke. The ABO allele frequencies of the latter fall within the wide range of frequencies found in Bantu populations (they do not differ significantly from those of the Duala and Ewondo) and so do also their MN frequencies. Their haemoglobin S allele frequency of 4 per cent is considerably lower than that of the Bantu populations to the south of them in Cameroun, but this may be explained by the different selective pressure exercised by malaria, which strikes the Bamileke much less severely [10, 88, 84].

To have remained so similar to the Bantoid populations of Nigeria and Cameroun the Bantu peoples of the circum-forest ring must not only have been submitted to similar environmental pressures, they must also have kept free of any significant admixture with genetically different populations. Their present territory was formerly occupied by Late Stone Age peoples; apparently these were not absorbed in large numbers by the newcomers, or else they were not very different from them. In Rwanda and western Uganda, which were forested in Early Iron Age times, most probably these indigenous inhabitants were the ancestors of the present Twa. The traditions of many Bantu people south of the forest tell of small hunters who roamed the country at the time of their arrival. These may have been Twa-like bands at the periphery of the forest.

It may be supposed, however, that during Late Stone Age times the southern savanna between the territory of the Twa and that of the Bushmen was inhabited by descendants of the West-Central African stock who did not differ much from the pre-Bantu. If the Dama of South West Africa really are relicts of the pre-Bantu hunter-gatherers in the southern savanna, this view is supported by their morphology and blood groups. In measurements they are near to the Luba of Shaba (Katanga) and Kasai, the Lega of eastern Zaire, the Hutu of Rwanda, the Nyamwezi of Tanzania, and the Duala, Basa and Ewondo of Cameroun. In their ABO, MN and Rh frequencies they resemble the Lega, the Hutu, the Thonga of Mozambique, the Eve of Ghana, and three populations of Liberia [122].

In the area between Lake Victoria and the Western Rift, at the latitude of Lake Kivu and the northern end of Lake Tanganyika, the biological distances to the anthropologically central Bantu rise. In this area live the Tutsi, Hima and related Elongated African pastoralists who differ profoundly from the local Bantu agriculturalists whose language they adopted. Their influence on their Bantu neighbours has been both cultural – in particular, the agriculturalists adopted many elements of the cattle complex – and genetical. The picture is especially clear in Rwanda and Burundi. Some interbreeding between Tutsi and Hutu has occurred in both countries, but the Hutu have been more influenced by the Tutsi in Rwanda than in Burundi, while the Tutsi have been more influenced by the Hutu in Burundi than in Rwanda. Tutsi genetic influence is still discernible in the Shi, west of Lake Kivu. These interbreeding processes have generated a cline – Rwanda Tutsi – Burundi Tutsi – Rwanda Hutu – Burundi Hutu – Shi – which is clearly expressed in the pattern of multidimensional distances between the five populations [92].

In Uganda, the Toro are closely similar to the Hutu of Burundi; the Nyoro and Nyankole, who strongly resemble each other, diverge from the Hutu in the direction of the Ganda; and the Ganda in turn differ only moderately from their eastern neighbours the Nilotic-speaking Luo. As stated in Chapter 10, Nilotic-speakers have recently founded the dynasty of the Bantu-speaking Nyoro, who stand at the most northerly frontier of the Bantu world, east of the forest. On the basis of present archaeological knowledge, it seems that this frontier has not changed much since the Early Iron Age. A contribution from the Nilotic-speaking area is apparently present in the gene pool of some of the populations of southern Uganda but, as stressed in Chapter 10, this component differs strongly from the Nilotes.

From Burundi to the east coast at the latitude of 5°–6°S, all the studied Bantu populations show very moderate distances to the Hutu of Burundi, and indeed to the Ewondo of Cameroun, as well as to the Haya west of Lake Victoria, the Sukuma and Nyamwezi south of it, the Nyaturu, and finally the Swahili. All these populations may be regarded as descendants of the nuclear Bantu, whose gene pool has been slightly influenced by the Elongated Africans who live intermingled with them or border them to the north.

Such an Elongated African component is conspicuous also in many Bantu populations of southern Africa. Most probably their ancestors picked it up in East Africa, together with pastoralism. However, Clark [33] is inclined to believe that the Elongated African pastoralists who were responsible for the Stone Bowl cultures of East Africa expanded as far as South West Africa in the first centuries AD. A few stone bowls have indeed been found in Rhodesia, Transvaal and South West Africa, but in the absence of associated artifacts their significance remains doubtful.

Wherever the contact of the ancestors of the Herero with Elongated Africans took place, these Bantu pastoral nomads of South West Africa show a marked influence of Elongated Africans in their physique [232]. It must however be stressed that the Herero's biotope is an arid one, climatically similar to that of the southern Sahara; under such conditions, selective pressures presumably favour a more elongated morphology, thus increasing the Elongated African look of the population over the generations. The linguistically related Kuanyama, who subsist on agriculture and stock-keeping in southern Angola in a less arid zone, may owe their broader head and face and lower face and nose to their adaptation to a different environment, as well as to a lower Elongated African component in their gene pool.

A markedly different stock, the Khoisan, has influenced the Bantu in southern Africa, especially in its eastern part; this has already been discussed in Chapter 8. The Elongated African and Khoisan admixture has not been the only factor of differentiation in the south-eastern Bantu. In particular, their migration into environments very different from that of the nuclear Bantu must have released differentiating selective pressures.

Renewed selective pressures were also released on those Bantu populations who migrated into the equatorial forest from the surrounding savanna and settled there during the present millennium. As concluded in Chapter 9, the pressures exerted by their new environment induced a shift towards the morphology of the Pygmies. In addition, the Bantu invaders of the forest came into contact with Pygmies and Pygmoids and some admixture may also be expected to have modified their gene pool. Where this occurs, it is synergic with climatic selection.

In eastern Zaire, west of the Great Lakes, a number of related Bantu populations have been studied. Some live in the savanna, others in the forest, but according to their traditions they all come from an area east of the Great Lakes which is now covered with savanna. There the Early Iron Age started in the first centuries AD, if not before, and was presumably introduced by the first wave of Bantu agriculturalists. The forest populations are in contact with the Mbuti or Twa, whereas the savanna ones may have been touched by a gene flow from the near-by Tutsi of Rwanda and Burundi. In multidimensional biometrical analysis, the set of forest populations is nearer to the Pygmies and farther apart from the Tutsi. It would, however, be wrong to interpret this situation as merely reflecting a differential gene flow (either the impact of a gene flow from the Mbuti on the forest populations, or from the Tutsi on the savanna populations, or both). The distribution of ABO allele frequencies, which differs greatly in the Tutsi and Mbuti, contradicts such an explanation: for the ABO system, the set of forest populations and the set of savanna populations are equidistant to the Tutsi and to the Mbuti. For the MN system, the set of savanna populations is not nearer to the Tutsi – on the contrary, in fact. Apparently only the influence of the environment can explain the anthropometric differentiation between the two sets of populations living under different ecological conditions [92, 107]. (See Tables 14 and 15 for a comparison of the savanna and forest Bira).

TABLE 15

Anthropometric means in five populations of the equatorial forest: three Bantu agriculturalist groups (the Lega, Bira and Oto Ekonda), one group of Pygmoids (the Twa Ekonda) and the Mbuti Pygmies

	100 Lega [92]	178 forest Bira [195]	66 Oto Ekonda [108]	163 Twa Ekonda [108]	510 Mbuti [78]
Stature (cm)	162	158	166	157	144
Lower limb length (cm)	93	89	93	87	78
Shoulder breadth (mm)	357	361	358	341	315
Hip breadth (mm)	246	245	240	232	240
Head length (mm)	193	188	191	187	184
Head breadth (mm)	148	146	147	145	142
Face height (mm)	118	116	120	116	104
Face breadth (mm)	139	139	139	134	133
Nose height (mm)	52	50	53	50	43
Nose breadth (mm)	46	45	45	44	45
Lip thickness (mm)	24	22	27	25	15
Relative lower limb length	55·7	56·6	55·7	55·4	54·5
Cephalic index	76·7	77·9	77·0	77·4	77·0
Facial index	84·9	83·9	86·9	86·9	78·3
Nasal index	89·3	90·3	84·0	87·8	103·8

Figure 20 shows how marked is the morphological differentiation between the savanna- and forest-dwelling Bantu populations of Zaire (marked respectively S and F); some of the latter, like the forest Bira, are near to the Twa of the Ekonda and of the Kuba.

However, in this figure the Oto caste of the Ekonda – a member of the Mongo group of Bantu tribes which occupies most of the forest of Zaire inside the bend of the Congo River – stands near to eastern savanna populations (compare also the Oto Ekonda, Lega and Bira in Table 15). Among other differences, body size is much higher in the Oto Ekonda than in the eastern forest populations of Zaire. There may be an environmental factor in this difference, but archaeological and historical data suggest another explanation. Deforestation in the Great Lakes area is recent; the Bantu populations who settled there some two thousand years ago, even those whose descendants live now in open country, must have spent many generations in the forest. On the other hand, the occupation of the central forest of Zaire by the Mongo seems very recent; although this group of some two million people covers a very large area, their languages display remarkably close relationships [81]. The linguistic zone to which they belong also includes the language of the Bushong, the hegemonous tribe of the Kuba. The Bushong, who live in the savanna south of the forest, show a low biometrical distance to the Luba of Kasai, themselves a recent offshoot of the Luba of Katanga. The mean stature of the Bushong is 170 cm, considerably higher than that of any savanna-dwelling population of eastern Zaire. The position of the Oto Ekonda in relation to the Bushong in Figure 20 is consistent with Guthrie's view of the recent migration and expansion of the Mongo into the forest from the nuclear Bantu area in the adjacent southern savanna. The Oto Ekonda occupy a lower position, which can be expected from an incipient adaptation to the forest biotope, possibly together with some genetic admixture from the Twa.

West of the Mongo area, in Congo-Brazzaville and Gabon, most populations have a shorter mean stature. This lies between 162 and 164 cm in the Yombe, Lari, Teke and Punu [29]. Here also, possible factors of the shorter body size are a stronger genetic admixture from Pygmoids and a longer time of occupation of the forest. The southern part of this area is covered with savanna, although it lies close to the equator. It was deforested long ago, perhaps by those Stone Age populations whose polished tools are found on the ground, and it had had no time to recover. Possibly these neolithic peoples were pre-Bantu, their archaeological remains marking the primary movement of Bantu expansion from north to south of the forest. Whatever their language, they may have contributed to the composition of the present populations of the area. Across the River Congo in the Lake Tumba area, the forest is not original virgin forest but is regenerated. In this region the early agriculturalists, presumably pre-Bantu, had disappeared before the recent arrival of the Ekonda, and the forest had time enough to grow up again after their departure.

13

Madagascar

Madagascar, one of the largest islands in the world, lies in the Indian Ocean about four hundred kilometres off the east coast of Africa between 11° and 25°S. It consists of three parallel longitudinal zones: the central plateau, at an altitude of between 800 and 1,500 metres, which descends in a great cliff to the east; a narrow littoral strip in the east; and a wider zone of hills and plains to the west. The climatic and vegetation zones are also longitudinal. The zone east of the great cliff has a high rainfall and, where not planted, it is covered with scrub or forest. The central plateau enjoys a tropical mountain climate and is now an area of grassland, but before human occupation it was partly forested. The whole of the western part of the island was formerly wooded with deciduous forest, but this has been largely replaced by savanna as a result of the action of man and cattle. The south-west receives scarcely any rainfall and is a semi-desertic area covered with spiny succulents.

The population of Madagascar, some five million people known collectively as Malagasy, is subdivided into eighteen ethnic groups which correspond with geographical regions or with former political units. On the plateau around the capital, Tananarive, live the Merina. This group of more than one and a half million people played a prominent political role in the nineteenth century and has settled in numbers in most parts of the island, especially in the towns. It consists of four castes: the nobles (Andriana), the commoners (Hova), the slaves (Andevo), and the Mainty, whose status is intermediary between the Hova and the Andevo. On the plateau south of the Merina the most numerous groups are the Betsileo and the Bara, while north of them are the Tsimihety. The major group on the east coast is the Betsimisaraka, and south of them on the coast live the Antaimoro, Antaisaka and Antanosy.

Figure 26. Localities of the ethnic groups of Madagascar mentioned
in the text

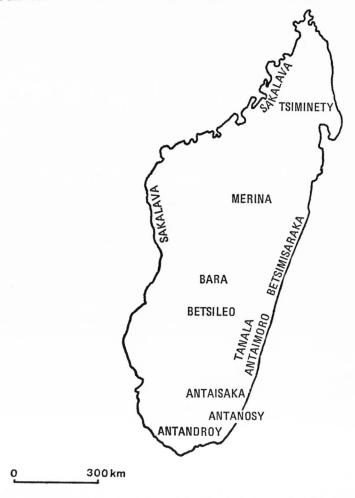

0 _____ 300 km

The Antaimoro and Antanosy claim Arab descent. In the forest
east of the Betsileo live the Tanala; the Sakalava occupy most
of the eastern region; and the extreme south is peopled by the
Antandroy.

All the groups of the island speak dialects of Malagasy. It is
closely related to the Indonesian languages, with some peculiarities
of its own such as the vocalization of final letters. Malagasy society

and culture show a blend of Indonesian and African traits. South-East Asian food plants predominate in the agriculture. Rice is the staple everywhere except in the west, with dry rice cultivation mainly on the east coast and irrigated rice cultivation on the plateau; taro and bananas are widely cultivated as well. However, several plants of the Sudanic complex assume an important place in some groups, especially sorghum and ground peas. Cattle, of African origin, are very numerous; the Sakalava and the Bara subsist mainly on cattle pastoralism. Fish is an important item of diet on both coasts.

When and how were the Indonesian and African elements of Malagasy culture introduced in the island? Archaeological evidence is absent: no Stone Age has been found in Madagascar, and the earliest dated Iron Age sites are around AD 1000. The oldest African element most probably belonged to the Early Iron Age population, presumably Bantu in language, who occupied the east coast of Africa from the first centuries AD. As stated in the last chapter, there is ample evidence that very early on the eastern Bantu adopted a number of cultural items of Indonesian origin. Most probably these were introduced by Indonesian seafarers who extended their trade to Ceylon, the west coast of India, southern Arabia, and ultimately the east coast of Africa. From there they would have discovered Madagascar. The already mixed Indonesian-African communities would have settled on the virgin island, which was ideal for the cultivation of dry rice and Indonesian root and tree crops [157].

This historical reconstruction must remain hypothetical as long as it is not confirmed by archaeology. The written Arab sources tell of a fleet of a thousand ships which, after one year of sailing from the east, conquered the African coast around Sofala in Mozambique in AD 945. They were searching for ivory, tortoise-shell, leopard skins and slaves both for their own country and for trade with China. This formidable expedition was probably organized by the Crivijaya empire of Sumatra, which had been Hinduized for centuries. Since the Malagasy culture shows no trace of Brahminism or Buddhism, this expedition could not have accounted for the earliest Indonesian influence in Madagascar. It could have been introduced at any time from Borneo, which remained pagan. According to Idrissi, the famous Arab geographer who wrote in the middle of the twelfth century, the Africans on the east coast had no ship which would have allowed ocean travel. Seafarers from the Zajab islands (Java and Sumatra) traded with the east coast, where they met local people and traders from Madagascar whose language they could understand [52].

In the second millennium, Arabs and Islamized peoples dominated the western part of the Indian Ocean and founded trade cities on the coast of Madagascar. Islam disappeared from the island, but the Arab calendar has been generally adopted. The Comoro Islands, between Africa and Madagascar, were occupied by an Islamized population speaking an Arabicized Bantu language; these were the Antalaut (in Malagasy *Antaloatra*, the sea peoples), who founded trading posts on the north-west coast of Madagascar [52].

The biological characters of the Malagasy have been little studied. It may however be stated that they are such as would result from the interbreeding of Indonesian (or Malay) and African populations. Only a small sample of Malagasy (95 Merina and 75 non-Merina) has been tested for the Rh system, which significantly distinguishes the two contributing areas. The sample has 43 per cent of R_0, 32 per cent of R_1, and 15 per cent of r. On the basis of the frequencies found in Java and the Celebes (6 per cent R_0, 83 per cent R_1 and 0 per cent r) and in the Bantu, a rough estimate of two-thirds of African blood and one-third of Indonesian blood is obtained for this sample [191]. But, as the frequency of visible traits and anthropometry makes clear, the proportion of Indonesian and African components varies largely between Malagasy groups. The Indonesian component is the most conspicuous in the Merina and Betsileo, the least conspicuous in the Bara and Antaisaka. For example, straight or wavy hair is observed in more than 20 per cent of the Merina, whereas it rarely occurs in the two latter groups, in which the typically African spiralled hair predominates. The frequency of eyefolds and skin colour varies in the same way; the Merina show the lightest skin colour and the highest frequency of eyefolds [30].

On the basis of the scanty data available, the proportion of Indonesian and African components therefore appears to be a major factor of variation between the Malagasy groups, but it does not seem to be the only one. The climatic zonation might have induced some differentiation through climatic selection (for example, stature is lower on the moist east coast than in the western drier zone). Some differentiation through the founder effect may also be expected to have taken place. Whatever the relative importance of the various factors of differentiation, the strong group endogamy which prevails in the island hinders the genetic homogenization of the Malagasy population.

14

Conclusions

The main conclusion to be drawn from this study of the biological diversity of man in sub-Saharan Africa is that the influence of the physical environment has been of paramount importance. In addition, geographical barriers – the Sahara in the north, the rapids and cataracts descending from the plateau to the coast – have very efficiently prevented any large-scale invasion of the sub-continent. Blood groups show that the incorporation of North African elements has been very modest. Only in the Horn of Africa is an important Arab element conspicuous, although it has often been over-estimated (Chapter 5). An Indonesian element is evident in the population of Madagascar, but on the continent itself, although a number of African cultures have been clearly influenced by Indonesia, no trace of this element has been detected in the living populations.

Although sub-Saharan Africa is so closed to outside penetration, it does not present any strong geographical barrier to internal migration (Chapter 1). In fact, large-scale migrations and expansions have been conspicuous in the history of man in Africa since the earliest times. The latest of these movements, the Bantu expansion, started only a little more than two thousand years ago and is still causing genetic changes in several areas (Chapter 12). Among others, one of its consequences was interbreeding between the Bantu invaders and the local Khoisan populations of southern Africa, who had developed markedly distinctive biological features in the geographical cul-de-sac where they had remained isolated for many thousands of years (Chapter 8).

The area from where the Bantu expansion started – the savanna/ forest mosaic north of the equatorial forest – had previously seen other migratory movements towards the south, those which brought the ancestors of the Pygmies and of the various groups of Pygmoids into the equatorial forest. There these groups were subjected to strong selective forces from the climate, which modelled their morphology into its present extreme form (Chapter 9). The Pygmies and Pygmoids have now been joined by some waves of the Bantu expansion, whose members have been submitted to similar selective forces from the equatorial forest biotope. As a consequence, two main mechanisms of genetic change, selection and interbreeding, are intensively at work in the area.

Selection by climate is not active only in the equatorial forest, although that is where its effects are most obvious. Associated with the climatic cline, from hot and wet to hot and dry, is a cline in human morphology, with the Pygmies at one extreme and at the other the populations called the Elongated Africans in this book (Chapter 10). Any migration along the climatic cline releases selection once again and causes evolution towards a new genetic equilibrium. This process appears to be active in several populations of the western Sudan and the Guinea rainforest (Chapter 11).

All this makes it clear that the population of the sub-Sahara is evolving rapidly today, mainly as the result of those two mechanisms of genetic change, interbreeding and selection, which have been released by the recent processes of migration and expansion. Very probably these processes will continue and increase in the immediate future. In order to follow man's biological evolution in the sub-continent and to define its factors, we need many more data than we have on the living populations of the area. Anthropobiology has an immense task ahead in Africa.

But however important it is for theoretical and practical reasons to follow the biological evolution of man, the immediate concern of millions of Africans today, especially in the Sahel, is to survive famine. Moreover, in many areas, malnutrition affects the children and permanently stunts their physical and mental development (Chapter 6). The anthropo-biologist has an important role to play in assessing the effects of malnutrition; his task is not only to study the genetic heritage – the genome – but also to determine how it is expressed in individuals and populations.

References

1 ADAM, A. *et al.* 1962. 'A survey of some genetical characters in Ethiopian tribes.' *Amer. J. Phys. Anthrop.* **20**: 172–204.

2 ALLISON, A. C. 1954. 'The distribution of the sickle-cell trait in East Africa and elsewhere and its apparent relationship to the incidence of subtertian malaria'. *Trans. Roy. Soc. Trop. Med. Hyg.* **48**: 312–18.

3 ALLISON, A. C. 1956. 'The sickle-cell and haemoglobin C genes in some African populations'. *Ann. Hum. Genet.* **21**: 67–89.

4 ALMEIDA, A. de. 1965. *Bushmen and Other Non-Bantu Peoples of Angola* (Johannesburg: Witwatersrand University Press.)

5 ANDERSON, J. E. 1968. 'Late palaeolithic skeletal remains from Nubia'. In F. Wendorf (ed), *The Prehistory of Nubia*, vol. II, 996–1040 (Dallas: Burgwin Research Center and Southern Methodist University Press).

6 ANDRE, L. J. and ANDRE-GADRAS, E. 1957. 'Etude des rapports entre la siklémie et la lèpre.' *Méd. Trop.* **17**: 596–9.

7 ARKELL, A. J. 1949. *Early Khartoum, an Account of the Excavation of an Early Occupation Site Carried Out by the Sudan Government* (Oxford University Press).

8 ARKELL, A. J. 1966. 'The Iron Age in the Sudan.' *Current Anthrop.* **7**: 451–2.

9 ARMATTOE, R. E. G., IKIN, E. W. and MOURANT, A. E. 1953. 'The ABO, Rh and MN blood groups of the Ewe and the Ashanti of the Gold Coast.' *West Afr. Med. J.* **2**: 89–93.

10 AUGER, F. 1967. 'Analyse de la variation morphologique de quelques populations du Sud-Cameroun.' Thèse de Doctorat de 3e cycle (Paris: Faculté des Sciences).

11 BAKER, P. T. 1958. *A Theoretical Model for Desert Heath Tolerance.* Natick, Mass.: US Army, technical report EP–96.

12 BARNICOT, N. A., J. P. GARLICK, and D. F. ROBERTS, 1960. Haptoglobin and transferrin inheritance in Northern Nigerians.' *Ann. Hum. Genet.* **24**: 171–83.

13 BARRAI, I. 1968. 'Dermatoglyphics in Babinga Pygmies.' *Atti Assoc. Genet. Ital.* **12**: 92–4.

14 BAUMANN, H. and WESTERMANN, D. 1948. *Les Peuples et les Civilisations de l'Afrique* (Paris: Payot).

15 BLUMBERG, B. S., IKIN, E. W. and MOURANT, A. E. 1961. 'The blood groups of the pastoral Fulani and the Yoruba of Western Nigeria'. *Amer. J. Phys. Anthrop.* **19**: 195–201.

16 BOULE, M. and VALLOIS, H. 1932. *L'Homme Fossile d'Asselar* (*Sahara*) (Paris: Arch. Inst. Paléontologie Humaine, mém. IX).

17 BOULOUX, C., GOMILA, J. and LANGANEY, A. 1972. 'Hemotypology of the Bedik'. *Hum. Biol.* **44**: 289–302.

18 BRAIN, C. K., ROBINSON, J. T., CLARKE, R. J., HOWELL, F. C. and LEAKEY, M. D. 1970. 'New finds at the Swartkrans Australopithecus site.' *Nature* **225**: 1112–9 and 1217–25.

19 BRAIN, P. 1955. 'Problems of sickle-cell distribution in Africa.' *Ve Congr. Intern. Transfusion Sanguine* (Paris 1954): 436–40.

20 BROTHWELL, D. R. 1963. 'Evidence of early population change in central and southern Africa: doubts and problems'. *Man* **63**: 101–4.

21 BROTHWELL, D. and SHAW, T. 1971. 'A late Upper Pleistocene proto-West African negro from Nigeria'. *Man* **6**: 221–7.

22 BRUES, A. 1959. 'The spearman and the archer: an essay on selection on body build'. *Amer. Anthrop.* **61**: 457–9.

23 BUXTON, L. H. D. 1923. 'Note on the measurements of the Ashanti made by Capt. Rattray.' *In* R. S. Rattray (ed.), *Ashanti* (Oxford: Clarendon Press).

24 CABANNES, R., SY-BABA and SCHMITT-BEURRIER, A. 1968. 'Etude des hémoglobines en Côte d'Ivoire'. *Ann. Univ. Abidjan, Médecine* **2**: 108–15.

25 CABANNES, R. J. 1962. 'Etude des types hémoglobiniques rencontrés dans les populations de la partie occidentale du continent africain'. (Toulouse: Thèse de Doctorat es-Sciences).

26 CAMPBELL, B. 1966. *Human Evolution* (Chicago: Aldine).

27 CAVALLI-SFORZA, L. 1966. 'Genetic drift in popolazioni umane' *Atti Assoc. Genet. Italiana* **11**: 50 p.

28 CAVALLI-SFORZA, L. *et al.* 1969. 'Studies on African Pygmies. I. A. pilot investigation of Babinga Pygmies in the Central African Republic (with an analysis of genetic distances).' *Amer. J. Hum. Genet.* **21**: 252–74.

29 CHABEUF, M. 1959. 'Anthropologie physique du Moyen-Congo et du Gabon mériodonal'. *Bull. Mém. Soc. Anthrop. Paris* **10**: 97–185.

30 CHAMLA, M. C. 1958. *Recherches Anthropologiques sur l'Origine*

des Malgaches (Paris: Mém. Museum National d'Histoire Naturelle).

31 CHAMLA, M. C. 1968. *Les Populations Anciennes du Sahara et des régions Limitrophes. Etude des Restes Osseux Humains néolithiques et Protohistoriques* (Paris: Mém. Centre Recherches Anthropologiques, préhistoriques et ethnographiques).

32 CHAVAILLON, J. 1970. 'Découverte d'un niveau oldowayen dans la basse vallée de l'Omo (Ethiopie)'. *Bull. Soc. Préhist. Française* **67**: 7–11.

33 CLARK, J. D. 1964. 'Stone vessels from northern Rhodesia'. *Man* **88**: 69–73.

34 CLARK, J. D. 1970. *The Prehistory of Africa* (London: Thames and Hudson).

35 COBLENTZ, A. 1961. 'Goranes et Toubous des confins nord du Tchad'. Thèse de Doctorat en Médecine (Paris).

36 COLE, S. 1963. *The Prehistory of East Africa* (London: Weidenfeld and Nicolson).

37 COON, C. S. 1963. *The Origin of Races* (New York: Alfred A. Knopf).

38 COON, C. S. 1965. *The Living Races of Man* (New York: Alfred A. Knopf).

39 CRESTA, M. 1965. 'Antropologia morfologica e sierologica dei N'Zakara della Republica Centrafricana'. *Quad. Ric. Scientif.* **28**: 9–20.

40 CRESTA, M. 1965. 'Note antropologiche sui Baya e i Banda della Republica Centrafricana'. *Quad. Ric. Scientif.* **28**: 59–68.

41 CRESTA, M. 1965. 'Contributo alla connoscenza antopologica dei Fulbe Bororo'. *Quad. Ric. Scientif.* **28**: 69–80.

42 CRESTA, M. 1965. 'Contributo alla connescenza antropologica dei Babinga'. *Quad. Ric. Scientif.* **28**: 81–102.

43 CRESTA, M. and SPEDINI, G. 1968. 'Antropologia morfologica ed ematologica del basso Dahomey'. *Riv. Antrop.* **55**: 163–78.

44 CRIGHTON, J. M. 1966. 'A multiple discriminant analysis of Egyptian and African Negro crania'. *Papers Peabody Museum Archaeology Ethnology* **57**: 45–67.

45 CROGNIER, E. 1969. 'Données biométriques sur l'état de nutrition d'une population africaine tropicale: les Sara du Tchad'. *Biométrie humaine* **4**: 37–55.

46 CROGNIER, E. 1972 'Adaptation morphologique d'une population africaine au biotope tropical: les Sara du Tchad'. Université Paris VII: Thèse de Doctorat d'Etat ès-Sciences.

47 CZEKANOWSKI, J. 1972. 'Forschungen im Nil-Kongo-Zwischengebiet. Anthropologische beobachtungen,' In *Wissenschaftliche*

Ergebnisse der Deutschen Zentral-Afrika-Expedition 1907–1908, band I, pp. 145–473 (Leipzig: Klinkhardt und Biermann).

48 CZEKANOWSKI, J. 1962. 'The theoretical assumptions of polish anthropology and the morphological facts'. *Current Anthrop.* **4**: 481–94.

49 DANKMEIJER, J. 1947. 'Finger prints of African Pygmies and Negroes'. *Amer. J. phys. Anthrop.* **5**: 543–84.

50 DART, R. A. 1952 'A Hottentot from Hong-Kong'. *S. Afr. J. Med. Sci.* **17**: 117–42.

51 DAVIES, O. 1968. 'The origins of agriculture in West Africa'. *Current Anthrop.* **9**: 479–82.

52 DESCHAMPS, H. 1970. 'Histoire de la Grande Ile'. *In Histoire Générale de l'Afrique Noire,* H. Deschamps (ed.), pp. 477–98. (Paris: Presses Universitaires de France).

53 d'HERTEFELT, M. 1965. 'The Rwanda of Rwanda'. *In* J. L. Gibbs Jnr (ed.), *Peoples of Africa,* pp. 405–40 (New York: Holt, Rinehart and Winston).

54 DUPIRE, M. 1962. *Peuls Nomades* (Paris: Institut d'Ethnologie).

54A EVANS-PRITCHARD, E. E. 1940. *The Nuer* (Oxford: Clarendon Press.

55 FAGAN, B. M. 1969. 'Radiocarbon dates for sub-Saharan Africa: VI'. *J. Afr. Hist.* **10**: 149–69.

56 FAGG, B. 1968. 'The Nok culture: excavations at Taruga'. *West Afr. Archaeol. Newsletter* **10**: 27–9.

57 FIELD, H. 1952. *Contribution to the Anthropology of the Faiyum, Sinai, Sudan, Kenya* (Berkeley: Univ. of California Press).

58 FOURQUET, R. 1969. 'Etude hémotypologique ABO, MN et Rh de l'ethnie Afar'. *Méd. Trop.* **29**: 669–79.

59 FOURQUET, R. 1970. 'Etude hémotypologique des Somali Issa et Gadaboursi'. *Méd. Trop.* **30**: 353–62.

60 FRASER, G. R., GIBLETT, E. R. and MOTULSKY, A. G. 1966. 'Population genetic studies in the Congo. III. Blood groups (ABO, MNSs, Rh, Js^a)'. *Amer. J. Hum. Genet.* **18**: 546–52.

61 GALLOWAY, A. 1937. 'The skeletal remains of Mapungubwe'. *Mapungubwe,* ed. L. Fouché, pp. 127–74 (Cambridge University Press).

62 GALLOWAY, A. 1937. 'The characteristics of the skull of the Boskop physical type'. *Amer. J. Phys. Anthrop.* **23**: 31–46.

63 GARLICK, J. P. and BARNICOT, N. A. 1957. 'Blood groups and haemoglobin variants in Nigerian (Yoruba) schoolchildren'. *Ann. Hum. Genet.* **21**: 420–5.

64 GENET-VARCIN, E. 1969. *A la Recherche du Primate ancêtre de l'homme* (Paris: Boubée).

65 GESSAIN, R., RUFFIE, J., KANE, Y. and O., CABANNES, R. and

GOMILA, J. 1965. 'Note sur la séro-anthropologie de trois populations de Guinée et du Sénégal: Coniagui, Bassari et Bedik
(groupes ABO, MN, Rh, Kell, Gm et hémoglobines)'. *Bull. Mém.
Soc. Anthrop. Paris* **8**: 5–18.

66 GIBBS, J. L. Jnr. (ed.). 1965. *Peoples of Africa* (New York: Holt,
Rinehart and Winston).

67 GIBLETT, E. R. 1969. *Genetic Markers in Human Blood* (Oxford:
Blackwell).

68 GILLES, H. M., WATSON-WILLIAMS, J. and TAYLOR, B. G., 1960.
'Glucose-6-phosphate dehydrogenase deficiency trait in Nigeria'.
Nature **185**: 257–8.

69 GLANVILLE, E. V. and HUIZINGA, J. 1966. 'Digital dermatoglyphs
of the Dogon, Peul and Kurumba of Mali and Upper Volta'.
Proc. Koninkl. Nederl. Akad. Wetenschappen, sér. C, **69**: 675–95.

70 GLANVILLE, E. 1969. 'Digital ridge-counts of Efe Pygmies'.
Amer. J. Phys. Anthrop. **31**: 427–8.

71 GOLDSMITH, K. L. G. and LEWIS, I. M. 1958. 'A preliminary
investigation of the blood groups of the Sab bondsmen of Northern Somaliland'. *Man* **58**: 188–90.

72 GOMILA, J., PEE-LABORDE, L. and LESTRANGE, TH. DE. 1965.
'Dermatoglyphes digito-palmaires et plis de flexion dans l'isolat
Bedik, Sénégal oriental (*résultats préliminaires*)'. *Proc. VIIth
Czekoslovak Anthropological Congress* (Brno, 1965).

73 GOMILA, J. 1971. *Les Bedik (Sénégal oriental). Barrières Cultur-
elles et Hétérogénéité Biologique* (Presses de l'Université de
Montréal).

74 GREENBERG, J. H. 1963. *Languages of Africa* (The Hague:
Mouton).

75 GREENE, D. L., EWING, G. H. and ARMELAGOS, G. C. 1967. 'Dentition of a mesolithic population from Wadi Halfa, Sudan'. *Amer.
J. Phys. Anthrop.* **27**: 41–56.

76 GREENE, D. L. and ARMELAGOS, G. 1972. *The Wadi Halfa
Mesolithic Population* (Amherst: Department of Ahthropology,
University of Massachusetts, Research Report 11).

77 GROBBELAAR, C. S. 1956. 'The physical characteristics of the
Korana'. *S. Afr. J. Sci.* **53**: 97–160.

78 GUSINDE, M. 1948. *Urwaldmenschen am Ituri* (Wien: Springer-
Verlag).

79 GUSINDE, M. 1949. *Die Twa-Pygmaen in Ruanda.* (Wien-Mödling:
Missionsdruckerei St Gabriel).

80 GUSINDE, M. 1966. *Von Gelben und schwartzen Buschmänner*
(Graz: Akademische Druck-u. Verlagsanstalt).

81 GUTHRIE, M. 1948. *The Classification of the Bantu Languages*
(London: Oxford University Press).

82   GUTHRIE, M. 1962. 'Some developements in the pre-history of the Bantu languages'. *J. Afr. Hist.* **3**: 273–82.

83   HAMPATE BA, A. and DIETERLEIN, G. 1961. *Koumen. Texte Initiatique des Pasteurs Peul* (Paris: Mouton).

84   HAPPI, C. 1959. 'Recherches hématologiques chez les Bamileke (Cameroun)' (Paris: Thèse de Doctorat en Médecine).

85   HARDY, J. 1962. 'The ABO blood groups of Southern Nigerians and their relation to the history of the area'. *J. Roy. Anthrop. Inst.* **92**: 223–31.

86   HARRIS, R. and GILLES, H. M. 1591. 'Glucose-6-phosphate dehydrogenase deficiency in the peoples of the Niger Delta'. *Ann. Hum. Genet.* **25**: 199–205.

87   HEINZELIN, J. DE. 1957. *Les Fouilles d'Ishango* (Bruxelles: Institut des Parcs Nationaux du Congo Belge).

88   HENNINOT, E., POLAERT, J. and HAPPI, C. 1958. 'Recherches sur les groupes sanguins des populations Bamileke (Bafang, Cameroun)'. *Bull. Mém. Soc. Anthrop. Paris* **9**: 340–51.

89   HERTZOG, K. P. and JOHNSTON, F. E. 1968. 'Selection and the Rh polymorphism'. *Hum. Biol.* **40**: 86–97.

90   HIERNAUX, J. 1954. 'Etat de nutrition des Kuba (Kasai)'. *Zaïre* **8**: 719–27.

91   HIERNAUX, J. 1954. *Les Caractères Physiques des Populations du Ruanda et de l'Urundi* (Bruxelles; Institut royal des Sciences naturelles de Belgique).

92   HIERNAUX, J. 1956. *Analyse de la Variation des Caractères Physiques Humains en une Région de l'Afrique Centrale: Ruanda-Urundi et Kivu* (Tervuren: Musée royal du Congo belge).

93   HIERNAUX, J. 1962. 'Données génétiques sur six populations de la République du Congo'. *Ann. Soc. Belge Méd. Trop.* **42**: 145–74.

94   HIERNAUX, J. 1963. 'Heredity and environment: their influence on human morphology. A comparison of two independent lines of 'study'. *Amer. J. Phys. Anthrop.* **21**: 579–90.

95   HIERNAUX, J. 1964. 'Luba du Katanga et Luba du Kasai (Congo): comparaison de deux populations de même origine'. *Bull. Mém. Soc. Anthrop. Paris* **6**: 611–22.

96   HIERNAUX, J. 1965. *La Croissance des Ecoliers Rwandais* (Bruxelles: Acad. roy. Sci. Outre-Mer).

97   HIERNAUX, J. 1966. 'Les Bushong et les Twa du royaume Kuba (Congo-Léopoldville). pygmées, pygmoïdes et pygmésation; anthropologie, linguistique et expansion bantoue'. *Bull. Mém. Soc. Anthrop. Paris* **9**: 299–336.

98   HIERNAUX, J. 1968. *La Diversité Humaine en Afrique Subsaharienne. Recherches Biologiques* (Bruxelles: Institut de Sociologie de l'Université libre de Bruxelles).

99 HIERNAUX, J. 1968. 'Bantu expansion: the evidence from physical anthropology confronted with linguistic and archaeological evidence'. *J. Afr. Hist.* **18**: 505–15.

100 HIERNAUX, J. 1969. 'Investigations anthropologiques au Moyen-Chari (République du Tchad) préliminaires à des recherches multidisciplinaires'. *Homo* **20**: 1–11.

101 HIERNAUX, J. 1970. 'Croissance et maturation physiques post-natales'. *In* H. Gratiot-Alphandéry and R. Zazzo (eds.). *Traité de Psychologie de l'enfant,* 2. pp. 7–63. (Paris: Presses Universitaires de France).

102 HIERNAUX, J. 1971. 'Ethnic differences in growth and development'. *In* R. H. Osborne (ed.), *The Biological and Social Meaning of Race,* pp. 39–56 (San Francisco: Freeman and Co.).

103 HIERNAUX, J., DE LONGREE, E. and DE BUYST, J. 1971. *Fouilles Archéologiques dans la Vallée du Haut-Laulaba. I. Sanga, 1958.* Tervuren: Mus. roy. Afr. centr., Sci. hum. 73.

104 HIERNAUX, J., MAQUET, E., and DE BUYST, J. 1972. 'Le cimetière protohistorique de Katoto (vallée du Lualaba, Congo-Kinshasa)'. *Actes du 6e Congrès Panafricain de Préhistoire (Dakar 1967),* pp. 148–58 (Chambéry: Imprimeries réunies).

105 HIERNAUX, J. 1972. 'La réflectance de la peau dans une communauté de Sara Madjingay (République du Tchad)'. *L'Anthropologie* **76**: 279–99.

106 HIERNAUX, J. 1973. 'Numerical taxonomy of man: an application to a set of thirty-two African populations'. *In* A. Basu, A. K. Ghosh, S. K. Biswas and R. Ghosh (eds.), *Physical Anthropology and its Extending Horizons,* pp. 151–61 (Calcutta: Orient Longman).

107 HIERNAUX, J. unpublished. 'Adaptation of morphology to climate in Central Africa'. Paper presented at the IXth I.C.A.E.S. (Chicago, 1973).

108 HIERNAUX, J. and VINCKE, E. unpublished. 'Anthropobiological data on the Oto and Twa of the Ekonda (Zaïre).'

109 HOLAS, B. 1952. *Mission dans l'Est Libérien (P. L. Dekeyser – B. Holas, 1948). Résultats Démographiques, Ethnologiques et Anthropométriques.* Mém. IFAN 14.

110 HUFFMAN, T. N. 1969. 'The Early Iron Age and the spread of the Bantu'. *S. Afr. Archaeol. Bull.* **25**: 3–21.

111 HUGOT, H. T. 1968. 'The origins of agriculture: Sahara'. *Current Anthrop.* **9**: 483–8.

112 HUIZINGA, J. 1967. 'Description and carbon-14 dating of Tellem cave skulls from the Mali Republic: a comparison with other negroid groups. I and II.' *Koninkl. Nederl. Akad. Wetenschappen, Proc.* **70**: 338–67.

113 HUIZINGA, J. 1968. 'New physical anthropological evidence on the

relationships between Dogon, Kurumba and the extinct Tellem population'. *Koninkl. Nederl. Akad. Wetenschappen, Proc.* **71**: 16–30.

114 HUIZINGA, J. 1968. 'Human biological observations on some African populations of the thorn savanna belt'. *Koninkl. Nederl. Akad. Wetenschappen, Proc.* **71**: 356–90.

115 HUNT, E. 1966. 'The developmental genetics of man'. *In* F. Faulkner (ed.), *Human Development*, pp. 76–122 (Philadelphia: Saunders).

116 INTERNATIONAL INSTITUTE OF AFRICAN LANGUAGES AND CULTURES. 1933. 'Proceedings of the 12th meeting of the Executive Council'. *Africa* **6**: 479–80.

117 JADIN, J. 1940. *Les Groupes Sanguins des Pygmoïdes et des Nègres de la Province Equatoriale (Congo Belge)* (Bruxelles: Inst. roy. colon. belge, Sci. nat. méd. 10).

118 JENKINS, T., ZOUTENDYK, A. and STEINBERG, A. G. 1970. 'Gammaglobulin groups (Gm and Inv) of various South African populations'. *Amer. J. Phys. Anthrop.* **32**: 197–218.

119 JENKINS, T., HARPENDING, H. C., GORDON, E. *et al.* 1971. 'Red cell enzyme polymorphisms in the Khoisan peoples of Southern Africa'. *Amer. J. Hum. Genet.* **23**: 513–32.

120 JENKINS, T. and CORFIELD, V. 1972. 'The red cell acid phosphatase polymorphism in Southern Africa: population data and studies on the R, RA and RB phenotypes'. *Ann. Hum. Genet.* **35**: 379–91.

121 KANE, Y. and RUFFIE, J. 1963. 'Etude hémotypologique de quelques groupes Peul, Toucouleur, Ouloff, et Sérère du Sénégal occidental'. *Bull. Mém. Soc. Anthrop. Paris* **4**: 545–53.

122 KNUSSMANN, R. and R. 1969/70. 'Die Dama – eine altschicht in Südwestafrika?' *J. S. W. Afr. Wissench. Gesellschaft* **24**: 9–32.

123 KOERBER, R. and LINHARD, J. 1951. 'Note sur la répartition des groupes sanguins AB, A, B et O dans divers groupes ethniques de l'A.O.F.' *Bull. Mém. Soc. Anthrop. Paris* **2**: 158–60.

124 KOSSOVITCH, N. 1934. 'Recherches séro-anthropologiques chez quelques peuples du Sahara français'. *C. R. Soc. Biol. Paris* **116**: 759–61.

125 LALOUEL, J. 1950. 'Les Babinga du Bas-Oubangui. Contribution à l'étude anthropologique des Négrilles Baka et Bayaka'. *Bull. Mém. Soc. Anthrop. Paris* **1**: 60–98.

126 LANDAUER, T. and WHITING. J. W. M. 1964. 'The effect of infant stress upon the adult stature of the human males'. *Amer. Anthrop.* **66**: 1007–28.

127 LAWICK-GOODALL, J. VAN. 1971. *In the Shadow of Man* (London: Collins).

128 LEAKEY, R. E. F., BUTZER, K. W., DAY, M. H., THURBER, D. L.

FITCH, F. J. and MILLER, J. A. 1969. 'Early *Homo sapiens* remains from the Omo River region of South-West Ethiopia'. *Nature* **222**: 1132–43.

129 LEAKEY, R. F. F., BEHRENSMEYER, A. K., FITCH, F. J., MILLER. J. A. and LEAKEY, M. D. 1970. 'New hominid remains and early artefacts from northern Kenya'. *Nature* **226**: 223–30.

130 LEE, R. B. 1968. 'What hunters do for a living, or how to make out on scarce resources'. *In* R. B. Lee and I. De Vore (eds.), *Man the Hunter*, pp. 30–45 (Chicago: Aldine).

131 LEFROU, G. 1943. *Le Noir d'Afrique* (Paris: Payot).

132 LEHMANN H. and NWOKOLO, C. 1959. 'The river Niger as a barrier in the spread eastwards of haemoglobin C: a survey of the haemoglobins in the Ibo'. *Nature* **183**: 1587–8.

133 LEITE, A. S. and RE, L. 1955. 'Contribution à l'étude ethnologique des populations africaines'. *Arch. Inst. Pasteur Algérie* **33**: 344–9.

134 LESCHI, J. 1948. 'Empreintes digitales chez quelques peuples d'Afrique Occidentale Française'. *Bull. Mém. Soc. Anthrop. Paris* **9**: 143–50.

135 LESTRANGE, M. DE. 1050. 'Contribution à l'anthropologie des Noirs d'A.O.F. II. Anthropométrie de 1023 Coniagui, Bassari, Badyaranke et Fulakunda de Guinée française'. *Bull. Mém. Soc. Anthrop. Paris* **1**: 99–136.

136 LEWIS, H. S. 1962. 'Historical problems in Ethiopia and the Horn of Africa'. *Ann. N.Y. Acad. Sci.* **96**: 504–11.

137 LEWIS, I. M. 1964. 'Somali Republic'. *In Encyclopaedia Britannica* **20**: 966–9.

138 LEWIS, I. M. 1965. 'The northern pastoral Somali of the Horn'. *In* J. L. Gibbs Jnr (ed.), *Peoples of Africa*, pp. 320–60 (New York: Holt, Rinehart and Winston).

139 LIVINGSTONE, F. 1967. *Abnormal Hemoglobins in Human Populations* (Chicago: Aldine).

140 LOBSIGER-DELLENBACH, M. 1951. 'Contribution à l'étude anthropologique de l'A.O.F. Haoussas, Bellahs, Djermas, Peuls, Touaregs, Maures'. *Arch. Suisses Anthrop. Générale* **16**: 1–86.

141 MANN, G. V., ROELS, O. A., PRICE, D. L. and MERRIL, J. M. 1962. 'Cardiovascular disease in African Pygmies'. *J. Chreon. Diseases* **15**: 341–71.

142 MAQUET, J. J. 1962. *Les Civilisations Noires* (Paris: Horizons de France).

143 MATEUS, A. M. 1953. 'A estatura de alguns grupos etnicos da Guiné'. *An. Junt. Invest. Colon.* **5**: 21–47.

144 MATEUS, E. DE OLIVEIRA. 1963. 'Analise de variancia e teste t de caracteres metricos da cabeça de alguns grupos etnicos da Guiné Portuguesa'. *Garcia de Orta* **11**: 11–25.

145 MATZNETTER, T. 1964. 'Hautleistenuntersuchung an sechs africanischen negerstammen'. *Z. Morph. Anthrop.* **55**: 315–34

146 MAUNY, R. 1971. 'The Western Sudan'. *In* P. L. Shinnie (ed.), *The African Iron Age,* pp. 66–88 (Oxford: Clarendon Press).

147 MEEK, C. K. 1925. *The Northern Tribes of Nigeria* (London: Oxford University Press).

148 MEINHOF, C. 1912. *Die Sprachen der Hamiten* (Hamburg).

149 MERIMEE, T. J., RIMOIN, D. L. and CAVALLI-SFORZA, L. L. 1972. 'Metabolic studies in the African Pygmy'. *J. Clin. Invest.* **51**: 395–401.

150 MONOD, T. 1963. 'The late Tertiary and Pleistocene in the Sahara and adjacent southerly regions', *In* F. C. Howell and F. Bourliere (eds)., *African Ecology and Human Evolution,* pp. 117–229 (Viking Fund Publications in Anthropology 36).

151 MORI, F. 1965. *Tradart Acacus. Artre Rupestre e Culture del Sahara Preistorico* (Torino: Einaudi).

152 MOTULSKY, A. G. 1960. 'Metabolic polymorphisms and the role of infectious disease in human evolution'. *Hum. Biol.* **32**: 28–62.

153 MOULLEC, J., LINHARD, J. and SUTTON, E. 1952. 'Quelques données sur les groupes sanguins des populations d'Afrique Occidentale Française.' *Rev. Hématol.* **7**: 512–18.

154 MÜLLER, E. W. 1964. 'Die Batwa. Eine kleinwüchsige jägerkaste bei den Mongo-Ekonda. *Z. Ethnol.* **89**: 206–15.

155 MUNSON, P. J. 1968. 'Recent archaeological research in the Dhar Tichitt region of south-central Mauritania'. *West Afr. Archaeol. Newsletter* **10**: 6–13.

156 MUNSON, P. J. 1972. 'A survey of the neolithic villages of Dhar Tichitt (Mauritania) and some comments on the grain impressions found on the Tichitt pottery'. *In Actes 6e Congres Panafricain de Préhistoire (Dakar 1967),* p. 91 (Chambéry: Imprimeries Réunies)

157 MURDOCK, G. P. 1959. *Africa. Its Peoples and their Culture History* (New York: McGraw-Hill).

158 NEEL, J. V., HIERNAUX, J., LINHARD, J., ROBINSON, A. ZUELZER, W. W. and LIVINGSTONE, F. B. 1956. 'Data on the occurrence of haemoglobin C and other abnormal haemoglobins in some African Populations'. *Amer. J. Hum. Genet.* **8**: 138–50.

159 NENQUIN, J. 1963. *Excavations at Sanga, 1957* (Tervuren: Mus. roy. Afr. centr., Sci. hum. 45).

160 NEWMAN, R. W. 1970. 'Why man is such a sweaty and thirsty naked animal: a speculative review'. *Hum. Biol.* **42**: 12–27.

161 N'GATCHOU HAGOUA, J. 1965. 'Contribution à l'étude séro-anthropologique des Mossi (Haute-Volta)' (Université de Lille: Thèse de Doctorat en Médecine 311).

162 OLIVER, R. 1966. 'The problem of the Bantu expansion'. *J. Afr. Hist.* **7**: 361–76.

163 OLIVIER, G. 1946. 'Documents anthropométriques pour servir à l'étude des principales populations du Sud-Cameroun'. *Bull Soc. Etudes Camerounaises* **15/16**: 17–86.

164 OSCHINSKY, L. 1954. *The Racial Affinities of the Baganda and other Bantu Tribes of British East Africa* (Cambridge: Heffer).

165 PALES, L. 1949. 'Raciologie comparative des populations de l'A.O.F. II. Les Diamate d'Effoc et les Floup d'Ossouye (Casamance-Sénégal).' *Bull. Mém. Soc. Anthrop. Paris* **10**: 210–20.

166 PALES, L. 1953. 'Raciologie comparative des populations de l'Afrique occidentale. V. Stature – indice cormique – indice céphalique'. *Bull. Mém. Soc. Anthrop. Paris.* **4**: 183–497.

167 PAULO, L. F. 1957. *Impressoes Digitais nos Indigenas da Guiné Portuguesa* (Lisboa: Junta Investig. Ultramar 37).

168 PHILLIPSON, D. W. 1970. 'Notes on the later prehistoric chronology of eastern and southern Africa'. *J. Afr. Hist.* **11**: 1–16.

169 PORTER, I. H. et al. 1964. 'Variation of glucose-6-phosphate dehydrogenase in different populations'. *Lancet* **April 25**:, p. 895.

170 POSNANSKY, M. 1967. 'Excavations at Lanet, Kenya, 1957'. *Azania* **2**: 89–114.

171 POSNANSKY, M. 1968. 'Bantu genesis-archaeological reflexions'. *J. Afr. Hist.* **9**: 1–11.

172 POSNANSKY, M. 1969. 'Yams and the origin of West African agriculture'. *ODU* **1**: 101–7.

173 POSNANSKY, M. 1970. 'African prehistory and geographical determinism' in *Geographical Essays in Honour of Professor K. C. Edwards*, pp. 215–23 (University of Nottingham).

174 PUCCIONI, N. 1917. 'Studi sui materiali e sui dati antropologici ed etnografici raccolti della missione Stefanini-Paoli nella Somalia Italiana meridionale'. *Arch. Antrop. Etnol.* **47**: 13–161.

175 RIGHTMIRE, G. P. 1970. 'Iron Age skulls from southern Africa re-assessed by multiple discriminant analysis'. *Amer. J. Phys. Anthrop.* **33**: 147–68.

176 RIGHTMIRE, G. P. 1970. 'Bushmen, Hottentots and South African Negro crania studied by distance and discrimination'. *Amer. J. Phys. Anthrop.* **33**: 169–96.

177 RIMOIN, D. L., MERIMEE, T. J., RABINOWITZ, D., MCKUSICK, V. A. and CAVALLI-SFORZA, L. L. 1967 'Growth hormone in African Pygmies'. *Lancet* **Sept. 9**: 523–6.

178 ROBERTS, D. F., IKIN, E. W. and MOURANT, A. E. 1955. 'Blood groups of the Northern Nilotes'. *Ann. Hum. Genet.* **20**: 135–54.

179 ROBERTS, D. F. 1957. 'Contribuzione alla etnologia dei "Pre-Niloti": i Mabaan a paragone dei Niloti'. *Riv. Antrop.* **44**: 317–24.

180 ROBERTS, D. F. 1962. 'Serology and the history of the Northern Nilotes'. *J. Afr. Hist.* **3**: 301–5.

181 ROBERTS, D. F. and BOYO, A. E., 1962. 'Abnormal haemoglobins in childhood among the Yoruba'. *Hum. Biol.* **34**: 20–37.

182 ROBERTS, D. F. and BAINBRIDGE, D. R. 1963. 'Nilotic physique'. *Amer. J. Phys. Anthrop.* **21**: 341–70.

183 SCHAPERA, I. 1926. 'A preliminary consideration of the relationship between the Hottentots and the Bushmen'. *South Afr. J. Sci.* **23**: 833–66.

184 SCHOTT, L. 1962. 'Eine betrachtung zum wachstumablauf im kindersalter bei Negritos und Bambuti'. *Artz. Jugendkunde* **53**: 359–66.

185 SCHREIDER, E. 1950. 'Les variations raciales et sexuelles du tronc humain'. *L'Anthrop.* **54**: 228–61.

186 SCHULTZE, L. 1928. 'Zur kenntnis des körpers der Hottentotten und Buschmanner'. *Jenaische Denkschriften* **17**: 147–228.

187 SELIGMANN, C. G. 1910. 'The physical characters of the Nuba of Kordofan'. *J. Roy. Anthrop. Inst.* **40**: 505–24.

188 SELIGMANN, C. G. 1966. *Races of Africa* (London: Oxford University Press, 4th edn).

189 SHAW, T. 1970. 'The analysis of West African bronzes. A summary of the evidence'. *Ibadan* **28**: 80–9.

190 SHAW, T. 1972. 'Finds at the Iwo Eleru rock shelter, Western Nigeria'. *In Actes 6e Congrès Panafricain de Préhistoire (Dakar 1967)*, pp. 190–2.

191 SINGER, R., BUDTZ-OLSEN, O., BRAIN, P. and SAUGRAIN, J. 1957. 'Physical features, sickling, and serology of the Malagasy of Madagascar'. *Amer. J. Phys. Anthrop.* **15**: 91–123.

192 SINGER, R. 1958. 'The Boskop "race" problem.' *Man* **232**: 173–7.

193 SINGER, R., WEINER, J. S. and ZOUTENDYK, A. 1970. 'Investigations on the biology of Hottentot and Bushman populations in southern Africa. Serology'. *Materialy I Prace Antropol.* **78**: 37–40.

194 SPEDINI, G. and CRESTA, M. 1968. 'Antropologia morfologica ed ematologica del basso Dahomey. II. Caratteri emotipologici'. *Riv. Antrop.* **55**: 179–88.

195 SPORCQ, J. 1972. 'Les Bira de la savane et les Bira de la forêt; étude comparative de deux populations de la République Démocratique du Congo'. *Bull. Mém. Soc. Anthrop. Paris* **9**: 97–120.

196 STEINBERG, A. G. 1966. 'Correction of previously published Gm(c) phenotypes of Africans and Micronesians'. *Amer. J. Hum. Genet.* **18**: 109.

197 STENNING, D. J. 1965. 'The pastoral Fulahi of northern Nigeria'. *In* J. L. Gibbs Jnr. (ed.), *Peoples of Africa*, pp. 361–402 (New York: Holt, Rinehart and Winston).

198 STROUHAL, E. 1971. 'Anthropometric and functional evidence of heterosis from Egyptian Nubia'. *Hum. Biol.* **43**: 271–87.

199 STRUCK, B. 1933. 'Anthropologische ergebnisse aus Portuguiesisch-Guinea'. *In* H. A. Bernatzie (ed.), *Äthiopen des Westens,* Band I, pp. 249–303. (Wien: Weidel und Sohn).

200 SUTTON, J. E. G. 1966. 'The archaeology and early peoples of the highlands of Kenya and northern Tanzania'. *Azania* **1**: 37–57.

201 SUTTON, J. E. G. 1972. New radiocarbon dates for eastern and southern Africa'. *J. Afr. Hist.* **13**: 1–24.

202 TALBOT, P. A. and MULHALL, H. 1962. *The Physical Anthropology of Southern Nigeria* (Cambridge University Press).

203 THILMANS, G. 1968. 'Recherches craniométriques sur l'origine des Pygmées d'Afrique'. *Bull. IFAN* **30, B**: 401–28.

204 THOMA, A. 1971. 'Évolution et différenciation du Polymorphisme ABO', *In Génétique et population. Hommage à Jean Sutter,* pp. 129–40 (Paris: INED).

205 TOBIAS, P. V. 1955. 'Physical anthropology and somatic origins of the Hottentots.' *African Studies* **14**: 1–15.

206 TOBIAS, P. V. 1957. 'Bushmen of the Kalahari'. *Man* **36**: 1–8.

207 TOBIAS, P. V. 1962. 'On the increasing stature of the Bushmen'. *Anthropos* **57**: 801–10.

208 TOBIAS, P. V. 1964. 'Bushman hunter-gatherers: a study in human ecology'. *In* D. H. S. Davis (ed.), *Ecological Studies in Southern Africa,* pp. 67–86 (The Hague: Junk).

209 TOBIAS, P. V. 1968. 'Cranial capacity in anthropoid apes, *Australopithecus* and *Homo habilis,* with comments on skewed samples'. *South Afr. J. Sci.* **64**: 81–91.

210 TREMEARNE, A. J. N. 1912. 'Notes on the Kagoro and other Nigerian headhunters'. *J. Roy. Anthrop. Inst.* **42**: 136–99.

211 TURNBULL, C. M. 1961. *The Forest People : a Study of the Pygmies of the Congo* (New York: Simon and Schuster).

212 TURNBULL, C. M. 1965. *Wayward Servants: the Two Worlds of the African Pygmies* (Garden City: Natural History Press).

213 TURNBULL, C. M. 1968. 'The importance of flux in two hunting societies', *In* R. B. Lee and I. DeVore (eds.), *Man the Hunter,* pp. 132–7 (Chicago: Aldine).

214 TWIESSELMANN F. 1958. *Les Ossements Humains du Gîte Mésolithique d'Ishango.* Exploration du Parc National Albert, Mission J. de Heinzelin de Braucourt, 1950. Vol. 5. (Bruxelles: Institut des Parcs Nationaux du Congo belge).

215 TWIESSELMANN, F. 1965. 'Expédition anthropologique du Dr J. H. Nyéssen. II. Les Oromo-Gallas, les Anouaks, les Chillouks, les Nouers'. *Bull. Soc. Belge Anthrop. Préhist.* **75**: 121–62.

216 VALLOIS, H. V. 1941. 'Recherches anthropologiques sur les Peuls

et divers Noirs de l'Afrique occidentale'. *Bull. Soc. Anthrop. Paris* **2**: 20–74.

217 VALLOIS, H. V. 1970. 'Observations anthropologiques sur les Pygmées Baka du Cameroun'. *Bull. Soc. Anthrop. S. O.* **5**: 1–7.

218 VAN DE GINSTE F. 1946. 'Anthropometric study on the Bapende and the Bakusu of the Belgian Congo'. *Amer. J. Phys. Anthrop.* **4**: 125–51.

219 VANSINA, J. 1965. *Les Anciens Royaumes de la Savane.* (Kinshasa: Institut de recherches économiques et sociales).

220 VILLIERS, H. DE. 1969. 'The morphology and incidence of the tablier in Bushman, Griqua and Negro females'. *Proc. VIIIth intern. Congress Anthrop. Ethnol. Sci.* (Tokyo-Kyoto 1968) **1**: 48–51.

221 VINCKE, E. 1969. 'Pratiques d'eugénique chez les Luba du Katanga'. *Bull. Mém. Soc. Anthrop. Paris* **12**: 259–69.

222 VOGEL, F. and CHAKRAVERTTI, M. R. 1966. 'ABO blood groups and smallpox in a rural population of West Bengal and Bihar, India'. *Humangenetik* **3**: 160–80.

223 VOLKOV-DOUBROVINE, V. P. and ROGUINSKY, J. I. 1960. 'Guipisténotse falia kak prisspossobitelnyi priznak v tropitcheskoï zonié'. *Voprossy antrop.* **1**: 45–55.

224 WALTERS, J. H. and LEHMANN, H. 1956. 'Distribution of the S and C haemoglobin variants in two Nigerian communities'. *Trans. Roy. Soc. Trop. Med. Hyg.* **50**: 204–8.

225 WASHBURN, S. 1963. 'The study of race'. *Amer. Anthrop.* **65**: 521–31.

226 WASSERMANN, H. P. and HEYL, T. 1968. 'Quantitative data on skin pigmentation in South African races'. *S. Afr. Med. J.* **42**: 98–101.

227 WEINER, J. S. 1954. 'Nose shape and climate'. *Amer. J. Phys. Anthrop.* **12**: 1–4.

228 WEINER, J. S. and ZOUTENDYCK, A. 1959. 'Blood-group investigation on Central Kalahari Bushmen'. *Nature* **4664**: 843–4.

229 WEINER, J. S., HARRISON, G. A., SINGER, R., HARRIS, R. and JOPP, W. 1964. Skin color in Southern Africa. *Hum. Biol.* **36**: 294–307.

230 WENDORF, F., SHINER, J. L. and MARKS, A. E. 1965. 'Summary of the 1963–1964 field season'. *In* F. Wendorf (ed.), *Contributions to the Prehistory of Nubia.* pp. 9–35 (Dallas: Southern Methodist University Press).

231 WENDT, G. G., ERMERT, A., KIRCHBERG, G. and KINDERMANN, I. 1967. 'ABO-blutgruppen und serumgruppen bei den negerstämmen Peulh und Marka'. *Humangenetik* **4**: 74–80.

232 WEININGER, M. 1965. 'Chimba und Vatrwa, bantuide vielzüchter

und nichtbantuide wildbeuten'. *Mitt. Anthrop. Gesell. Wien* **95**: 180–90.

233 WIERCINSKI, A. 1965. 'The analysis of racial structure of early dynastic populations in Egypt'. *Materialow I Prac Anthropologicznich* **72**: 3–47.

234 WILLETT, F. 1971. 'Nigeria'. *In* P. L. Shinnie (ed.), *The African Iron Age*. pp. 1–35 (Oxford: Clarendon Press).

235 WORKMAN, P. L. 1968. 'Gene flow and the search for natural selection in man'. *Hum. Biol.* **40**: 260–79.

Index